1988 Cowboys Schedule

Date	Opponent	Kickoff (Dallas Time)
Preseason		
Aug. 6	at San Diego	8 P.M.
Aug. 13	at L.A. Raiders	3 P.M.
Aug. 22	Salesmanship Game I	7 P.M.
	Chicago	
Aug. 27	Salesmanship Game II	8 P.M.
	Houston	
Regular Season		
Sep. 4	at Pittsburgh	Noon
Sep. 12	at Phoenix	8 P.M.
Sep. 18	N.Y. Giants	3 P.M.
Sep. 25	Atlanta	Noon
Oct. 3	at New Orleans	8 P.M.
Oct. 9	Washington	Noon
Oct. 16	at Chicago	Noon
Oct. 23	at Philadelphia	Noon
Oct. 30	Phoenix	Noon
Nov. 6	at N.Y. Giants	Noon
Nov. 13	Minnesota	7 P.M.
Nov. 20	Cincinnati	Noon
Nov. 24	Houston	3 P.M.
Dec. 4	at Cleveland	Noon
Dec. 11	at Washington	Noon
Dec. 18	Philadelphia	Noon

THE OFFICIAL
1988 DALLAS
COWBOYS
BLUEBOOK
VOLUME IX

by Carlton Stowers
and Jarrett Bell

Taylor Publishing Company
Dallas, Texas

Photographs courtesy of

The Dallas Cowboys
The Dallas Cowboys Cheerleaders
The Dallas Cowboys Weekly

Published in cooperation with the Dallas Cowboys

ISBN 0-87833-642-7

Printed in the United States of America

CONTENTS

WHAT TOMORROW BRINGS

Roger Staubach's retirement in 1980 may have started the Cowboys' slide.

There are those, of course, who fiercely continue to refuse acceptance of the current state of Dallas Cowboys affairs. They cling gamely to the days when the good times rolled and refuse to acknowledge that their team has tumbled from the NFL mountain and is now faced with the task of dusting off their backsides and beginning the long climb back. Memories, like the song says, will do that to you.

Those loyalists who blindly believe in miracles their heroes are not presently capable of providing have, quite simply, not grasped the reality of the times. Once considered an automatic Super Bowl contender, the Cowboys now hope to rebuild to a point where modest goals like a winning season and contending for the NFC East title are again within reach.

They are, in a sense, victims of their own success, their own celebrated polish and poise PR. In a decade now stowed away in the history books, the Cowboys worked for and earned the role of professional sport's model team. They won with near-boring regularity, their front office served as a textbook example of how a first-class business should be run, and their coach and players generally symbolized the clean-cut, red-white-and-blue image the powers-that-be of the National Football League would like the public to buy in large quantities.

It is Tex Schramm, president and general manager of the Cowboys, who has long preached that "the fans want their players to be heroes; they want them to be model citizens. And they want them to win." Anything less, he says, is a disappointment to many.

Which is to say being "America's Team" hasn't always been easy. The spotlight seldom dims, win or lose. The nation has watched closely, some in unbridled admiration, others in the eternal hope that something would happen to derail the winning machine and spoil the spit shine image.

With back-to-back losing seasons, that derailment has now become official. And the howling criticism from far and wide has been scattershot at every part of the organization.

Which is to say the world has changed since those days when Roger Staubach, the squeaky-clean Cowboys quarterback, was directing his team to those almost magical come-from-behind victories that paved the way to Super Bowl glories. More so than any player before him or since, Staubach represented the image that elevated the Cowboys a notch above most others in professional sports. In a manner of speaking, he was too good to be true. And, as a byproduct, so was the team he so artfully guided.

There are those who will insist that the slide of the Cowboys began on March 31, 1980, when a tearful Staubach stood before a press gathering the size of which most politicians only dream about and announced his retirement.

For the Cowboys, and those who followed them, things would never be the same—at least not until another Staubach came on board to capture the public imagination with the same blend of remarkable talent and public image. Only then, the experts surmised, could the Cowboys' star regain its brightness.

And now, eight years after Staubach's final appearance in a

Eight years after Staubach stepped down, the new hero on the Dallas horizon appears to be Herschel Walker.

blue and silver uniform, a new hero looms on the Dallas horizon. The burden attached to the mega-bucks contract under which he labors is weighty. Whether he realizes it or not, likes it or not, he is the individual charged with the responsibility of repolishing the public's perception of the Dallas Cowboys. His name is Herschel Walker.

Last year, in his second season with Dallas, the former Heisman Trophy winner's niche was finally carved. Weary of trying to design an offense wherein Walker and the club's all-time rushing leader Tony Dorsett could share time and glories, Landry and his staff reached the decision to turn the tailback job over to the former Georgia and USFL superstar. For the first time in his brilliant career, 34-year-old Tony Dorsett found himself listed No. 2 on someone's depth chart.

The results speak for themselves.

Walker led the Cowboys in rushing (891 yards on 209 attempts) and receiving (60 catches for 715 yards) to become the first NFL player ever to account for over 700 yards in each department in consecutive seasons. For his efforts he was picked to the Pro Bowl and was named to several All-Pro second teams. Those who like to tinker with projections point out that he would have easily attained 1,000 yards in each category and qualified for even greater postseason honors had the job been his all year and the strike not interrupted the flow of the season.

"What we're doing now," says Landry, "is counting on Herschel to play the dominant role in our rebuilding process. He's our foundation. He's the guy people are going to have to stop if they're going to beat the Cowboys. And if he stays healthy, we're going to be okay."

But not everyone is convinced.

There are those critics who now insist the franchise is leaning too heavily on the abilities of one man. O.J. Simpson, for all his brilliance, never turned Buffalo into a champion. The Chicago Bears didn't begin to flex their muscles until the gifted Walter Payton was finally blessed with a strong supporting cast. Likewise, Herschel Walker, regardless of his multitude of talents, cannot carry the Cowboys alone.

No one knows that better than Landry, a man who has seen pro football stars come and go for almost three decades.

Which is to say his point is being missed. By focusing the spotlight squarely on a new hero, the Cowboys have made a statement long overdue. Staubach, it has now been realized, will never throw another "Hail Mary" touchdown. Tony Dorsett's string of 1,000-yard seasons are history and something which the NFL Hall of Fame must now

Walker, the Heisman Trophy winner, is being counted on by Tom Landry to play a dominant role.

consider. There will be no more circus catches from Drew Pearson or bone-crushing tackles from Cliff Harris.

Those days are gone. End of story. Retired players and colorful history won't win games for you this Sunday. And, so, the Cowboys have put their scrapbooks into storage.

It is a bittersweet task long overdue. Landry now preaches of a three-year plan to return the team to championship level. Even Schramm, who is perhaps more history-conscious than most politicians and military leaders, has made it clear that the most important item on the Cowboys' agenda is the future. In the aftermath of the troubled seasons past he weighed the problems with the organization over which he has presided since Day One and came to a difficult conclusion. Yesterday's successes had seduced the entire organization—from front office to scouting, PR department to coaching staff—into a stubborn refusal to change. While holding too long to a "it worked in days past so it should work today" philosophy, his Cowboys lost a precious step. Once the recognized league innovator, Dallas spent too much time polishing the fenders while not bothering to check under the hood.

"What has happened to us in recent years," Schramm now admits, "is our own doing."

That, perhaps, is the most important admission to come out of the administrative offices of the Cowboys since the new decade began. In a manner of speaking, Schramm is saying, 'We have met the enemy and it is us.' And now that the adversary has a face he can be met head-on. There is evidence of a new direction in virtually every office one enters at Cowboys Center.

Thus, the book now in your hands is not another rehashed celebration of the past. Rather, it is one that focuses squarely on the future, providing hints and hopefully a little insight into what tomorrow holds. And that, in its own way, is vastly more exciting than reading history.

Gone are the days of "Hail Mary" touchdown passes . . .

. . . and of Tony Dorsett's 1,000-yard seasons.

PROMISE FOR THE FUTURE... HERE AND NOW

Jim Jeffcoat (left) and Randy White signal the blend of youth and experience on the defensive line.

"You can't idly say you're going to eliminate all of the older players and bring in youngsters, because if the youngsters can't play at a high level you've really got a problem."
—Cowboys president and general manager Texas E. Schramm

A h, finally, Year Two of Tom Landry's self-projected three-year rebuilding plan. Year One was certainly an interesting experience. By season's end, though, there were enough positives, which included the fresh faces and a little bit of that phenomenon called momentum, to allow the reasonable assumption that the transition was on track.

You know the story line. Let's review. The Dallas Cowboys, after an NFL-record 20 straight winning seasons—18 of which ended with a playoff berth—presumably bottomed out at 7–9 in 1986.

A losing season? Katie, bar the door, the Fat Lady's coming to sing. What was going on in Dallas? That was the biggest question in these parts since, "Who Shot J.R.?" After that face-slap '86 campaign, it was as if three alarms went off, sirens sounded, flares shot up and the firemen rushed in to survey the extent of the damage to a house that was once the prettiest in the neighborhood.

Landry, as if he were a fire inspector himself, certainly sifted through the rubble, looking for causes. He nobly determined that there was something still left to the structure, and that he wanted to do something about it.

"I like the Cowboys," Landry said shortly after the end of the Cowboys' first losing season since 1964. "The Cowboys have been my life for 27 years. I don't like the Cowboys in this position. If I can help get them out, that is fine. That is what I intend to do."

Soon after, Landry issued his estimate of the damage: three years. Thus, the start of the restoration project to return the Cowboys to contending status. It was another in a series of different types of coaching challenges for Landry, who signed a three-year contract extension in case anyone wondered if he was serious. Back in the early

"Too Tall" Jones still plays a key role in the defensive plan.

'60s, the mission was to build a winner from scratch. Done. In the mid-'70s, the object was to develop a second Super Bowl winner, with a completely different cast than the first. Done. Now the dare is to bring a franchise back to life. Done? Not yet.

Year One had the bottom line look of the previous season. The Cowboys finished it by watching the playoffs on the networks, and they had a losing record again. The 7–8 mark gave Dallas its first back-to-back losing seasons since 1963 and '64. Take away the 2–1 replacement-season input, and it's two games under .500. But the signs were apparent toward the end of the season that the transition period was well underway.

The Cowboys won their final two games, eliminating the Rams and the Cardinals from the NFC playoff picture, while already being mathematically eliminated themselves from the hunt. They did so with an assortment of youngsters in the lineup—filling in after injuries to veterans or playing because they earned the extended

game-situation looks from the coaching staff. It was the first time the Cowboys had won their final two regular-season games since 1979. Whoa! That was an encouraging sign for Landry, who saw his team suffer through seven losses in the last eight weeks the previous year.

"Anytime you finish strong against teams that are going for the playoffs, it tells your players they're not far from being playoff contenders themselves," said Landry. "We left last season with a lot of hope for this season."

The key to the current campaign, naturally, rests with the development of the younger players. Herschel Walker said at one point last year that he felt part of the team's problem was that there were "a lot of older players and a lot of younger players, but not much in between." It's too late to do anything about the "in between" personnel, but players who might normally have to wait a few years to gain frontline experience are getting their chances without delay. If they hold up, they'll be the foundation for the future.

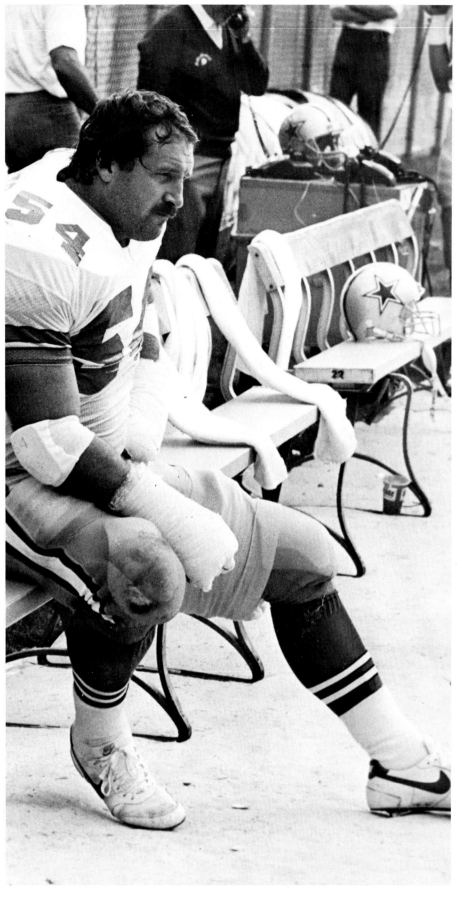

White may see work as a standup end, if Tom Landry does as promised and "loosens up the flex."

"We have to mature, especially on offense where we have so many young players," said Landry. "And we need to strengthen the defense. We have enough good, young players on offense now that we should score points if they continue to develop as we expect. On defense we need a stronger pass rush and we need more depth, so that when older players like Randy White, Ed Jones and Mike Hegman are ready to step down, we have quality replacements for them. Because of injuries and age, we need immediate help at those positions. If we can get a few more top prospects we could improve fairly quickly because we've already got a pretty good nucleus of young players. We probably finished last year with more young guys playing than ever before. I can't remember winning a couple of games with that many young players on the field. That's encouraging."

In recent years, Landry has admitted to tinkering with the idea of scrapping the flex defense—the stiff-against-the-run, gap-controlled scheme that he invented—and installing a 3–4 defense. But Landry continues to subscribe to the notion that the flex will still work effectively if the players play it properly. No argument here. They gave up a measly 3.5 yards per carry against the run last year, a figure tied for second best in the NFL.

Still, the Cowboys ranked next-to-last in the league in pass defense last year, an indication perhaps that opposing quarterbacks weren't pressured enough, the coverage wasn't good enough or a combination of the two. The head coach has said he will loosen up the flex a bit, may use Randy White as a standup end, and continue to use some of the variations of other defenses that were employed at times last year. But the Cowboys will still be the team with the flex defense.

"It's going to take a lot of changes to put us in the 3–4," Landry said. "It is a matter of the quality and size of the linebacker crew."

Offensively, the Cowboys will rely on the multiplicity of Walker to spark the unit. Less pressure will be applied on the quarterback position. Also, Landry has given himself back the role of offensive coordinator, and will use less of the 49ers-type controlled passing game that pass offense coordinator Paul Hackett brought with him to Dallas two years ago. The Cowboys moved the ball well between the 20-yard lines, and ranked 11th in the league in total yards—but the team was still plagued by roughness when it got inside plus territory. That may be the reason Landry wants to shake up the offensive system a bit.

"It will be a little more balanced attack," Landry said. "We had been leaning more toward the passing game, but now we'll blend the running a little more. We will be geared to a bigger offensive line with Herschel as the strength of our running game."

Added Landry, "I have always been able to coordinate the offense so I will be going back to the offense after two years. My game plans will still have a lot to do with bringing the game plan to the table. I will coordinate the offense and the defense. If we're going to have another losing season, it's going to be my fault."

Here's a position-by-position look at the '88 Dallas Cowboys:

Quarterback

Cowboys coaches were disappointed last summer when Steve Pelluer didn't mount more of a training camp challenge for the No. 1 job. He is getting another shot this year, with the job basically his to lose.

The emergency appendectomy he underwent in the early offseason, while vacationing in West Germany, provided a scare, but didn't cost Pelluer much preparation time. Hopefully, it didn't cost him any of the momentum and confidence he gained during his starts in the final two games of last season.

In the victories over the Rams and the Cardinals, Pelluer performed basically error-free, completing about half of his passes and staying out of the interception column. In fact, Pelluer starts the new season with an impressive streak of 94 passes without an interception. While Pelluer will never be a quarterback in the mold of a John Elway or Dan Marino, his efforts late last year did plenty to support the notion that a team can go far as long as the quarterback is in control.

In the past, Landry complimented Pelluer for displaying an even-keeled demeanor. That was before the eight-week education during the '86 campaign, when Pelluer took over the offense in the stead of Danny White, who was lost for the second half of the season with a broken wrist. Pelluer, an innocent, inexperienced victim that year of a broken down offensive line, was sacked an unmerciful 47 times in '86. He admitted that as the team went 1–6 while he directed the offense, he lost a tremendous amount of confidence. Credit the man for being honest.

For 1988, Steve Pelluer is being counted on as the No. 1 quarterback.

The extremely mobile Pelluer has regrouped since then, and is in the position to silence the critics who have already tried to write him off as a failure. At 26 and entering his fifth year, though, the former University of Washington star is approaching a crossroads: starter or support player.

Danny White knows all about critics, and how they love to point fingers at the quarterbacks. His career has been filled with controversy, doubt and blame, along with a fair amount of success. With White approaching his 13th season with the Cowboys and already having passed his 36th birthday, the need for another quarterback to emerge as the No. 1 man is evident.

However, White will tell you that he'd like to go out in style. But first, there's the matter of the right wrist that last year hampered the Cowboys' career record-holder for completions and touchdown passes. At times, White would attempt to throw a pass 10 yards to the receiver's right side, and the ball would sail 15 yards to the left. The control factor in his wrist—although it got stronger as the season progressed—was as unpredictable as some recreational golfers' tee shots. So as he enters the '88 season, the wrist and the assurance of it holding up an entire season remain key concerns.

"He wants to play and he thinks he can start and win for us," said Landry. "It's a question of whether he can be consistent in his throwing motion, which is where he had trouble last year."

If White is healthy, he will be valuable as either the experienced starter who can read a defense as well as any quarterback, or as the crafty reserve who provides better insurance than Allstate. But again, the key "if" is in the wrist.

"We have quarterbacks who can win for us," said Landry. "Steve Pelluer is the front-runner, mainly because he won the last two games, he's young and he's got his confidence back. We just feel he's the one to get the shot.

"Naturally, you lean towards

The key "if" for quarterback Danny White is his wrist. If White is healthy, he'll play a big role.

Pelluer because he's younger and healthier, but he's going to have to earn the job," added Landry. "There won't be any guarantees at the quarterback position going into training camp. But even if Pelluer is the starter, Danny could play an important role as a backup."

The wild card player at this position is Kevin Sweeney, the strong-armed seventh-round draft pick last year who starred in the replacement games. Sweeney is only 5–11, and Landry has said he is too short.

Okay, well, why did Dallas draft him if he was too short? Why did Landry personally call Sweeney after the draft (customary for high-round-draftees, and not middle- to late-round picks) to congratulate him? Sweeney is also only a quarter-inch shorter than Chicago's Jim McMahon. Landry says he will give the NCAA's all-time leading passer for yards (10,623 at Fresno State) a better look in '88, but he still needs to be convinced that the spirited and confident young man can

withstand the Mike Tyson-type blows delivered in the big leagues.

"He has some awfully good qualities," Landry admitted, "as we saw in the replacement games. He can really throw the football. It's a matter of whether he's strong enough to hold up under the punishment you have to take as an NFL quarterback. We're going to see what he can do this summer."

Paul McDonald, the former Cleveland Browns lefthander, will also try to figure into the team's plans. He has yet to take a single snap in the regular season, since being signed midway through the '86 season when White was injured.

Running Back

The big transition here took place last November when Herschel Walker moved from fullback to replace Tony Dorsett as the tailback. Dorsett was a brilliant player in 11 seasons with the Cowboys. He is fourth on the NFL's all-time rushing list, only 276 yards away from catching Jim Brown. But at 34, his days as a bread-and-butter back are numbered.

Since joining the Cowboys in '86 after three standout seasons in the USFL, the 26-year-old Walker has gained 3,180 yards from scrimmage. Only the Colts' Eric Dickerson can boast a higher mark. Last year, Walker became the first NFL player to total more than 700 yards rushing (891) and receiving (715 on a team-high 60 catches) twice in his career. Over a full, 16-game slate, that would project to over 1,500 yards rushing and more than 1,000 yards receiving. And the man can also do ballet. With Dorsett's departure to Denver, there is no question that the offense will revolve around Walker in '88, even moreso than last season.

"We're counting on Herschel to play the dominant role because he has that kind of ability," Landry said. "We are building for the future with Herschel as the foundation. If he can stay healthy, we're going to be okay."

What the Cowboys would like to avoid, though, is overburdening

Walker to the point where opposing defenses are able to key on him. Walker's versatility as a great pass-catcher who can line up from several different positions is a great asset, but the best way to keep pressure off Walker and to keep opposing defenses guessing is to have a suitable number of other offensive threats.

Ninth-year man Timmy Newsome returns at fullback, and he will again be counted on as the key blocker in the backfield and a prime receiving threat. Newsome, 6–1, 235, doesn't get enough credit for being a fine blocker, but teammates and coaches rave about his ability to level defenders.

Todd Fowler, heading into his fourth season, is the backup fullback, but has only rushed for 30 yards and caught just seven passes for 49 yards since becoming a Cowboy. Although he is an excellent special teams player, Fowler's challenge is to push Newsome for playing time.

Backup tailback Darryl Clack has had very little opportunity to display his running ability. But from what he has shown in training camp, preseason games and as a kickoff returner, Clack has something to bring to the picnic. A second-round draft choice in '86, he should play a bigger role in the offense this year. "We made a mistake last year by not playing him more," Landry said. Although he is listed as a tailback, Clack may also be a fullback candidate. Gerald White, a replacement player who was re-signed after last season, will also get another look at fullback.

Wide Receiver

The addition of enthusiastic Miami wideout Michael Irvin should do wonders for the position, and fill the deep-threat void created when Mike Sherrard broke his leg. The Cowboys' No. 1 draft pick, and the 11th player chosen overall, the 6–2, 202-pound Irvin has the size, speed (4.52 in the 40), sure hands and overall athletic ability that should make him a star.

Irvin is also a tough-nosed type

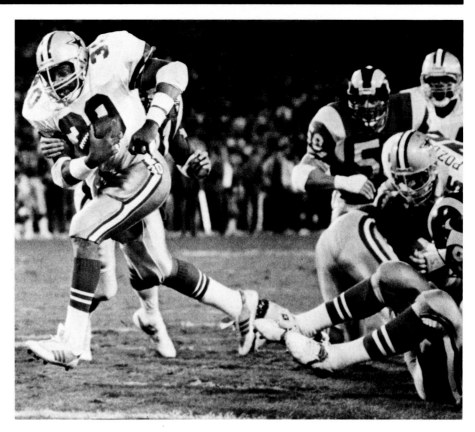

Veteran fullback Timmy Newsome returns as the key backfield blocker.

who is not afraid to go over the middle, and has never lacked for confidence.

"I think he has the potential to be a starter," Landry said of Irvin's possible rookie-season contribution. "He has that much ability."

Landry also said he isn't concerned with the reputation Irvin brings with him as a hot dog. "We don't feel like that's a problem," he said. "We covered that area pretty strong. (Scout) Walt Yowarski covers in his area consistently. The guy's a leader, and he performs extremely well in practice and in games. He's a hard worker. He has a few things that he says and so on, but he still performs."

Unfortunately, the talented Sherrard will begin the season where he spent all of last year—on the injury list. While jogging on a California beach last February, Sherrard refractured the right leg that caused him to miss the entire '87 season and won't be able to return until midseason at the earliest.

Without Sherrard, the Cowboys

lose a player who had established himself as one of the top up-and-coming receiving threats during his rookie year, when he grabbed 41 passes for 744 yards. The team's No. 1 pick in '86 will certainly work hard to come back. He has the determination and attitude that coaches love.

"It's really a shame what's happened to Mike," said Landry, "who is such a great talent. We can't count on him for this season, but that doesn't rule anything out. All we know right now is he'll definitely miss camp and preseason. Beyond that, we'll just have to wait and see, and hope for the best."

Still, there are a lot of promising young faces at this position. Kelvin Edwards, the fourth-round draft choice of the Saints in '86, dominated during the replacement games and earned a job with the regulars after the strike. A few weeks later, he was the starter and primary deep threat. He finished the '87 season with 34 catches for 521 yards, but needs to find a comfort zone. The benefit of a training camp could

Dallas is set at tight end with Thornton Chandler (left) and Doug Cosbie.

make a tremendous difference for Edwards, who has run a 4.2 40-yard dash.

Reliable Mike Renfro returns for his 11th season, after mulling over retirement. Never a fast player, Renfro has lost a step or two at age 33, but there's no denying his ability in the clutch. Case in point: the fourth-and-13 with just over a minute to play in the fourth period at New England, and the Cowboys trailing. Renfro caught a 43-yard pass from White to set up the game-tying field goal, setting the stage for Walker's dramatic 60-yard run in overtime. Renfro's experience is valued, but can the Cowboys afford not to have another younger starter gaining experience?

Gordon Banks, a player who has simply done well in whatever role he has been asked to perform, will try to wrestle away a starting job. Banks started early last year after Sherrard was injured, and early in '86 after Renfro was hurt. Do coaches have enough confidence in him to be a legitimate starter? Rod Barksdale, acquired in the Ron Fellows-to-the-Raiders trade last summer, will be in a battle to make the team. With sprinter's speed, though, he should compete strongly.

The fourth-round pick a year ago, Kelvin Martin was impressive late last year as both a punt returner and a tough-nosed receiver. Coaches like his style. Ray Alexander— a former star in the Canadian Football League who had a great camp last summer until he broke a wrist—will also compete, as will Everett Gay. The team's fifth-round pick last year, Gay also spent the year on injured reserve after injuring an ankle. Cornell Burbage, who played well during the strike games, has also been invited back.

Tight End

With Doug Cosbie healthy and coming back for his 10th season, the job is in good hands. Now it's a matter of how he's used. Two years ago, Cosbie was virtually taken out of the offense after catching 124 passes the two previous seasons. There were signs early last year that the 6-6 target would resume his former role as one of the primary options, but passes thrown his way tailed off as the season progressed. He finished with 36 receptions last year, but is still capable of catching over 60 passes.

The emergence of Thornton

Chandler continues to be a bright spot. He appears to be the heir apparent to Cosbie's position, and at 6-5, 245, might be a Cosbie clone. Steve Folsom, an excellent blocking tight end, also returns.

Offensive Line

The Cowboys' line used to be known as small, finesse types that relied on trap blocking. Last year after Jim Erkenbeck came over from the Saints, the Dallas line began taking on a different personality. Man-on-man, zone blocking is the philosophy, and big bodies are in demand. In fact, in the past 10 years, the size of the Cowboys' starting linemen has grown from an average of 255 pounds to 295. Indeed, they like the big bodies these days.

Hold it right there, buddy. Big, yes. A body to rival Shamu the Killer Whale, no. Hold it, Nate Newton. After using a crash-course diet last summer to drop almost 50 pounds and get into training camp shape at 298 pounds, Newton turned in a solid season in his first year as the starting left guard. Then came the offseason, get-togethers with family and friends

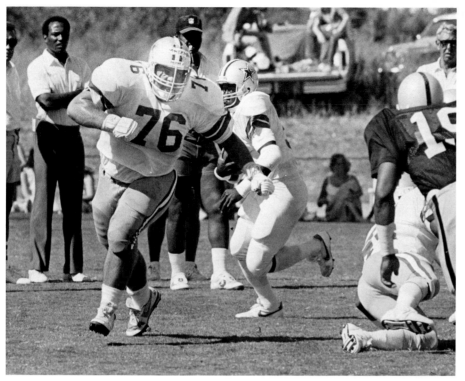

Jeff Zimmerman starts camp as the No. 1 left guard.

and lots of grub.

Newton checked into the first veterans' mini-camp last spring bigger than he was last year, at a whopping 354 pounds. The nickname "The Kitchen" fit a lot better than his pants. Again, it would take a crash-course diet to reach his playing weight of 300 pounds (give or take a dozen). Erkenbeck has called Newton his best lineman, and a potential All-Pro when in shape, but after the drastic weight gain, he wondered for the fourth-year veteran's health. "I'm going to treat him like he's got a disease," Erkenbeck said during that first mini-camp last spring.

Landry awarded 310-pound Jeff Zimmerman, last year's third-round draft pick, Newton's starting job during the offseason. But it is clearly a battle that will be staged in Thousand Oaks. Returning to his starting job at right guard will be 290-pound Crawford Ker, a strong, fourth-year vet. Ker comes off a steady season, and has developed well. "He's been our only steady player at any of the offensive line positions over the last two years," said Landry. If he improves even more, he may be thought of as the potential Pro Bowler on the line.

And making the Pro Bowl would be something for a Dallas lineman. The last offensive lineman for the Cowboys to earn a Pro Bowl berth? Tackle Pat Donovan in 1982. Seventh-year pro Glen Titensor, who was out with an injured knee last year, and Bob White also return to compete at guard.

One of the brightest spots for the Cowboys last year was the contribution delivered by a pair of rookie tackles—Kevin Gogan and Daryle Smith. Gogan, the eighth-rounder last year, was thrust into the starting lineup after the sudden retirement of Phil Pozderac in October. Smith, who first signed with Dallas for the replacement squad, took over at left tackle for an injured Mark Tuinei and performed admirably the final six weeks of the season. "It will be interesting to see how much those young guys improve," says Landry. "They showed a lot of potential last year. And they were so green."

Tuinei will try to hold off Smith's challenge for his job, after returning from a knee injury. The sixth-year veteran bounced around from the defensive line to center, and even played some guard, before finding a home at left tackle. The

bad luck was that he was injured after showing consistent progress. If he can return to the level he was at before he was injured, the Cowboys may have finally solidified left tackle. Steve Cisowski will also try to stick as a tackle.

The center position is another experiencing transitional winds. Tom Rafferty has been a valued member for 12 years, but will play a reduced role this year. George Lilja, a sixth-year man, moved in last year and is expected to pose a stiff challenge for the starting job. Gary Westberry is another candidate.

There's one bottom line number to remember: 52. The Cowboys, who gave up 60 sacks in '86, only cut the total by eight last year, in one less game. Obviously, they still need to dramatically improve their pass protecting as a unit.

Other pieces to the Cowboys' offensive line puzzle may be found in the form of 6–3, 289-pound Oklahoma guard Mark Hutson and 6–6, 297-pound Boston College tackle David Widell, Dallas' third- and fourth-round picks, respectively. The presence of the two high-round picks will certainly pose a serious challenge for spots on Dallas' line of the future.

Defensive Line

This unit has had an infusion of youth recently, and will continue to go through a transition period. Former No. 1 draft picks Kevin Brooks and Danny Noonan, aged 25 and 23, respectively, have moved into prominent tackle roles the past two years and will anchor Dallas' line of the future.

Longtime force Randy White was bothered by a neck injury last year, and may play a reduced role this season, his 14th with the Cowboys. The 35-year-old White, will probably also be used as a stand-up defensive end in pass-rushing situations, as the Cowboys try to improve a pass rush that, despite 51 traps last year, softened during critical situations. Noonan, who spelled the future Hall of Famer more often as his rookie season progressed in '87, will likely inherit White's right tackle spot this season. Landry is impressed with what Noonan brings to the line.

"He has two great assets— strength and speed," Landry said. "He's fast for a lineman and he's powerful. He's stronger than anyone I've seen on the line of scrimmage since Bob Lilly. He can move people."

Brooks led all linemen with 67 tackles last year, after winning the left tackle job from John Dutton (since-released) in training camp. Coaches would like to get a better pass rush from Brooks, but the same can be said for the entire line.

Ed Jones led the Cowboys with 10 sacks last year, and despite constant references to his age, keeps getting rejuvenated and turning in solid seasons. With Jones at 37 and entering his 14th season, it is evident that the Cowboys need to prepare for an eventual replacement at left end. Jones had a great game against the Giants last November—with four sacks, two batted passes (including one to Jim Jeffcoat, which was returned for a touchdown) and a forced fumble—to earn NFC Player of the Week honors. But he finished the year with just one sack in the final six weeks. Jones is still the best the Cowboys have at left end, and won't likely be seriously challenged.

One candidate as a left end of the future may be right end Jim Jeffcoat. The sixth-year pro was shifted in some situations last year, but may not be the quick pass-rusher coaches desire at right end. The Cowboys are not disappointed in Jeffcoat, though, who plays the run exceptionally well. That trait could make him a natural.

A group that includes returnees Don Smerek, Mark Walen, Randy Watts and Robert Smith will compete for spots on the line. Smerek, an eighth-year veteran, has never challenged for a starting job, but can play all four line positions. Walen, the third-round pick in '86, missed his rookie season with a broken foot and was seldom used last year. It could be a proving

Eugene Lockhart hopes to rebound from a broken leg.

year for the tackle.

Watts was impressive at end on the replacement squad, but did not stand out after finishing the year with the regulars. Smith, a former USFLer, was a standout during camp last summer, but spent the '87 season on injured reserve after breaking a forearm. Smith may give the Cowboys a boost as a pass-rushing end.

Linebacker

One of the reasons Landry won't switch to a 3–4 is personnel. In other words, he doesn't have the players to use in a linebacker-dominated 3–4 defense. Last year, the Cowboys' starting linebackers didn't turn in enough big plays.

Starters Mike Hegman, Eugene Lockhart and Jeff Rohrer combined for nine sacks, one interception and zero forced fumbles. On top of that, a broken leg jinx visited the position as Lockhart, Hegman and backup Jesse Penn suffered broken bones in the final month of the season.

Lockhart was having a Pro Bowl-type season before his injury, and finished the year with 80 tackles. He also became comfortable assuming a leadership role on the defense. And whenever he's on the field, aggressiveness is not far away. Entering just his fifth season, he may yet reach a higher level of ability.

If the Cowboys did play a 3–4, they would have little problem finding capable inside players. Steve DeOssie, a fifth-year man, is another solid hitter. His biggest contributions over the years have come on special teams and in short-yardage situations. He has proved in fill-in stints for Lockhart that he is plenty capable.

The third middle linebacker last year was Ron Burton, the free agent from North Carolina who was the surprise addition last year. In three games at the end of the season, he won a vote of confidence with his determined play, and demonstrated he can make an impact with his ferocious hits, too. Burton has been penciled in at Hegman's left linebacker spot, and, as a former end, figures to be fast enough to move to the outside.

Hegman has seen his best days, and this is the year he could be moved out of his starting position. Last summer, he said he thought he was beginning his final season. Then he changed his mind, and decided to come back to try a 13th season. He will get competition from all directions—Burton, former No. 2 pick Jesse Penn and this year's No. 2, Ken Norton, Jr.

Rohrer comes off a solid season and has always played the run well. Still, he is not the quick, active type that teams now seek at right linebacker. Penn could compete for the job, but comes off a slow-healing broken foot. Some have Penn, who enters his fourth year, written off as a disappointment. The chance to earn some respect was cut short, though, when he broke his leg during a strong showing against the Rams. Penn's physical tools have never been questioned.

Garth Jax and Jeff Hurd will also vie for positions. Jax, a third-year man, will try on the left side. Hurd, a replacement player last fall, will line up on the right side.

In Norton, the son of the former heavyweight champion, the Cowboys have a player noted for his hitting. The 6–2, 230-pounder played inside at UCLA, but will be tried outside. He has the quickness to do it, having been timed at 4.58 in the 40-yard dash. He fits the mold of the productive, aggressive type the

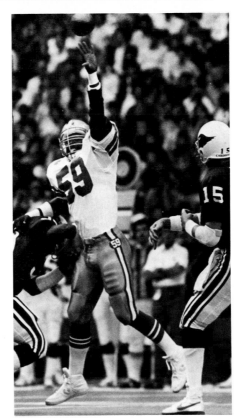

Jesse Penn also suffered a broken leg, spoiling his chance to earn respect.

Cowboys have longed for in recent years.

Defensive Back

Another area that needs to be upgraded, although it may be accomplished from within is defensive back. The Cowboys were 27th in the league in passing yards allowed, a traumatic 229.6 yards per game. Even worse, Dallas allowed a league-high 14.06 yards per catch.

The leader and most dependable player in the secondary is cornerback Everson Walls, the former free agent who is 11 interceptions away from surpassing Mel Renfro as the club's all-time leader. Solid is how Landry desribes the left corner spot.

The Cowboys invested a second-round pick for a cornerback last year, and former Baylor star Ron Francis didn't disappoint. He had his embarrassing moments at times, as all rookies do, but also demonstrated the traits that led to his high-draft position. Among them, the 5–9 Francis displayed a

mental toughness that is needed in order to excel. Some insiders say Francis has the potential to be better than Walls, a three-time All-Pro. Indeed, Francis has a promising future.

"Ron Francis got beat by some good receivers," Landry said, "but he has the speed, the closing ability and the competitive nature to be a top guy. Now he just has to do it."

Manny Hendrix, the former Utah basketball star, and ex-replacement player Robert Williams return to compete. Charles Wright, a free agent from Tulsa, is another cornerback possibility.

Strong safety Bill Bates and free safety Michael Downs are the incumbent starters. But with Vince Albritton and Victor Scott in the wings, the safety jobs may still offer a new look in '88.

Bates, who has long been making it as an overachiever, is being pushed by Albritton. Both are fearless, reckless types, only Albritton is bigger, stronger and faster. He is one of the team's best athletes, and it will take a lot to keep him off the field. Coaches have been gaining more and more confidence in Albritton, a fifth-year man who fought off injury problems early in his career. Beating Bates out won't be easy. Bates made the Cowboys as a longshot free agent in '83 because of his competitiveness, and has always been a favorite of Landry's because of his hustle. Still, he may be another player who will have to adjust to a new role.

Tommy Haynes, one of the best players on the replacement team, will also compete at strong safety.

Downs, the seventh-year vet, picked up his game toward the end of last season, but has yet to return to the near-Pro Bowl level he once played at. The Cowboys seemed to have tried to hand the job to Victor Scott in recent years, but he has had bad luck with injuries. Downs is another who won't give up his job without a stiff challenge. Downs' experience and role as defensive signalcaller gives him points. But Scott, if healthy, scores points because of aggressiveness—his tackling and hitting ability.

Special Teams

What a difference a year makes. Last year, the Cowboys special teams were in a state of confusion. Longtime kicker Rafael Septien had to be replaced. There was no punt returner to speak of. And the Cowboys were just average when it came to coverage squads.

The Cowboys enter the current season hoping to have continued fine performances from key special teams members. Dallas improved from 18th on the NFL's composite special teams list in '86 to seventh last year, under first-year special teams coach Mike Solari.

Kicker Roger Ruzek led the impressive efforts, setting a club record by hitting an amazing 86.2 percent of his field goal tries. That was the only statistical category the Cowboys led the NFL in last year. And this from a free agent who was released during the early stages of

Roger Ruzek gave the Cowboys consistency in field goal situations.

Kelvin Martin emerged as the Cowboys' best punt returner in several years.

Mike Saxon has made adjustments to his punting style during the offseason.

Ron Francis was one of several rookies who played key roles in 1988.

Jesse Penn is a key performer on Dallas' coverage teams.

camp last summer, but re-signed several days later when he revealed to Cowboys coaches that he had been flirting with a new kicking style the first time out. If nothing else, Ruzek has probably learned to experiment after he's made the team. But if it were up to Landry, he wouldn't change a thing with Ruzek's style.

"He has a real consistent, mechanical style," said Landry, a former kicker himself. "He doesn't have the quirks in his kicking that inconsistent kickers have. So he has a chance to be a top kicker for years."

Consistency is what punter Mike Saxon seeks in his fourth season. The pattern for Saxon thus far has been to start the seasons kicking well before watching his average spiral downward as the season progresses. Saxon, whose 39.5 yard average last year was 10th-best in the NFC, adjusted his offseason routine in order to preserve his leg more for the log haul. Results pending.

Kelvin Martin emerged as the best punt returner the Cowboys have had in years. Dallas drafted Martin for punt return duty, and after battling minor injuries, he responded with a 9.8 yard average return that ranked seventh in the

NFC. The darting moves that Martin possesses led to the highest average for a Dallas punt returner since 1980, when James Jones averaged 10.1 per return.

The kick return game was also reliable, led by Darryl Clack. The 21.9 mark Clack earned last year was seventh best in the NFC. It also proved to be a good stage to display his running ability, as coaches have promised to use him more as a running back. Kelvin Martin and Kelvin Edwards will also help on kickoff returns.

Dallas' coverage teams include several enthusiastic performers who spearhead aggressive units. Ron

Bill Bates will try to hold off the challenge of the youngsters.

Burton, Bill Bates, Vince Albritton, Jesse Penn and Steve DeOssie were all vital to the coverage teams last year, and give the Cowboys a very solid nucleus.

Summary

The addition of Michael Irvin is a tremendous boost to the offense, and will take pressure off Herschel Walker. Irvin could be the steal of the draft. Steve Pelluer's development is another key, with the emphasis on not making the mistakes to hurt the offense. Third- and fourth-round draftees Mark Hutson and David Widdell should help the offensive line depth.

The defense should be strong on the inside, with the questions at end. Norton is another name for the linebackers crew, where an emerging player can really make an impact. A transition at safety would give the Cowboys a more aggressive secondary.

It won't be easy for the Cowboys to earn a playoff spot in Year Two of Landry's rebuilding plan. The Redskins and Giants are considered the frontrunners in the NFC East, with the Eagles figured to be another tough division foe. And the Cowboys get no breaks from a schedule that is rated as the third-toughest, based on last year's records. Dallas has seven games against teams that made the playoffs last year, including three teams that advanced to the two conference championship games.

Still, the rebuilding process is well underway, and there is an optimistic breeze felt in the Cowboys camp. Landry says the team is not far away from being a playoff team again.

"We had a chance to win every game we played last year, but we lost quite a few tough ones," said Landry. "We just need to continue to do what we did last year, which was add good, young players and let them play.

"We're developing the personality of a physically tough and tough-minded team. As soon as these young guys learn how to win consistently, we'll be back in the playoffs."

TEX & TOM

Tom Landry (top) and Tex Schramm look back on 1987 . . . and ahead to the 1988 season.

QUESTION: Coach Landry said during the 1987 season that he signed a three-year contract because he thought it would take three years to get the team back to where it should be. Are you closer or farther away than you were a year ago to getting this team back to where you want it to be?

LANDRY: I think we made good progress last year as far as turning over some things that we had to turn over. We had a good draft, which was a key to it, with (Danny) Noonan and (Ron) Francis and (Jeff) Zimmerman. With a few of those early choices we were able to bolster not only the defense but some of the offense.

And we made major changes in the offense in the line with (Daryle) Smith and (Kevin) Gogan and really we swung over to a little bit more of a running offense with Herschel Walker featured.

They were all good changes. They were the first step. I wouldn't say we were further along than I thought we would be or whether we were behind. I think we are pretty much on schedule. This year's draft was a fairly critical one again. If we can come up with two or three players who can start for us or be ready for the retirements of people like Ed Jones or Randy White or Mike Hegman, then we will have made more progress.

SCHRAMM: I feel a lot better about us being closer to where we want to be. I feel we have helped ourselves in the last two or three drafts and feel very confident that this year's group could be very pivotal.

The loss of Mike Sherrard was a very difficult blow because it affected our entire focus on offense. We felt it was very important to have a strong deep passing game to complement Herschel Walker. Now we again have that with Michael Irvin and can only excitedly dream of the time when Sherrard and Irvin can line up together. I think we have the makings of a fine offensive team on the board. One that can be a strong playoff caliber.

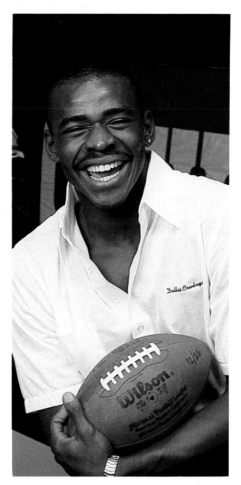

Michael Irvin is expected to electrify the offense.

However, you have to remember that a quarterback plays a very key role when you start playing the big games. And we still have to learn definitely whether we have the quarterback who can take us into that atmosphere and be successful in it.

QUESTION: Tom, do you have a quarterback on your roster who can get you deep in the playoffs and perhaps into the Super Bowl?

LANDRY: I think right now the unknown factor is Pelluer. Steve is a guy who was pushed into the arena too quick in 1986 with a new offense. We had a new passing game that year, predicated on a lot of experience and a lot of know-how.

Then, when Danny got hurt, Steve was pushed in prematurely. That will leave him with a stamp that he has to overcome. Anytime you lose as a quarterback, you

think it is your fault. I wouldn't blame him at all for what happened in 1986 because he wasn't ready for the offense. Now if he had been in our old offense at that time, he would have handled it much better.

That's why the last few games last year were so important to him. If he can start out with that kind of success this year, he has a chance to keep winning.

Of course, Danny always has that capability if he is healthy and ready to play. But that is an unknown factor. Kevin (Sweeney) is an interesting young man. The fans like him because of the replacement games. The guy does have some ability. He has an excellent arm and a good feel of the game. We are going to take a good look at him this summer.

One thing about quarterbacks is that you have to have one who can take you to the playoffs. If you don't, you are going to spend a lot of time going nowhere. So that's the key. Does he have the spark that can take you to the playoffs?

QUESTION: One of the goals last year was to see a return of the winning attitude which many felt was lost the year before. How important were the two season ending victories in that regard?

LANDRY: I believe the last two games were pretty significant to start a new year. It doesn't necessarily mean it is there. We lost a lot of games during the last two years from the midseason of 1986 through the strike year.

Those last two games were significant in that both clubs—the Rams and the Cardinals—really had a chance to get in the playoffs if they went out and won those games. Whether they took us lightly, I don't know. But I don't know how you can do that when you are trying to win a playoff berth.

Still, we won and we played solid and it gave us some encouragement in the (quarterback) Pelluer situation. He was able to go into those two games and win them after taking some earlier losses, not only the ones he had in 1986 but the couple of times we put him in during 1987. I think it will give Pelluer a little encouragement and that is important.

SCHRAMM: I think they could be a tremendous step because it showed that we have the capability of beating playoff teams when those playoff teams have a great deal at stake, as both the Rams and Cardinals did. It should encourage everybody from the standpoint that we have the personnel.

It's a matter now of going out and playing winning football.

QUESTION: Tom, during the offseason, have you said to yourself that if we can get better in this one particular area, the whole team will be clearly improved. And, if so, what area would that be?

LANDRY: I don't know that I have felt that way. What happened at the end of last year was that we played the type of game we need to play for a little while.

We had a low number of errors in those two wins. We had few interceptions, few traps, few fumbles. That is the kind of game we have to play. We can't beat ourselves. We had teams in the '70s that made mistakes and still won. We can't do that anymore. When we make mistakes, we are beaten.

To me, that is a significant thing. We must create that situation again to start off with. We set high goals for the last four or five games in the areas of traps and interceptions and penalties and we met those goals.

But back to the original question, if we could have had a healthy Danny White for the whole year in 1987, we would have been in the winning column. That, of course, is still a question mark. He seems to be throwing well, but we will have to wait and see how he does as time goes on.

QUESTION: Do you anticipate any hangover from the 1987 strike?

LANDRY: The strike was devastating for football. We played our first football game after the strike against Philadelphia and we couldn't have beaten SMU, even though they don't have a team.

That's as low as I've ever seen a team play a football game.

When you have that kind of a mental down, you don't get rid of it in a hurry. It took us several years to shake off the 1982 strike. We still don't have a contract. It has to come up again and again until it is settled. All those scars are going to be felt again any time you talk about a new contract.

SCHRAMM: I don't think there will be another strike. But there can still be distractions from the standpoint that there is a great possibility there will not be a bargaining agreement this year.

I don't think there will be a bargaining agreement because the union has apparently elected to choose the courts rather than the bargaining process. And when you talk about that process it can be a very long time. The last time this happened, in the mid-'70s, it took three years to settle.

Schramm hopes to avoid distractions this time out.

QUESTION: If someone without a great knowledge of football came along and asked you why you used to win all the time and now you don't, would you feel comfortable in simply telling them that you just don't have the players you used to? Or is it more complicated than that?

LANDRY: The key to the whole thing is the players and the draft. The purpose of the draft is to do exactly what it is doing to the teams of the '70s—teams like the Raiders and the Steelers and ourselves and Miami. It is making us struggle.

The young clubs like Denver, with John Elway, and Cleveland, with Bernie Kosar, have been able to draft key players along the way. The New York Giants are the best example. There was a team that was down for a long time and when they were able to get players like Lawrence Taylor they climbed to the top and won a Super Bowl.

The draft is the thing that does it. Washington is one of the exceptions. Washington has done a remarkable job to hold its club together after being high in the standings year after year. They've made some excellent moves. And Joe Gibbs has managed to get people who some people didn't think could play and they played well.

Still, if we had not had players like (Robert) Shaw and (Billy) Cannon see their careers end so quickly, and if we had had Mike Sherrard last year, it would have been a different story.

All of them would have been starting and playing well. Sherrard was a gem. If we had had him last year, who knows? We would probably have been over .500. But we need more than one player to get in the playoffs.

SCHRAMM: It's more complicated. I don't think that's the sole reason, but it's easy to lean on.

QUESTION: Are there other factors then, Tex, that you think have played a critical role over the last two years?

SCHRAMM: I just think we might be on the way to breaking an attitude that winning would just automatically happen. I think that attitude creeped into a lot of levels and perhaps subconsciously affected people's efforts.

One thing is certainly true. In the final analysis, you win with players and the player has to have the determination to beat the individual he is facing personally in addition to having a burning desire to be a winner.

QUESTION: Because it has become so difficult to stay on top in the NFL, do you think the 20-year streak of winning seasons may not be appreciated as much by the average fan as it should be.

LANDRY: Perhaps so. That streak, well, I don't know if it ever will be duplicated again. I don't know whether it can be accomplished. I doubt it. The Clint Murchison era was a unique one for the Cowboys. We worked within ourselves and Clint was the type of owner who took the pressure off everybody. He didn't put pressure on, he took it off. Therefore, you could do the things with confidence that you had to do to keep the team up.

Usually, teams panic long before they make the necessary changes they need to make. That's the nature of the beast, I guess. I haven't traced the Yankees and Celtics trend, but I would say they stayed at the top right on through. We struggled from time to time, but we could pull it out because of the confidence shown by Clint and management to correct those things.

SCHRAMM: I don't think it is recognized for the accomplishment that it is.

This was brought home to me when someone pointed out that when we were completing our 20th (winning) year that the closest team to us at that time was Miami.

If they had continued to have winning seasons, and they have since had a losing one, they would have broken the record in the year 2,000. That all of a sudden put in perspective to me what it would have meant if back in 1965 somebody said you will not have

a losing season until 1986.

It didn't come easy and like so many things that you accomplish, they may be put in perspective and recognized in later years. After two losing seasons, another 20-year streak would feel pretty good.

QUESTION: Tex, in addition to worrying about the product on the field, you have had to contend with a great many off-the-field league matters in recent years. The last two seasons couldn't have been too enjoyable for you.

SCHRAMM: It wouldn't be very hard to go along with that conclusion.

Many of the things I personally have been involved in aren't the most pleasant. The sale of the club and the death of Clint Murchison—who had been very important to the Cowboys and to me personally for many, many years from the beginning—and, obviously, the distraction of another league such as the USFL and the resulting lawsuits, and labor problems culminated by a somewhat bitter strike, and an obvious decline to our own success on the field, doesn't give you very much to smile over.

QUESTION: Tom, considering the difficult times the team has experienced the last few years, have you sensed that any of the fun has gone out of what you do?

LANDRY: I think right now the challenge is the thing that makes it interesting.

When you are trying to overcome a lot of odds, everybody is on the same page. When you go to the playoffs every year, it becomes harder and harder to get the players to recognize that they might not be in the playoffs. That's the only problem with winning every year. You assume you are going to go to the playoffs. There's nothing wrong with that, assuming you are good enough to go.

But the fact is you get kind of complacent in that area. Now there is no doubt for us we have to fight and scratch and do everything we can to get someplace. And I don't have any trouble doing that right

Landry looks forward to another coaching challenge.

now because the challenge is there every morning when you get up.

It's not like—let's wait and see where we end up in the playoffs. That's the trouble with having too many playoff teams like some of these sports to do. It's not hard for them to make the playoffs. For us, though, it's going to be tough. It's going to be tough to get over .500.

The schedule this year is harder than any I've seen in a long time and it couldn't come at a worse time. For the New York Giants to play the schedule they are playing and for us to play the one we're playing is kind of a mockery of the scheduling process. But that's the way it is.

If we had not won the last two games last year we would have been down there with an easier schedule. But I'd much rather have won those two games and had a harder schedule.

ANYTHING BUT ORDINARY

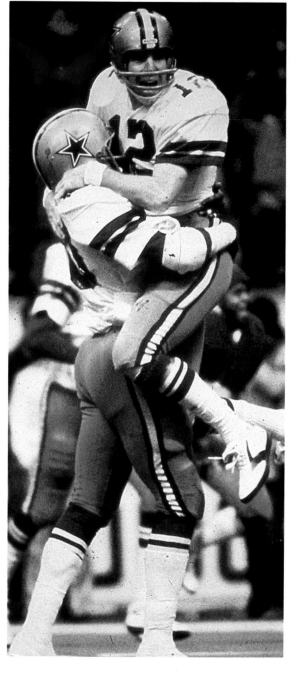

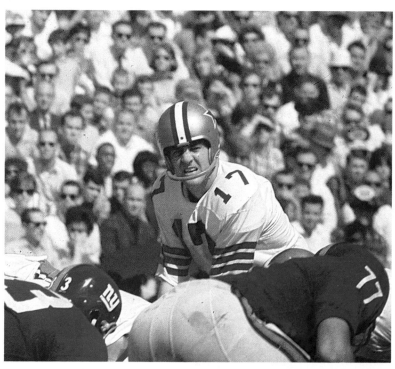

Roger Staubach (left), Don Meredith (top) and Danny White are three of the many great quarterbacks who have worn the Silver and Blue.

Nothing is easy about playing quarterback in the National Football League. There's the risk factor and the responsibility element. There's that playbook the size of a telephone book. And the expectation that the quarterback know precisely when each of his receivers will run a slant pattern toward the nearest concession stand. Next, the pressure to produce. That goes hand in hand with the ability to withstand blame.

Nobody said it was easy.

A glance through the pages of the storied history of the Dallas Cowboys reveals that there is nothing particularly *ordinary* about the different quarterbacks who have played for this team, either. An interesting collection, those Dallas Cowboys quarterbacks. A group prone to unpredictability. Each with a story of his own.

Remember the first one? Well, he was almost the first one, coming to Dallas figuring without a doubt that he'd be the quarterback for the baby franchise when it began play in 1960. Then there was the one who would sing in the huddle. There were also two who alternated, one of whom went on to become the king of comebacks. There was a rattlesnake hunter among the group, too. And who can forget the ultimate challenger? The history of Dallas Cowboys quarterbacks even includes one would-be signalcaller who wound up in an administrative position within the organization, and another who literally came out of the stands.

Don Heinrich was a top professional prospect when he graduated from the University of Washington in 1952. He had led the nation in passing twice, and was the holder of the NCAA record for pass completion percentage at the time. After leading Fort Ord to the service championship in 1953, Heinrich joined the New York Giants in 1954.

The six years in New York were frustrating for Heinrich, as the leading role he had been used to playing belonged to Charley

Meredith was on hand the first year, but didn't play a big role.

Connerly with the Giants. Following the 1959 season, Giants owner Wellington Mira asked Heinrich if he were interested in going to the league's newest franchise in Dallas.

Heinrich eagerly accepted the opportunity, as he would be reunited with former Giants teammate Tom Landry and be able to serve as player-coach. Also, he'd be the established No. 1 quarterback . . . finally.

In the spring of 1960, Heinrich helped Landry design the Dallas offense. At the time, the only other quarterback in town was a rookie from SMU, Don Meredith, who would later be known as Dandy Don. Heinrich knew that the kid quarterback had a solid future, but also figured that the job was his at least until Meredith developed further.

But just prior to the opening of the Cowboys' first training camp in

Eddie LeBaron came out of retirement and was the starter for most of the first season.

Forest Grove, Oregon, the Cowboys lured former Redskins quarterback Eddie LeBaron out of retirement. "Right then," Heinrich said, "I began to wonder just where I fit in."

LeBaron began the season as the starter, but Heinrich did see action throughout the course of the Cowboys' inaugural year. "It seemed to me," he said, "that the tougher the opponent was, the more I was called on to play.

"We were playing the Chicago Bears in Wrigley Field one Sunday and Eddie went down with an injury in the first quarter so I went in. We were working out of the Shotgun that day—only we called it the spread formation—because the Bears' rush was so good. Still, I got killed. Then killed some more. Late in the game I remember Doug Atkins breaking through for about the hundredth time. Instead of

really putting it to me as I threw the ball, he just ran on by, laughing. 'Man,' he said, 'you've been down enough for one day.'"

Heinrich had had enough for a career, retiring after the Cowboys' winless campaign. Looking back on his season with the Cowboys, Heinrich sees it a lot differently than he did at the time.

"I just went to Dallas expecting too much," he said. "I really didn't understand what they were trying to do there. At the time I was pretty upset, but, looking back, it makes more sense to me. The funny thing about it all is that even when I felt I was getting the short end of the stick I had a lot of respect for Landry and LeBaron. Both are good friends to this day.

"And Meredith, he was fun. I knew he was going to keep Tom guessing for a lot of years. I'll never

forget one morning in a quarterback meeting when Tom was giving us certain situations and asking what play we'd call. He dealt a lot of attention to Meredith since he was a rookie and had so much to learn. So he asked Don, 'If we're on the opposition's 20 and it's second-and-three, what are you going to do?'

"Don stood up and said, 'Well, I think I'd go to my five-iron and hope to hell I didn't hook it.' Landry turned red as a beet."

The Cowboys gave up a lot to land LeBaron, of most importance the No. 1 pick in the first draft they were to participate in. Dallas also dealt a sixth-round choice and even offered its first starting quarterback, who had earned his law degree at George Washington University, a position with the law firm Wynne and Wynne (Bedford

Don Heinrich, another veteran, was the backup to LeBaron in 1960.

Wynne was a minority owner in the team at the time).

"What it boiled down to was I was a big fan of Tom Landry and he was a great friend," LeBaron said of his decision to come out of retirement.

After a three-year stint with the Cowboys, though, LeBaron went to Reno, Nevada, where he began his career in law. Ironically, the former Cowboys quarterback worked with the father of then-future Cowboys quarterback Glenn Carano. And in one of the true "Ripley's Believe It Or Not" Cowboys stories, it was LeBaron who coached the Pop Warner team that Carano played on as a youngster.

LeBaron practiced law for several years before returning to the NFL, eventually becoming the general manager of the Atlanta Falcons. "One of the amazing things to me," he said, "is that I was out of football

for 13 years and when I came back and started looking around the league, there were the same people running the Dallas club who had been there in 1960 when I was with them. Tex Schramm, Tom Landry, Gil Brandt. That says a lot for the way they've run their business."

While LeBaron and Heinrich were counted on to provide the experience at quarterback during that first season, Don Meredith was to be brought along slowly. He played some, in Landry's shuttle system, and even started a game or two. But the offensive team was still LeBaron's to direct, and Meredith was Dallas' first "quarterback of the future." That's why the night before the season finale in Detroit, Meredith decided to make it a trip to remember. He partied until dawn. "In fact, by the time the sun came up, I wasn't

even feeling the cold anymore," he recalled a few years ago.

When he arrived at the stadium, Landry informed the former SMU All-America that he would make the start. Meredith, despite the need for a quick nap, became excited at the thought. Landry, though, had a change of heart, and decided to start LeBaron. He told Meredith to warm up on the sideline in case he wanted to make a switch. Three quarters later, Meredith was still warming up—and he literally had to. The temperature that afternoon was below freezing, a 17-mile-per-hour wind blew in and it snowed harder as the game progressed. In the fourth quarter, Landry told Meredith to start warming up again. Meredith refused.

"I didn't play any football that day," he said, "but I learned a couple of things. First, I found out that all-night partying is okay if you don't have to play a football game the next day. And it was on that afternoon that I first began to realize that Tom and I were going to really have a lot of fun together."

Meredith would later become famous for singing "The Party's Over" on *Monday Night Football* telecasts, but he was singing long before then. Teammates became used to Meredith singing a few choruses of "The Great Speckled Bird" in the huddle, before calling the play. A lock to make any all-character team, Meredith would not leave his persona off the field. He took his wit and humor with him everywhere.

For example, there was the preseason game against the Giants. With the Cowboys holding a 7–3 fourth-quarter lead, Meredith stepped to the line and noticed middle linebacker Sam Huff settled in the hole where the play was called. Meredith audibled. Huff moved to the spot where the next play was called. Meredith looked at Huff and said, "Aw, hell, Sam, get back over there where you're supposed to." Huff couldn't help from laughing. The play went for a first down.

Moreso than any quarterback

in the history of the club, Meredith played with pain. Knees. Shoulders. Ribs. Abdomen. Ankles. Concussions. No one ever questioned the man's courage. Don Cochren, who joined the Cowboys' training camp in 1965, remembers Meredith as a player who would always try to maintain his sense of humor, even in situations that were far from funny.

"I remember one time we were playing in Washington, and he picked up a max blitz," said Cochren. "Dan Reeves had slipped off on the left side, and was wide open on the sideline. So he lays a pass in the air, and Chris Hanburger comes in, and just as his arm is up in the air, Hanburger hits him right in the chest. He knocked him down and left him in a heap.

"Reeves scored the touchdown and Meredith is still laying out there. So I run out there, and he's on the ground going, 'Oh man, why did I do it? Why did I do it?' I thought maybe he had a concussion or something. So I get down there and whisper, 'Why'd did you do what, Dandy?' He said, 'Why did I ever leave Mount Vernon? Why didn't I stay home with Hazel?' The guy's out there in pain and the trainer's out there laughing. You just never knew what he was going to pull."

"Meredith was a wonderful personality," remembers veteran *Dallas Times Herald* columnist Frank Luksa. "One of those who was carefree. He didn't take football ultra-seriously, and I think that's where he and Landry never seemed to get on the same wave length. It's a very serious business to Tom, and to Don, it wasn't. If there was a flaw in his game and his personality, perhaps it was that lack of killer commitment."

Still, Meredith was Dallas' first superstar quarterback, leading the team from expansion to its NFL title game in 1966.

While Meredith established himself, several other quarterbacks made pit stops in Dallas, providing backup support. Among them, former Baylor star Buddy Humphrey (1961), ex-TCU standout Sonny Gibbs (1963), a second-round future pick of the Cowboys in 1962, and John Roach.

In 1964, Roach came out of the stands to play for the Cowboys. A former star at Highland Park High School and SMU, Roach returned to Dallas to pursue life after football after a six-year NFL career as a backup with the Chicago Cardinals and the Green Bay Packers. He had no thoughts of returning to the game, but was at the Cotton Bowl to watch the preseason game between the Cowboys and the

Playing with pain was a Meredith trademark.

Craig Morton was the only quarterback Dallas drafted in the first round.

Packers. The Packers stomped Dallas, 35–3, that afternoon. In the process, Meredith injured a knee. With LeBaron having retired after the '63 season, the Cowboys quarterback position could certainly be termed as shaky.

After the game, Roach bumped into Dallas receiver Buddy Dial. "John, we sure can use you," Dial suggested. Roach burst into laughter.

The following Tuesday, Tex Schramm called with the same suggestion, adding that Dallas had made arrangements with Green Bay to acquire the rights. Roach was not in football shape, but he was an insurance policy that the Cowboys had to take out.

The Cowboys' quarterback position became a bit more stable in 1965, after the drafting of California star Craig Morton. To this day, Morton is the only quarterback the Cowboys have drafted in the first round. The presence of the youngster, who threw a 56-yard touchdown to Bob Hayes on his first NFL pass, also provided fuel for the first major quarterback dilemma Landry would face with the Cowboys. Fans and media pushed for the young hopeful to replace Meredith, as the team had suffered through five straight losing seasons. But this call was one that belonged to Landry.

Reflecting recently on his career, Landry rated the decision as the most difficult one he has encountered, pertaining to the quarterback position.

"Meredith-Morton was the toughest because I didn't have very many people on my side," Landry said last December, while pondering another quarterback switch, Steve Pelluer for Danny White. "I remember it so well because the press conference we had was so similar to the one this week. Everyone was upset because they thought we weren't making the progress that we should have been. And everybody expected me to dump Meredith and go with Morton."

Landry made up his own mind, and later proved to make the right choice. The Cowboys advanced to the NFL title games in 1966 and 1967 behind Meredith.

"I thought Meredith at that time was the one we could win with because those were the years where we had our great drafts," he said. "When those players came in, Meredith was ready, and in '66 and '67, we had those great seasons with Meredith at quarterback."

Meredith suddenly retired after the Cowboys lost to Cleveland in the Eastern Conference final. The move was totally unexpected, as the 31-year-old was in the prime of his career and his skills had not deteriorated.

"It was a total shock," Landry remembered. "He didn't even come back on the plane."

"For some reason he had soured on the game," says Luksa. "It was no longer any fun for him. He apparently got no pleasure from it, so he decided to quit. Interestingly enough, though, after a year out of the game, he contacted Tex Schramm and inquired about coming back." The comeback never materialized, though, paving the way for the start of his most entertaining football analyst career.

"The hell of it was, the better we got, the more serious everybody became," he said. "Back when we were 1–11, everybody was singing. Everybody was loose. When we started putting it together and got to be 11–1, I looked around and realized I was the only one still singing."

Morton took over the reigns in 1969, leading Dallas to an 11-2-1 mark, and another Eastern Conference title game appearance. But a young quarterback drafted as a future pick in 1964, Roger Staubach, joined the club that year after honoring his commitment to the Navy.

The 1970 season began the second quarterback dilemma for Landry. As the '71 campaign got underway, that dilemma turned into a full-scale controversy. What the head coach decided to do was alternate the quarterbacks each series, stating that he had confidence in both of them. That experiment

Morton assumed a backup role when Staubach took over.

reached a peak in the seventh game of the season, when Landry alternated his quarterbacks on every play at Chicago.

"To me, alternating quarterbacks is still the ultimate," Landry says. "But quarterbacks just don't accept it because they feel like robots going in and out."

Staubach was named the starter after the Chicago game, and proceeded to spark the team to 10 straight victories, including the Cowboys' first Super Bowl title, a 24–3 win over Miami. Staubach was injured for much of the 1972 season, but came off the bench to spark an outstanding comeback in the divisional playoff game at San Francisco.

Morton played a backup role until he was traded to the Giants in 1974. He would reunite with many of his former teammates in Super Bowl XII, but by the time the 1978 game came around, Morton was a Denver Bronco. He is still the only quarterback to have led two different teams to the Super Bowl, having directed the Cowboys

offense during their first appearance following the '70 season.

The feats Staubach accomplished in the '70s remain among the proudest moments in franchise history. He earned the tag "Captain Comeback" while directing the Cowboys to 23 come-from-behind victories.

That Staubach actually played for the Cowboys is even more remarkable considering he was a bit unsure if his football ability would remain up to par during his commitment to the Navy. He had starred for the Academy and won a Heisman Trophy in 1963, but the layoff triggered the uncertainty he felt when he took a leave of absence to attend the Cowboys training camp in 1968. For the Cowboys, it was a good thing that Staubach set the camp on fire with his brilliance.

"I had been away from football for so long," Staubach remembered. "My last game was with the College All-Stars in '65. I wanted to use those couple of weeks of leave to find out about myself, what I could

Staubach became a legend—for the Cowboys and in the NFL. He won three NFL passing titles and a Super Bowl MVP Award—and made four Pro Bowl appearances.

still do. If I'd fallen on my face out there, it wouldn't have been the end of the world. I liked the Navy. My wife liked it. We had some great friends. Hey, I would have gone for the career."

In his 10-year career with the Cowboys, Staubach became a legend. His accomplishments on the field—which included three NFL passing titles, a Super Bowl MVP Award, four Pro Bowl appearances, various All-Pro selections and the clutch performances—speak for themselves. Off the field, the Staubach image was just as impressive. With a strong commitment to his Christian beliefs and to family values, Staubach was a hero to those in all segments of society. Underneath the clean-cut image, though, was a man with an acute sense of humor.

Sitting on the team bus after the Cowboys narrowly defeated the Eagles one afternoon, Staubach was informed that the key 33-yard third-down scramble he had was the longest of his career. Staubach

appeared blank. "Frankly," he said, "I was amazed that anyone was able to catch me. I don't know who it was who finally caught me, but he must be some fast dude. In fact, I wouldn't be surprised if the game films don't show that it was one of those illegal off-the-bench tackles or something."

One training camp story involves Staubach and center Tom Rafferty. To break Rafferty's habit of eating all of the mixed nuts he kept in his dormitory room, Staubach sprinkled dry dog food in with them. A few days later, Rafferty complained of a stomach ache. "Gosh, Tom," Roger said, "that's too bad. Maybe we'd better get you to the vet right away."

When Staubach announced his retirement on March 31, 1980, it marked the end of an era. It also provided Danny White, who rode the bench for four years behind Staubach, a chance to realize his goal of being the next Cowboys quarterback.

For White, it turned out to be a smooth transition, as he helped the

Cowboys to three straight NFC title game appearances in his first three years as the starter.

"The good thing was that it was my team," said White. "There was no question about it. It was a good situation because the coaches had a lot of confidence in me, the players displayed a lot of confidence in me. We just went out and won games. It was great.

"The thing I didn't enjoy about it was continually being asked if it was tough following in his footsteps. Because it wasn't something that I had even thought about. It was a non-issue as far as I was concerned, yet everywhere I went, that's what they all wanted to ask about. We'd go to St. Louis, New York or Minnesota, and that's all they wanted to ask about. What's it like following in Roger's footsteps? And I didn't have an answer. I got kind of tired trying to figure one out. So that part of it got kind of old, although I never grew tired talking about him."

The queries about the shadow of a legend were nothing in terms of

White had to hold off Gary Hogeboom's challenge . . .

pressure, compared to the White-Gary Hogeboom controversy that began after the NFC championship game in early 1983. Hogeboom, who was the up-and-coming quarterback, replaced an injured White in the title game at Washington and threw two third-quarter touchdown passes to put the Cowboys back in the game.

Although the Cowboys lost the game and Hogeboom threw two fourth-quarter interceptions, a controversy was born. Add to that White's role in the '82 strike (he was openly against the walkout) and a newspaper poll that indicated a majority of the players favored Hogeboom over White, and Landry had quite a mess on his hand. White retained his starting job in '83, but lost it to start the '84 season.

In what was one of the funniest incidents in recent club history,

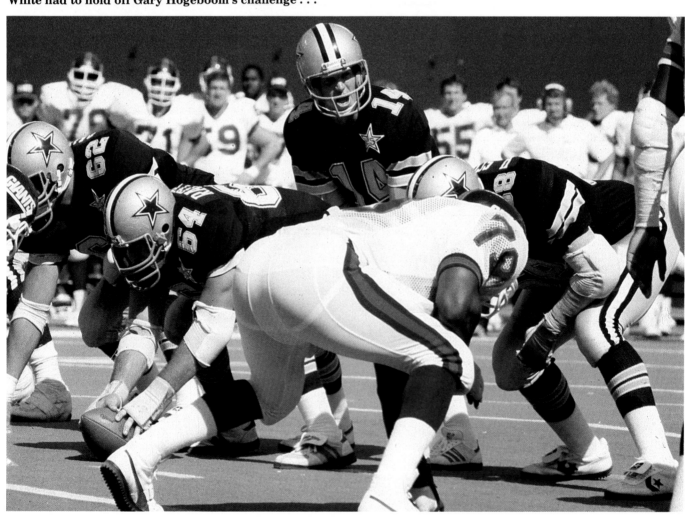

. . . as the up-and-coming quarterback battled to take over the No. 1 spot.

Landry—never one known to be great with names—announced the switch this way: "At quarterback, we're going to go with Pozderac." Landry meant Hogeboom, but was a bit ahead of himself. The 6–9, 285-pound Phil Pozderac would be in the lineup for the season opener . . . but at tackle.

"With the Hogeboom thing, I felt like the coaches had lost confidence in me," White recalled. His tour back to the bench didn't last long, though, as Hogeboom lost the job toward the end of the '84 slate, and was later traded to Indianapolis.

"You have to give him credit," Landry said of White, "because he fought back and won them (his teammates) back. And that's why Hogeboom went and he stayed."

There have been other, mild "controversies" of sorts over the years involving Cowboys quarterbacks. When Dan Reeves joined the Cowboys as a free agent from South Carolina in 1965, his hope was to continue to quarterback. But of several teams interested in signing him, only the Detroit Lions wanted him to play quarterback. Landry first envisioned Reeves as a safety, but running back wound up as Reeves' new position. He later became one of the most productive backs in club history.

"To this day, he probably still thinks he should have been a quarterback," Cowboys vice president for personnel Gil Brandt says of Reeves, who is now head coach of the Denver Broncos.

Reeves did get to play a bit of quarterback, spending the 1971 season listed as the No. 3 quarterback. It was a dream come true for Reeves. Late in a game against Philadelphia, Landry decided to let Reeves direct the offense. Reeves drove the team to the Eagles' 17-yard line before a penalty wiped out the drive.

"Looking back, I wish I'd been able to get us in the end zone on that drive," Reeves later said. "Shoot, if I had, people might never have heard of Roger Staubach."

Perhaps the most unique quarterback to play for the Cowboys

Now, Steve Pelluer is being counted on to spearhead the Cowboys' resurgence.

was Clint Longley. He earned the moniker "The Mad Bomber" after coming off the bench to fire a 50-yard touchdown pass in the final seconds to beat Washington on Thanksgiving Day in 1974. At the time, he was Dallas' future quarterback hope. Longley's stay in Dallas was short-lived, though, ending on a most ugly note. Twice in the final week of camp in 1975, Longley and Staubach commenced to delivering blows to each other. On the final day of camp, Longley ignored a meeting request with Landry and went to wait for Staubach in the training room. There, he hauled off on Staubach again before bumming a ride to the airport.

The once-promising future faded fast for Longley. But he did leave behind a unique distinction: he was the only Cowboys quarterback—the only Cowboys player ever—to hunt rattlesnakes. He claimed he and some friends once captured 230 snakes after locating a prize den. While with the Cowboys, he offered several teammates the opportunity to join him on a snake-hunting mission. None accepted.

"One time during the offseason," remembers Cochren, "he brought two sacks of rattlesnakes that he took and threw them out there on the practice field. It was a little cool, but it was a sunny day.

"After about an hour, he said he wanted to show me something. I went out there and there were about six rattlesnakes out on that field, with their rattles going, and I told him I had seen all that I wanted to see. He had another guys with him. After they left, (locker room attendant) Otis Jackson got the old lawn mower and mowed across there where they had been. He said he wasn't going to take any chances if they forgot one."

Since Longley's days, there have been others who have been labeled with the "quarterback of the future" tag. Glenn Carano was a fascinating, strong-armed prospect who joined the Cowboys as a second-round pick in 1977. He played with the Cowboys through the '83 season, but never seriously mounted a challenge to the starting positions held by Roger Staubach and Danny White. By the time he

Clint Longley had his day—but didn't stick around after decking Staubach.

left Dallas for the USFL, Carano was frustrated that he had played so long without starting. Carano's career ended shortly after his departure from the Cowboys.

Steve Pelluer, a fifth-round draft choice in 1984, must know what it feels like to be called a "quarterback of the future." After the trade that sent Hogeboom to Indianapolis in 1985, Pelluer stepped into the No. 2 spot, always within a crushing hit of having to take over the team's offense. Midway through the 1986 season, that "opportunity" became a reality. White fractured his right wrist against the Giants, forcing him to miss the second half of the season.

As he filled in for the next seven games, the man that Landry once said reminded him of himself because of his cool demeanor underwent an education so severe that he later admitted he lost much confidence. It took a while for Pelluer to regroup, but toward the end of last season, began to show signs that he was again ready to be Dallas' "quarterback of the future." He played virtually mistake-free football in leading the Cowboys to wins over the Rams and Cardinals in the season's final two weeks. He also gained a measure of confidence from the coaching staff, and entered the 1988 season as the man to beat for the starting job.

There are still a few other quarterbacks on the team's all-time list, their distinction being the little or no time they spent on the field. Brad Wright earned a job in 1982 as the clipboard-carrier, but unfortunately for him, it just happened to be a strike year. Two months after making the Cowboys as a free agent, Wright was waiting tables in a Mesquite restaurant to support his family.

Paul McDonald joined the Cowboys in 1986, as insurance after White's injury. The lefthander, who was the starter for Cleveland before Bernie Kosar arrived, was hailed upon arrival as an extremely intelligent type who would pick up the offense quickly. McDonald also made the squad in 1987. Through a year-and-a-half, though, McDonald never

Dan Werner, now director of the Cowboys' travel agency, even had a shot at quarterbacking the team in 1973.

played a single down during the regular season.

Such was the case for Bob Belden, a quarterback for the Cowboys in 1969–70. In fact, Belden never even started at Notre Dame. Many wondered why the Cowboys used a 12th-round pick on him. Belden's story was simple. He gave it his best shot to make it as a pro, but never made it.

Dan Werner's break from the game wasn't as clear-cut. After sitting the bench for the better part of his career at Michigan State, where he was unfortunately matched as a passing quarterback in an option offense, Werner was drafted by the Cowboys in the eighth round in 1973. Today, Werner is still with the Cowboys— as the director of the team's travel agency, having risen from scout to business manager to his current position.

Werner lasted about four weeks in camp in the first of two tryouts with the Cowboys. The New England Patriots then picked him up, and he spent three weeks in their camp. Next came a stop

as a film-grader in the Cowboys' scouting department. He soon quit that job and tried out for the World Football League's Houston franchise. Cut. In 1974, the NFL experienced a strike, and Werner was asked to try out with the Cowboys again. Cut. The Saints picked Werner up, and he lasted about four weeks before being released.

It was about that time that Werner met a career crossroads: to continue trying to play or to make a living some other way.

"I think five training camps with double sessions every day finally helps you along in that decision," Werner reflected recently. "But the unique experience for me was to be able to see four different, distinct operations. To see the personalities of the organizations as well as the coaches and players. That certainly contributes to a perspective going in."

As history proves, there really isn't anything easy or ordinary about being a Dallas Cowboys quarterback.

ADVICE FROM THE ELDERS

Elders for the defense: "Too Tall" Jones, Randy White and Mike Hegman.

Among the many benefits to be accrued by having played in the NFL for many seasons is for a veteran player to find himself in a position to share years of accumulated knowledge with those who are just beginning their careers.

While experiences gained on a personal level are invaluable for youthful players, so, too, are those acquired after listening to or watching the seasoned vets.

For some of the older Cowboys, the decision to counsel a junior teammate and offer some well-chosen words of advice on how to handle various situations is easy to handle. Other vets prefer to wait until they are questioned before providing their recommendations.

A longtime characteristic of cornerback Everson Walls' personality has been to openly relay his thoughts to players having considerably less than his seven seasons of NFL experience.

"I tried to give it (advice), even my first year," he says. "I remember when I was in college, I always tried to help guys because I didn't like the way upperclassmen treated the freshmen. I don't like the way the veterans treat the rookies. It's best to be treated with respect than to always be over a person or to order them around."

The Walls' technique has earned him long-lasting friendships, including that of New Orleans Saints' defensive back Bobby Johnson who had a free agent tryout with the Cowboys in 1982. "He calls me to this day, just praising me to death: 'Man, you were bad. You were this, you were that. I remember when you first talked to me.'

"I don't think anyone had ever approached him with such friendliness or openness," explains Walls. It surprised him. Now, he calls me to see how I'm doing."

The solid traits that Walls hopes to see displayed in youthful additions to the Cowboys roster starts with "a foundation," he hopes they've developed "as a solid person, overall." He encourages them to

Twelve-year veteran Danny White has gained valuable insight.

think of the team first, saying: "Selfishness has no place in a team game."

Being well-versed in the ups and downs of a 12-year career with the Cowboys, quarterback Danny White has a reservoir of guidelines to call upon. He is comfortable in talks to guys who are struggling or who are going through a difficult time. He tells them, 'Hey, this is just something that's temporary. You can overcome it. This isn't anything that's going to be a permanent type of setback.'"

When White joined the Cowboys as a 24-year-old—after two years of experience in the old World Football League—he became part of a team that had just participated in Super Bowl X. But, in the ensuing four seasons, he would gain valuable insight in learning how to handle adversity by observing Roger Staubach.

"He was right at the top of the

list of successful people that I've learned a great deal from. I watched him as he struggled," offers White. "He came a long ways and climbed a big mountain to get where he finally got in professional football. I'm convinced that his faith and his love for his family . . . those kinds of qualities enabled him to do it. He didn't have to say anything to me, it was obvious, written all over his face."

When center Tom Rafferty came to the Cowboys in the same year as White, he found a veteran offensive line that included tackles Rayfield Wright and Ralph Neely, guard Blaine Nye and center John Fitzgerald; a line that "set the pace" for the young players. Rafferty, who has tried to maintain that standard, was surrounded by vets who "were serious and didn't slough off, and all had to work hard to get where they were. They all studied real hard and were intelligent."

And no matter whether it's the grinding pace of training camps or the day-to-day headaches of practice, he finds that these are times when the older players need to step forward and set an example, "just to keep things going and make sure everything's snappy. It keeps you sharp and that's where leadership comes in, where the things everybody really doesn't want to do you've got to do to be a good football player."

Training camp is where vets get an intensified view of the rookies, and a time for Walls to develop a rapport with the would-be pros, often passing on a word or two of logic.

"We talk to a lot of younger players in camp. It's mostly talk about practice, sharing experiences that we've had with them on and off the field. And, depending on what their gripe is, I'll try to give them advice, accordingly. Mostly, it's just trying to portray to them what I did . . . the things that I have seen happen, the things that have happened to me, and try to get them to make up their own mind and own decisions."

Eventually, most of the wide-

eyed rookie defensive backs find time to observe Walls' style—not necessarily the wise thing to do, he cautions. "I think the curious thing about them is when the coaches tell them not to do what I do because they know my technique is all wrong. So, they watch me more out of curiosity than anything else.

"You don't really want to jump the gun with a guy. You want to make sure he's on the team before you start giving him advice on what to do as a Cowboy player."

Rafferty's primary advice for a young player is not to look for any substitutes to replace hard work and knowledge. His message is to "push it up a notch," no matter how hard the work load seemed in college. "You've got to be in better shape and be bigger and stronger."

It's always been Rafferty's manner of handling his job to carefully learn his assignments, always asking as many questions as possible. Then he is well-versed when unproven players look to him "to provide the solutions. I know that when we're out on the field guys look to me for answers, if they have questions and are uncertain."

Some questions about opponents' defenses have become increasingly more difficult for Rafferty to find concise answers to, no matter how many years he has been studying the same team. The changing nature of the defenses has resulted in "a different look every week. You have to be on your toes more than you used to be. In just the last few years they're going from containing to pressure defenses with a lot more blitzing.

"So," advises Rafferty, "you just have to be that much more prepared."

For a future NFL Hall of Famer like defensive tackle Randy White, it matters not at all that the youngster he takes under his wing today may take his job tomorrow. The nine-time All-Pro has "enjoyed helping guys out," in particular rookie Danny Noonan last year, "when he was in there playing with limited knowledge of what was going on but with a tremendous amount of ability. There's a lot of

"Too Tall" Jones (top) has a simple bit of advice: "Go hard on every play." Tom Rafferty says to put the emphasis on hard work and knowledge.

little things I can help him with."

The tips that White passes along become especially gratifying when "a guy really enjoys the game and enjoys playing. They want to learn," says White. "They want to be good and that makes it fun.

"The main thing is to work as hard as you can at conditioning . . . get as strong as you can, then learn as much as you can." By cutting through the chaff, White tells the young player that "you just go out there and play. I try and help anybody out with any knowledge that I have or experience that I can relate to help them."

Too much knowledge—as a beginning professional—can sometimes lead to an increased amount of "thinking," says White. "Then you have to work your way through that to where it just becomes your natural instincts, again. That's one of the toughest things, I think, for a young player.

"If you're going to be successful you've got to dedicate a lot of time and work into it. If you want to be good you've got to put the time in. You can't leave it," observes White. "It stays with you 24 hours a day. Basically, the guys who block and tackle the best and hustle . . . work together the best are going to be the ones who are going to be successful."

The challenge that 13-year veteran Ed "Too Tall" Jones issues the unseasoned Cowboys is "to go hard on every play, all the time, regardless of mistakes and that way you'll never hear anything negative from coaches or anyone else. Also, no matter what happens, you've got to remember not to get too discouraged."

While a healthy supply of intensity has highlighted his unforgettable career with the Cowboys, Jones, who has yet to miss an NFL game, attaches great significance to the importance of "studying and staying in the best shape possible," adding, "I've seen too many players around the league who get hurt not being prepared."

As Mike Hegman enters his thirteenth and final season with the Cowboys, he cannot forget some

Everson Walls offered advice even in his first year.

early advice he received from fellow linebacker D.D. Lewis. The only problem with that came when Hegman didn't know if Lewis was "serious" or not. "He used to kid me all the time, but also helped me a whole lot when I was coming up."

One area that Hegman sees as warranting some counseling is the impatience that often results from not becoming a starter soon enough. "I tell them that I went through the same thing for three years and I just say: 'Your time will come.' Mostly I had to do that with Jesse (Penn). I could see how Jesse was when I was young.

"I used to get upset . . . just go crazy," notes Hegman. "I used to worry coach (Jerry) Tubbs to death and I can see that happening now to (Steve) DeOssie and Jesse. They've (Cowboys) got a good group . . . the best group I've seen. A couple years from now they might have one of the best linebacker groups in the league."

Anytime Rafferty sees a talented young player join the Cowboys with immediate starting aspirations, he welcomes it.

"If a young guy comes in and has enough confidence to think he can play, I think that's good. Guys like

that usually have a lot of good traits. It's tough to come in and play in your first year," says Rafferty, a starter since his second season. "I really don't say anything to the young guys about starting and playing. I think most of the guys are more concerned about making the team."

As the calendar has ticked off 12 seasons in a Dallas uniform for Danny White, one of the aspects of being a player that has pleased him the most is to have earned the respect of his teammates. "One of the gratifying things happens when you've been in the league for a long time and players look up to you. We've got a lot of young players on this team who are eager to learn."

It's the type of willingness that Hegman displayed a dozen years ago and is "now seeing the same thing in reverse. When they (today's young Cowboys) get older, they'll see the same thing."

"One piece of advice that was given to me," says Danny White, "when I was very young and has always been important as I've dealt with different situations . . . unexpected things, is really advice for life rather than just as a football player. It's that you need to keep your priorities in line and try to maintain a balance in your life.

"By that, I mean, don't get too caught up in striving for the wrong kind of success—temporal success. If you maintain a balance between that and things that are permanent—your family, your friends—then it seems like the disappointments go away a lot quicker and don't affect you quite as much.

"Throughout my life, there have been circumstances that I could not have dealt with if it hadn't been for the fact that I'd put so much emphasis on my family," says White.

The ongoing process of veteran Cowboys giving advice to their youthful counterparts represents "a chance"—as Walls terms it—for them "to go further in life than a person with a hard head and stopped-up ears."

YOUTH MUST
BE SERVED

Ron Burton symbolized the emphasis on youth during the 1987 season.

Tom Landry loathes the word. He'll go through all manner of verbal gymnastics to avoid its use.

It's the "R" word. As in Rebuilding. As in the Cowboys' current project, which they hope will end with a return, if not to the playoffs, then at least to a break-even posture.

For 20 years the Dallas Cowboys never had a losing season, an unprecedented NFL run. Whenever a key starter was ready to ride off into retirement, a young player was poised to step in.

Rebuild was a dirty word because it carried the stigma of failure. To rebuild, you first must strike bottom.

Then came the early '80s when the Cowboys' draft well began to dry up. Bad decisions and bad luck left the Cowboys without that young pool of potential starters that they once drew upon.

Then, late last season came a glimmer of hope. The Cowboys were among the NFL's strongest regular-season finishers of 1987, shoving two teams on the verge of a playoff berth into oblivion on the final two weekends.

And the Rams and Cardinals were dispatched with a decided Dallas accent on youth.

"We probably finished last year with more young guys playing than ever before," Landry said. "I can't remember winning a couple of games with that many young players on the field. That's encouraging."

Landry sets sights on a modest goal: a .500 season. Coming off the Cowboys' first back-to-back losing seasons since 1963–64, that is well within their grasp despite a demanding schedule.

The kids will lead them.

"We had a chance last year to win every game," Landry said. "We just need to continue doing what we did last year, which was to add good, young players and let them play. We're developing the personality of a physically tough and tough-minded team. As soon as these young guys learn how to win

Burton made his big impact during the final three games.

consistently, we'll be back in the playoffs."

Tick off the names of the aging Cowboys superstars: Danny White enters his 13th season; Randy White's in his 14th year; Ed Jones starts his 14th year.

All will assume different roles this season as younger players begin to take over.

Thus, further improvement will hinge on the development of youngsters like cornerback Ron Francis; offensive linemen Kevin Gogan, Jeff Zimmerman and Daryle Smith; wide receivers Kelvin Edwards and Kelvin Martin; defensive linemen Danny Noonan and Kevin Brooks; safeties Victor Scott and Vince Albritton; and, from the guy who symbolized last year's youth movement, linebacker Ron Burton.

"We have to mature, especially on offense where we have so many young players," Landry said. "And we need to strengthen our defense. We have enough good, young players on offense now that we should score points if they continue to develop as expected.

"On defense we need a stronger pass rush and we need more depth,

so that when older players like Randy White, Ed Jones and Mike Hegman are ready to step down, we'll have quality replacements for them."

Let's take a more detailed look at a few of the new faces who have emerged as future Cowboys stars.

Ron Burton certainly made an impression at the end of last season.

Ron Brown of the Rams remembers. Burton nailed Brown twice with such a fury that Brown eventually decided to retire and return to the track circuit.

George Rogers of the Redskins remembers. So does the Cardinals' Stump Mitchell.

Burton may have played extensively at middle linebacker in only the final three games last season (starting two of them), but he made enough big hits to become a major part of the Cowboys' highlight film.

So who is this studious-looking fellow often mistaken for Chicago Bears' Pro Bowler Mike Singletary?

Burton began to draw attention almost as soon as he arrived at training camp in the summer of '87. One of a battalion of rookie free agents, Burton made a fast impression as a young man who knew how to deliver a blow.

"The main reason I like to play the game is because I like to hit," Burton said. "When I get out on that field, I change. I really run my mouth, talking to my opponent. It's a totally different me."

Wearing a polo shirt and jeans, Burton hardly fits the role of a thug. He's friendly, quiet and religious.

But after you study his face, you stop at the neck. And what a neck!

"I guess that's another reason people sometimes think I'm Mike Singletary, other than the fact that we wear the same glasses," Burton said. "People look at this guy with this neck. The neck really shows up.

"It's a compliment (the Singletary comparison), I guess because of the hitting aspect and that we're the same size. But right now I'm just trying to be Ron Burton."

And there's nothing at all wrong with that. Starting middle linebacker Eugene Lockhart still owns the reputation as the biggest hitter on the Cowboys defense, but Burton is closing fast.

"When he's playing he's got that funny look in his eyes that Singletary does," said Cowboys scout John Wooten, who signed Burton. "I call it wildness, for lack of a better word. You look at his eyes, then look at film clips of Singletary as he's about to make a hit, and it's that same look."

Burton's had that hitting ability since he was in high school at Highland Springs, Va., a Richmond suburb.

"He was always a competitor, right from when he was a 138-pound freshman," said Highland Springs coach Rudy Ward. "It was always life and death. By the time he was a senior, he was easily the dominant player on the field.

"His senior year he played fullback and defensive end. We made the state semifinals against Hampton but he sprained a knee and was out for the game. It was like losing our two best players and our chances went out the window."

The competitive fires always burned deep in Burton's gizzard.

Baseball was his first love. He started as a Little League power-hitting catcher and stayed with baseball for seven years.

He wrestled in the seventh and eighth grades. He was on the high school track team. He played basketball until his senior year, a rebounder who enjoyed the physical contact of rebounding.

And, of course, there was football.

"I had to work at it but sports came pretty easy to me," Burton said. "I was able to compete with guys older than me, below me, around me. My younger brother Tony and I were always playing some sport and we played against one another a lot."

Burton grew to 220 pounds and blossomed as a player by the time he was a senior. When the Highland Springs offense had trouble moving the ball, Burton was moved from tight end to fullback. Suddenly, the offense was putting up 30 points per game.

Burton made every local, area and state all-star team. Several college recruiters showed interests but the offers weren't pouring in either.

The University of North Carolina recognized something in Burton that the other schools did not see and Burton was off to Chapel Hill the next fall.

Burton's impact was far from immediate. He was redshirted, then tore a major shoulder muscle while bench-pressing 370 pounds in the spring of 1983, forcing him to miss the entire '83 season.

After regaining his health, Burton was switched from outside linebacker to defensive end prior to his senior year. Previous questions about his stamina and consistency were soon laid to rest as Burton led the Tar Heels with eight sacks and was named the team's outstanding defensive player.

NFL scouts began to notice. One play in particular stayed with Wooten.

During a game against Maryland, Burton crossed the width of the field in pursuit of Terrapin quarterback Dan Henning, Jr. Burton stalked

Ron Francis left Baylor . . .

Henning and finally caught his man, bouncing him head-first in front of the Maryland bench.

"It was like Lilly chasing Griese in the Super Bowl," Wooten said. "That's what I saw that made me like him."

Other scouts also liked Burton, but they liked a lot of other guys more. On draft day Burton's name was never called. The Steelers flew him to Pittsburgh the next day and attempted to keep him away from the phone while they tried to persuade him to sign a free agent contract.

But Burton was not sold on the Steelers and returned to Chapel Hill. Wooten called and gave his pitch. Linebacker coach Jerry Tubbs also called.

The Cowboys and Raiders were the finalists for Burton's services and Burton picked Dallas based on a larger signing bonus and a better opportunity to make the team.

Landry soon became aware of

. . . and became a starter for the Cowboys in his first season.

Burton because of his productive special teams play. Then Burton received his opportunity when Eugene Lockhart went down for the season with a broken fibula.

In his first start at middle linebacker, a narrow loss to the Redskins, Burton distinguished himself with two jarring hits on Rogers.

Burton twice flattened Brown in the Monday night victory over the Rams as the Cowboys knocked them out of the playoffs.

"Brown was really slow from that point on," Burton said. "I think he'll remember who I am."

Burton continued his flashy play against the Cardinals, helping eliminate them from the playoffs.

"Those teams came in on a roll," Burton said. "The young guys who played in those last three games showed some enthusiasm and that coupled with the experience of the older guys really riled everybody up. Everson Walls said that the

enthusiasm really rubbed off. Those last two games saved the season for us."

Burton set offseason sights on claiming a full-time job. With Lockhart's return to the middle, Burton moves to the outside. Although his size (6–1, 245) isn't ideal, there's no measuring his heart.

"He's not tall and lean like a lot of outside linebackers," Landry said, "but he's fast enough to play out there and he's a football player."

Wooten sees more and more Burtons joining the Cowboys as the team's personnel philosophy leans more heavily toward the competitive player rather than the super-athlete.

"Our system as we've known it would spit this kid out because his measurables didn't show that well," Wooten said. "But the NFL has become a kick-butt league. Our division is a very physical one. If we're going to get back in the hunt and compete with the physical teams like the Redskins, Giants and Eagles, we're going to do it with the Burtons."

The Cowboys will also do it with guys like Kelvin Edwards, a hungry player who was on the rebound when he joined the Cowboys during the player's strike of 1987.

Edwards, released by the Saints a few weeks earlier, quickly distinguished himself as one of the stars of the Cowboys replacement team. Hooking up with rookie quarterback Kevin Sweeney, Edwards was for a month the team's principal offensive threat.

When the strike ended, Edwards did not fade into oblivion as was the case with many of the productive strike-breakers. The rookie from Liberty Baptist remained and finished the season tied for fourth on the team in receptions.

Now he holds a solid position in the Cowboys' future. With Mike Sherrard out for a second season with recurring leg problems, Edwards is the starter at wideout.

Without Sherrard, Edwards figures on double-team attention from opposing defenses. But, he says, that doesn't matter. Let's give

this guy high marks for moxie.

"My goal is to lead the league in several categories this year," Edwards said. "I eventually want to be the number one receiver in the NFL."

To that end, he'll feel a lot more comfortable this season.

"Last year, right after the strike, I was trying too hard to make things happen," Edwards said. "Then toward the end ef the season I felt like I started to put things together like I needed to.

"Overall it wasn't a real good season for me. But it is something I can study and see what I did wrong. This year I think I can do the things that the team needs for me to do to help them on the field."

Without Sherrard, Edwards knows his job will be more difficult. But Sherrard re-injured his leg while jogging during the offseason, placing his career in jeopardy.

"I was looking forward to a good season with Mike," Edwards said. "If they had doubled up on him, it would have left me open and the same goes for him if they tried to double team me. I don't think they would have been able to stop us no matter what they did."

In New Orleans, stopping Edwards was no problem. That's because he rarely left the bench. He caught 10 passes in 1986 and the Saints made it abundantly clear he didn't fit into their long-range plans.

"That's past business," Edwards said. "I really wasn't unhappy that the Saints released me. I asked them to. I played very little at New Orleans and I wasn't used to that. In college and high school, I was used to the ball coming my way all the time.

"I felt like I would have a better chance somewhere else, and it was a business decision they had to make. I think I showed I can play, and they went on to have a great season. So I think it worked out best for both parties."

Having an entire offseason to work with quarterbacks Steve Pelluer, Danny White and Sweeney, Edwards entered the season brimming with confidence.

"I believe we can be the winning team Dallas has had in the past," Edwards said. "We just have to put our minds to it and go out and get the job done."

Ron Francis did just that in 1987, although not without several harrowing moments.

A rookie cornerback playing opposite former All-Pro Everson Walls, Francis knew he'd be treated by opposing quarterbacks as if he had a large red bull's-eye painted on his back.

Francis became the starter in training camp when Ron Fellows was dealt to the Raiders.

He was immediately placed under a microscope. While most teams play zone coverage, Cowboys corners must play man-to-man, often with no help from the safeties.

Walls has stood in Francis' shoes. As a rookie starter in 1981, Walls met the challenge head-on, leading the league in interceptions his first two seasons.

"It's tough," Walls said. "You're out there alone in front of all those

people. But that's not the thing you fear most. I worry most about what Tom (Landry) is going to say in front of everyone when we review the game films."

The pressure did not surprise Francis. He knew such treatment is standard for rookie cornerbacks.

"I knew they would be picking on me," he said. "I just try not to think about it. If they came my way, I just tried to do the best I could."

Francis survived a similar experience his junior year at Baylor, when he was switched from running

Kelvin Edwards joined the Cowboys during the strike—and was an instant success.

Burton (top) and Edwards could help make this rebuilding process go quickly.

back to cornerback. The word spread quickly through the Southwest Conference that the Bears had an easy mark on the corner. His senior season, Francis was SWC Defensive Player of the Year.

"My senior year they didn't come at me quite as much," he said. "When you make a few plays, it gets their attention."

Francis is quiet, almost disturbingly so. Walls says that's an ideal temperment for an NFL corner.

Francis isn't saying. That's part of the mystique.

"You could put Francis and Too Tall Jones in the same room for an hour and they probably wouldn't say 10 words," said secondary coach Dick Nolan. "Boy, is he quiet. But if something bothers him, you never know it. That's a great personality for a corner."

"It's scary sometimes, but that's part of the job of being a cornerback," he said. "Sometimes it seems like the world is against you. Everybody sees what you do. I like that."

"Nothing really seems to bother Francis," Walls said. "He takes things in stride and bounces back well. That's a good defensive back mentality. Emotion can hurt you out there if you get so keyed up you forget what your responsibilities are. Sometimes you're out there on your own."

Walls was free with his advice last season. He remembered his rookie season when veteran Charlie Waters took the raw free agent under his wing. Waters was so impressed with Walls' ability to make big plays that he swore the kid was from Mars.

"Charlie helped me a lot," Walls said. "Our lockers were close to each other and he gave me a lot of support. He got me not to worry about some of the bad plays I made. I offer advice to Francis. He just takes it, then goes about his business.

"He marches to a different beat, I'll say that. I just don't know what affects him."

HERSCHEL WALKER

DALLAS COWBOYS CHEERLEADERS

The 1988–89 season marks the seventeenth year of the Dallas Cowboys Cheerleaders. What began in 1972 with seven cheerleaders has become a one-of-a-kind American phenomenon that personifies class and professionalism.

Much like the football team they proudly support, the Dallas Cowboys Cheerleaders feature veterans training rookies who will someday take their place.

Initially, the dream is wearing the famous uniform and cheering at Cowboys home games. The dream enlarges once they become an actual participant and are afforded so many opportunities to broaden their lives.

The benefits include growth, sharing and learning as they are given a chance to travel and learn about people from all walks of life. Their perspective is expanded and a new thirst for adventure takes over. The young women develop a new understanding about themselves and the world they live in. It's a feeling that will accompany them for the rest of their lives.

The Dallas Cowboys Cheerleaders bring happiness to handicapped children on telethons across the country and to others on visits to nursing homes and hospitals. To make this kind of difference in the world is an opportunity few are given. These young women blossom as they gain poise and self-confidence by giving joy to others.

In a healthy, controlled

environment, they learn to work hard toward common goals and clarify personal goals just by being a part of this most unusual team.

It's an exciting time for the Dallas Cowboys Cheerleaders when preseason begins. The wondrous, exhilarating feelings of a rookie entering Texas Stadium for the first time are appreciated by the veterans who understand just what it means to be a part of the greatest cheerleader squad in America.

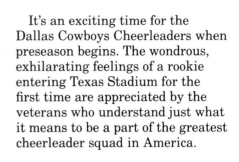

The Dallas Cowboys Cheerleaders have entertained U.S. military personnel throughout the world: Korea, Turkey, Beirut, Greece, Iceland, Greenland, Japan, Diego Garcia, West Germany and the U.S. Navy fleets in the Indian Ocean.

It's been seventeen years since the cheerleaders were formed. Special memories remain of the people they have met in nursing homes, veterans hospitals and Variety Club telethons.

PHOTOGRAPHER CREDITS
Ron St. Angelo
Robert Srenco
Randy Reinink, U.S. Army

WORKING OVERTIME

At the "Superstars" competition, Danny Noonan was in his element lifting weights.

For the most part, the setting on the north side of the Dallas Cowboys headquarters is all natural. There are trees, hills, insects, a narrow creek, and a peaceful seclusiveness that envelopes the surroundings. There are no distractions. Other buildings, traffic and curious onlookers are, by design, at a distance. Such is the view from the outdoor training facility at the Cowboys' home.

Hours earlier, the scene was completely different, noisy and taken over by Cowboys players who were participating in their offseason conditioning programs. But as the dinner hour winds down, there is hardly a soul on the premises. Still, there is a rhythmic sound that pierces through the quietness. Clank. Clank. Clank.

The weight room serves as an office, so to speak, for Danny Noonan, the massive tackle who was the Cowboys' No. 1 pick in 1987, and a man who is no stranger to these settings. Tonight, in the fashion of an overworked executive, he is putting in overtime. The rhythm is the result of Noonan's repetitions during a weightlifting exercise. There are grunts and groans that accompany each push.

It is Noonan's second visit of the day, but if you ask coaches, teammates or even the security guards who man the facility, there is nothing unusual about Noonan's after-hours presence in the weight training area.

At Nebraska, Noonan practically lived in the weight room. He is somewhat of a legend in Lincoln, and a model of sorts, when it comes to dedication in the weight room. He was known to have spent hours lifting after Nebraska games, despite wearing game-day bruises and being worn down mentally and physically. He pushed for the Nebraska weight room to be opened on weekends. In Dallas, he has already developed a reputation, too, as that same, restless, tireless worker from Lincoln who seems to breathe, eat and sleep weights. When the Cowboys called to inform Noonan that he was the 12th pick

overall in last year's draft, he was in the Nebraska weight room. In other words, he is a conditioning coach's dream.

"He works out so much," said one teammate, "I don't know how he does it. I just wonder if he ever gets sore. If he does, he never shows it."

"Yeah, I still get sore," Noonan said. "The more you work out, the less you get sore. But they have that old saying, no pain, no gain."

Noonan has gained plenty. When he entered the University of Nebraska as a freshman, he weighed all of 215 pounds. A couple of seasons earlier, he struggled to make 200. He realized at a young age that if Danny Noonan was to accomplish his goals of securing a

scholarship to play at Nebraska and then go on to become a pro football player, he would need the strength and the bulk. So he habitually labored in the weight room. Now that he has reached many of the goals that kept him motivated through high school and college, he remains driven.

Danny Noonan has a fear. It is not a nightmarish dream that haunts him, rather a reality that rests in the back of his mind. The fear is that he could someday wake up and be a 215-pounder again.

"I've always been thin," said Noonan, a man who now has a 21-inch neck, "even in high school. When I graduated I was about 215. So I've always had a fast

No. 1 draft pick Noonan was a lightweight as a college freshman.

If the Dallas Cowboys are to return to status among the upper echelon of NFL teams, they will do so because of players like Noonan.

metabolism. To this day, if I don't eat six meals a day . . ."

Hold it. *Six* meals per day?

"At least. People think I sit down and eat three hamburgers at each sitting. I don't eat like that. I may eat a hamburger every once in a while. But I eat every two or three hours. If I don't eat like that, I'll drop weight. I could be weighing . . . by the start of camp I could be weighing 225. I guarantee it. If I didn't work out, if I didn't eat like I normally do, I could weigh two-and-a-quarter."

"He's probably overplaying it with that estimate," says Cowboys conditioning coach Bob Ward. "To lose 50 pounds would be something. When he gets done playing football he probably could, but I don't know if he could lose that much in two or three months."

Noonan will take no chances, though, when it comes to his Charles Atlas-type body. "Different guys are different. Some guys can work out four days a week and still not overtrain. I like to work out six days a week. If I'm doing it right, I'm not going to burn out. And if I am run down or something, maybe I'll cut out a workout. I can pretty much tell."

Ward says the 6–4, 270-pound Noonan possesses all of the physical

qualities needed to succeed in a sport where so much is dependent on power and speed. In fact, Ward says the strength of Noonan—who bench pressed 500 pounds coming out of college—is awesome.

"His major weakness is his strength," said Ward. "That sounds foolish, but it's not. Because once you lose your strength, you have to rely on other qualities. If you don't develop the finer qualities of movement, which he needs to develop, I consider it a weakness. I think he needs to work on being soft."

The man is anything but soft. Sculptured may be the best descriptive word for Noonan. Ward's use of "soft" is not derogatory, though. To him, the usage means, "using somebody else's strength instead of your own. He can drive almost anybody back off the ball with his strength. He just needs to work on finesse."

Agreed. Noonan says the realization that he needs to be a better finesse player is among the chief lessons he learned during his rookie year with the Cowboys. He lists improving the finesse aspect of his game as one of his top priorities this year.

"What I learned last year?

Probably that I couldn't play like I did in college. In college, I just kind of ran over people. In the pros, it's a lot tougher to run over guys. It's a lot tougher to bull rush people and try and put them on their back. What I've got to do this year . . . what I've been working on, is using finesse. To try and give a head fake or something, instead of just trying to run over my opponent.

"If I mix that up, maybe one time bull rush him, then the next time use some type of finesse move, it will help me tremendously this year, especially as far as pass-rushing goes. Playing at Nebraska, we pretty much played running teams. So to become a better finesse player will no doubt help my pass rush."

If the Dallas Cowboys are to return to status among the upper echelon of NFL teams, they will do so because of players like Noonan—energetic young talents with a true love for winning. Aligned at the right tackle spot next to fourth-year man Kevin Brooks, Noonan looked extremely capable of being the heir to Randy White's right tackle position, when he was able to play toward the end of last season. Partly because of Noonan's potential (and also because of age and nagging injuries to White), coaches have been preparing to move White to a pass-rushing role on the defense. That could free up the right tackle spot for Noonan to claim as solely his.

In Noonan and Brooks, the Cowboys probably have the players who will anchor the defensive line for years. At least that is the hope. As for Noonan's part, there seems to be little doubt from those who watched him in his first year that he is the right man for the job. He may indeed, as one newspaper writer suggested, be the second coming of Randy White.

"You watch Noonan," White, a nine-time All-Pro, said late last season. "Noonan is a helluva player. In the 13 years I've been in this league, he's without a doubt as good as any young player I've seen."

While it might be expected that an aging vet would bristle when the thought of who will replace him is forwarded, such is not the case with White, as applied to Noonan. He genuinely looks excited when talking about Noonan, and does not

hold back encouraging words.

"Hey, time catches up with everybody," White said of the transition taking place at right tackle. "When you've got a guy like Danny who can make things happen, you get him out there."

Noonan will be the first to tell you that his second year in pro ball will be almost as beneficial as his first, in terms of what he will learn. For starters, he will attend his first pro training camp. Last year, Noonan held out of camp for 43 days, while his agent worked out the matter of a four-year, $1.7 million contract. In his absence, he may have become the first Cowboys rookie to earn a nickname before playing a single snap in camp.

Teammates-to-be called him Danny "No-No" Noonan. Each time, the story goes, one would ask if the No. 1 pick was coming in on any given day, the response would be, "No, no Noonan." By the time Noonan did join the team, they were back from Thousand Oaks, preparing for the preseason finale,

and the season opener against the Cardinals. A couple of months before the start of this year's session at Camp Landry, though, Noonan was looking at the month-long stint with optimism.

"It's not going to be as hard on me this year," Noonan predicted. "If I had gone to camp as a rookie, not knowing anybody, not knowing the system, then right there it would have been tough. This year, I know everybody and I know the system. So it's going to be easier."

Still, the '88 season will be similar to a rookie season for Noonan when considering the disappointing elements of his real rookie season. First, the holdout. Then, he played in just one game, where he saw limited action before a 24-day players' strike. Next, there was a position switch from end to his more natural tackle spot. By the time it was over, Noonan and Cowboys coaches were just trying to salvage as much time and experience as they could for the player Tom Landry had projected as a starter on draft day. So Noonan had a few things to put behind him, before settling in with his new surroundings.

Having recently purchased a house in Coppell, Noonan is already making major strides toward settling in his new area. "I feel like I'm settling into Dallas, getting to know the city. I'm enjoying it a lot more. Right after I signed, my rookie year, a lot of things happened really quick. So now I'm just kind of settling down."

Becoming more settled in the flex defense is the primary individual goal the 23-year-old Noonan hopes to accomplish this season. He admits that it is tougher for him to play on a four-man front, having spent his four years at Nebraska as the noseguard in a 3–4 defense. But he understands the basic concept of the flex, and figures he fits in well within the scheme.

"I like the flex," he said. "I still don't know the finer points of the flex. But there's not very many people around here who do. You ask people what the flex is, and nobody

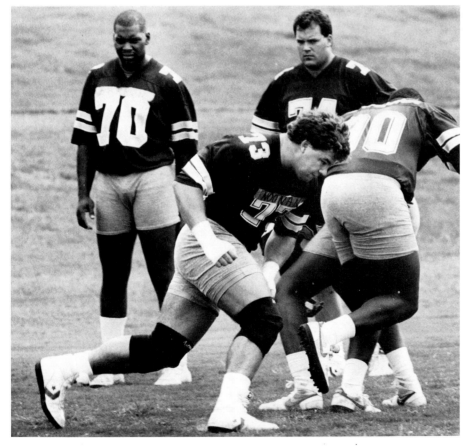

After mini-camp, Noonan became "no-no" when contract talks slowed.

At Nebraska, Noonan got used to winning.

really knows. I thought I picked it up pretty well last year. Randy really helped me out a lot.

Still, Noonan admits that the adjustment he is undergoing takes time. "I liked the nose better, but I feel I can play tackle pretty well, too. It's different at tackle, but I feel comfortable there, too. You're farther off the ball at tackle. And your opposing lineman is farther off. The guard is back two or three yards, whereas if you're over the center, you're right up on top of him and can get off the ball a little quicker. So that's different. Plus, in some of our defenses I'm backing off of the ball. Sometimes I'm maybe five yards away from the ball. So it's a little different for me, but I get more relaxed at tackle the more I play it."

When Noonan was a star at Lincoln Northeast High School, leading his team to the state championship game in 1982, the Dallas Cowboys were still among the premier teams in the league,

and a perennial playoff participant. He remembers watching and being impressed with a Dallas line that included current teammates White and Ed Jones, and since-retired John Dutton and Harvey Martin. While Noonan, who grew up just six miles from the University of Nebraska campus, joined the Cornhuskers' powerhouse program, though, the Cowboys began declining. By the time Noonan was drafted with the team's highest pick at the time since the second overall choice used on Tony Dorsett in 1977, the Cowboys had finished two of their last three seasons without a playoff berth. When Noonan's rookie year had ended, it was three of four, and two straight losing seasons.

Rebuilding is often an ugly word, but Noonan knows that it is exactly the predicament the franchise is in. He also admits that it is a personal challenge to him to do his part in helping restore the Cowboys' winning ways.

"It is a challenge," said Noonan, who Landry points to as the strongest Dallas lineman since Bob Lilly. "And I'm not used to losing. In four years at Nebraska, I lost five or six games. It makes me mad when we lose. I really don't know what it takes, though. You can have all the greatest players in the world, but there's got to be that extra something in your heart. That's where it comes from. You can have the best athletes ever, but you've got to have guys who deep down inside want to win. That's what we have to find out with this team."

Noonan has a gut feeling about this team. The season-ending victories over the Rams and Cardinals were boosts to the entire organization. Noonan says it was especially evident among the players.

"I really felt good towards the end of last year," he said. "We came out and won the last two games, and it gave us such a lift to go into the offseason with. I really felt good about the St. Louis game. We all played well together. Last year was such a difficult year to judge, but I think we'll do even better this year. We've been out of the playoffs three of the last four years. But I think we'll get back on top."

Although glamour, fame and a large sum of money are among the benefits of being a highly successful football player, Noonan says he will not become a changed person. He married his high school sweetheart, Penny, after the Nebraska-Oklahoma game in 1986. He still regularly visits with friends that he grew up with. And he has tried to keep a level head about his status in the business and sports worlds.

Indeed, Noonan feels he is being rewarded for years of hard work. "But I still play for fun," he said. "My paychecks are for practices. I play the game on Sundays for fun. That's the way I feel about it. I wouldn't play the game if I didn't play it for fun. Personally, I can't come close to performing right if I'm not having a good time out there. Some people may think that's crazy, but that's just the way I am."

What else would you expect to hear from a man who has so much fun in the weight room that he often visits twice a day? He just does things his way, and does them well. Noonan says that life in the weight room does have its boring moments and its dangerous obstacles, but he continues to stay inspired because of the desire to do well.

"There's a little bit of a mental challenge to lifting," he said. "It's in the back of your mind. You know you're working out, and you're thinking, 'What's the guy with the Redskins doing? Is he drinking beer while I'm here lifting? That just pushes me a little harder. I'm sure that's in the back of my mind.

"It gets boring sometimes," Noonan added of life with the barbells. "Especially when you get a lot of other things going on, and you have a hard time to work out. But you've got to find time. It's just that simple."

When the Cowboys drafted Noonan, he was busy in the weight room. Later, he was on hand in Dallas to meet the press.

PLAYERS

Vince Albritton — 36

Safety ★ Washington
5th Year ★ FA, 1984

Ht: 6-2, Wt: 217
Born: 7/23/62

One of the team's best overall athletes, Vince continued to make tremendous strides last year. Since joining the Cowboys as a free agent in 1984, he has raised his game a notch each season. He led all non-starters with 35 tackles, while playing mostly as an extra defender in the team's 4–0, pass-prevent defense. An extremely aggressive hitter, Albritton had positioned himself as a definite challenger by the end of the '87 season. "With Vince in there," says defensive backs coach Dick Nolan, "there's not much difference." Although he can play either safety position, he may be better suited for strong safety. Vince is also one of the team's most consistent cover men on special teams. Games/Starts: '84 (16/0), '85 (7/1), '86 (16/1), '87 (11/1). Total: 50/3.

Rod Barksdale — 80

Wide Receiver ★ Arizona
3rd Year ★ Trade, L.A. Raiders, 1987

Ht: 6-1, Wt: 193
Born: 9/8/62

The Cowboys acquired Rod from the Los Angeles Raiders for cornerback Ron Fellows, while trying to add speed to the receiver corps. Rod, who did not play football in high school or college, boasts world-class speed, and was a three-time track All-America at Arizona. He was also a semifinalist in the 100-meter dash at the 1984 Olympic Trials. In his initial season with the Cowboys, Rod caught 12 passes for 165 yards while adjusting to the Dallas offense. A native of Los Angeles, Rod attended Compton High School. Games/Starts: '85 (IR), '86 (16/15—Raiders), '87 (12/1). Total: 28/16.

Gordon Banks — 87

Wide Receiver ★ Stanford
6th Year ★ FA, 1985

Ht: 5-10, Wt: 170
Born: 3/12/58

The team's most experienced receiver after Mike Renfro, Gordon has proven to be a dependable player since joining the Cowboys. He has also proven to be a reliable starter when called on, as was the case four times last year. His diving, 34-yard catch at New York last year was one of the biggest plays in the victory over the Giants. A stress fracture to his foot, though, caused Banks to miss the final seven games last year. He signed with Dallas late in the '85 season after injuries decimated the receiver corps. Banks began his pro career with the Saints and played two seasons. Gordon hails from Los Angeles, where he attended Loyola High School. Games/Starts: '80 (7/0—N.O.), '81 (6/1—N.O.), '83 (18/18—Oak., USFL), '84 (18/18—Oak., USFL), '85 (2/0—Dallas), '86 (16/5), '87 (5/4). Total: 72/46 (36/10—NFL).

Bill Bates — 40

Safety ★ Tennessee
6th Year ★ FA, 1983

Ht: 6-1, Wt: 199
Born: 6/6/61

Another example of the Cowboys' tradition of developing free agents, Bill has worked hard to improve each season. After making the club primarily because of superb special teams play, he moved into the starting lineup in '86, and has added aggressive hitting, determination and intensity to the defense. Bates was second on the defense with 81 total tackles, while his three traps led the secondary. He was also third with 14 special teams tackles—evidence that his effort on the special teams did not decrease after he made the starting lineup. In '84, Bill made the NFC Pro Bowl squad as a special teamer. Before becoming a starter, Bill led all non-starters in tackles for three straight years. Games/Starts: '83 (16/1), '84 (12/2), '85 (16/0), '86 (15/15), '87 (12/11). Total: 71/29.

Kevin Brooks — 99

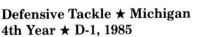

Defensive Tackle ★ Michigan
4th Year ★ D-1, 1985

Ht: 6-6, Wt: 278
Born: 2/9/63

Kevin took over the starting left tackle job during training camp in '87, replacing longtime starter John Dutton. He did not disappoint and continues to mature in his new role. Brooks led all Dallas defensive linemen with 67 tackles, while proving to be an excellent run-stopper. He also contributed four traps last year. Coaches are counting on Brooks to give Dallas another long-tenured anchor for the defensive line. The Cowboys had hoped that Brooks would crack the starting lineup sooner, but a knee injury and subsequent surgery stopped his bid in '86. Since being Dallas' No. 1 pick in '85, Kevin has played all four line positions, but left tackle appears to be his permanent home. Games/Starts: '85 (11/0), '86 (9/0), '87 (13/12) Total: 33/12.

Cornell Burbage　15

Wide Receiver ★ Kentucky
2nd Year ★ FA, 1987

Ht: 5-10, Wt: 181
Born: 2/22/65

Cornell stuck with the club until the final cutdown day in 1987, leading the team in receiving yards in the preseason with 88 on five catches. He rejoined the Cowboys as a replacement player last fall, and caught seven passes for 168 yards in three games. He also scored two touchdowns, including a 77-yarder that was the longest of the season for the Cowboys. While at Kentucky, Cornell finished third in the Southeastern Conference in kickoff returns his senior year (23.1) and fifth in punt returns (6.7). He finished his collegiate career with 64 receptions for 988 yards.

Steve Cisowski　70

Tackle ★ Santa Clara
2nd Year ★ FA, 1987

Ht: 6-5, Wt: 275
Born: 1/23/63

Steve gave the Cowboys solid play at right tackle during his three starts in the replacement games last fall. An eighth-round pick by the New York Giants in 1986, Steve signed with the Cowboys as a free agent and lasted until the final cutdown day before being released. At Santa Clara, Steve proved to be both a durable and versatile athlete. He started 43 straight games at either tackle or guard for the Broncos, and was an All-Western choice in 1986. He also lettered in basketball, wrestling and track at Santa Clara.

Ron Burton　57

Linebacker ★ North Carolina
2nd Year ★ FA, 1987

Ht: 6-1, Wt: 245
Born: 5/2/64

One of the team's biggest surprises last year, Ron emerged from training camp as a quiet, hard-working youngster who might be able to provide solid special teams play and emergency backup duty at linebacker. By the season's end, Ron had impressed coaches enough with his no-nonsense approach and bone-jarring tackles to be penciled in as a potential starter. A standup defensive end in college, Ron backed up middle linebackers Eugene Lockhart and Steve DeOssie for much of the season. Burton got an opportunity to show his ability when an injury bug hit the Dallas linebackers. He started the final two games of the season and was a hit . . . literally, making few mistakes and giving the Cowboys another tough competitor for the defense. Games/Starts: '87 (12/2). Total: 12/2.

Darryl Clack　42

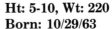

Running Back ★ Arizona State
3rd Year ★ D-2, 1986

Ht: 5-10, Wt: 220
Born: 10/29/63

Darryl Clack's opportunities to contribute while playing behind Herschel Walker and Tony Dorsett have been limited. But when the opportunity has presented itself, Darryl has shown why the Cowboys used such a high draft pick on him. He has a smooth, gliding style that produced the highest kickoff return average since 1982. He registered a 21.9 mark on kickoff returns last year that placed him seventh among NFC kickoff returners. The previous year, Darryl averaged 22.2 yards per return, which would have placed him fifth among NFC returners had he had one more attempt. Tom Landry says he'd like to see more of Clack as a running back. The Cowboys also like Clack's receiving traits. Games/Starts: '86 (16/0), '87 (12/0). Total: 28/0.

Thornton Chandler　89

Tight End ★ Alabama
3rd Year ★ D-6, 1986

Ht: 6-5, Wt: 242
Born: 11/27/63

Since making the Cowboys as the sleeper of the '86 draft class, Chandler has been a solid backup to starter Doug Cosbie. Primarily known as a blocker at run-oriented Alabama, Thornton has shown ability as a receiver with the Cowboys. Chandler has the prototype tight end features: good height, long arms, excellent hands and solid blocking ability. He is now looked upon as the eventual replacement for Cosbie. In his first two years with Dallas, Thornton caught just 11 passes. But of the 11 receptions, three went for touchdowns. Thornton's father, Tommy Chandler, played at Florida A&M with former Cowboys great Bob Hayes. Chandler hails from Jacksonville, Fla., where he attended Raines High School. Games/Starts: '86 (15/1), '87 (12/1). Total: 27/2.

Doug Cosbie　84

Tight End ★ Santa Clara
10th Year ★ D-3, 1979

Ht: 6-6, Wt: 242
Born: 2/27/56

The Cowboys' all-time leading receiver among tight ends, Doug earned that distinction last year, surpassing Billy Joe DuPree's mark of 267 catches midway through the '87 season. His 288 catches rank him fifth on the all-time list. While his role in the Dallas offense has diminished somewhat the past two years (28- and 36-reception seasons after 60- and 64-catch campaigns), Doug's abilities haven't. A Dallas newspaper once described Doug as "the consummate Cowboy—the diplomat, the hard worker, the willing learner, the unknown collegiate with the unlimited talent, the draft find." Games/Starts: '79 (16/1), '80 (16/0), '81 (16/0), '82 (9/9), '83 (16/16), '84 (16/16), '85 (16/16), '86 (16/15), '87 (12/12). Total: 133/95.

Steve DeOssie   55

Linebacker ★ Boston College
5th Year ★ D-4, 1984

Although he has been a backup player throughout his pro career, that hasn't stopped Steve from making valuable contributions. He is one of the team's best players in short-yardage and goal-line situations, and the Cowboys do not lose much when he steps in at middle linebacker. When Eugene Lockhart was injured last season and Ron Burton played the middle, Steve moved outside after Mike Hegman and Jesse Penn also suffered late season injures. Steve may have a future on the outside. Also, the aggressive DeOssie has been a consistent standout on special teams, finishing fourth in special teams tackles last year with 13. Steve grew up in Roslindale, Mass., where he attended Don Bosco High School. Games/Starts: '84 (16/0), '85 (16/0), '86 (16/0) '87 (11/2). Total: 59/2.

Ht: 6-2, Wt: 249
Born: 11/22/62

Steve Folsom   85

Tight End ★ Utah
3rd Year ★ FA, 1987

Provided solid backup support behind Doug Cosbie and Thornton Chandler, after emerging from camp last summer as a surprise roster addition. Although he did not catch a single pass last year, his value to the team was as a blocker. He had replaced Cosbie and wound up springing a key block during Herschel Walker's 60-yard run in overtime that beat New England last November. Steve previously played three seasons with the USFL Philadelphia/Baltimore Stars and was briefly with the Philadelphia Eagles (three games in '81) and the New York Giants ('82).

Ht: 6-5, Wt: 236
Born: 3/21/58

Michael Downs   26

Safety ★ Rice
8th Year ★ FA, 1981

For the seventh year in a row, Michael led the secondary in tackles, with his team-high 86 last year. After a slow start, Michael finished the '87 season on an extremely strong note. His four interceptions last year were second-most on the club. A starter since the first game of his rookie season, Downs has since established himself as one of the league's premier safeties. The Cowboys would like to see a return to the level he displayed in '84 and '85, when he was named to several All-Pro and All-NFC teams. Michael continues to climb on the team's all-time interception list. One of the team's top free agent finds, he finished the '87 campaign with 32 interceptions. Games/Starts: '81 (15/15), '82 (9/9), '83 (16/16), '84 (16/16), '85 (16/16), '86 (16/16), '87 (12/12). Total: 100/100.

Ht: 6-3, Wt: 212
Born: 6/9/59

Todd Fowler   46

Fullback ★ Stephen F. Austin
4th Year ★ S-1, 1984

By assuming a variety of roles for the Cowboys, Todd has demonstrated true value to the club. Since joining Dallas as its first-round pick in the '84 NFL supplemental draft of USFL players, he has played fullback, tight end and been solid on special teams. In two seasons with the USFL's Houston Gamblers, Todd rushed for 1,405 yards and 14 touchdowns, and caught 51 passes for another 540 yards and three touchdowns. A knee injury suffered in his final USFL season, after the Cowboys had selected him, has limited his progress. Still, Cowboys coaches like his competitiveness. Todd's father, Mal, was a fullback at Texas Christian University in the early '50s, and coached his son at Van High School. Games/Starts: '85 (8/0), '86 (16/0), '87 (12/1). Total: 36/1.

Ht: 6-3, Wt: 222
Born: 6/9/62

Kelvin Edwards   81

Wide Receiver ★ Liberty Baptist
3rd Year ★ FA, 1987

The star of the replacement team last year, Kelvin showed enough during the strike games to stick with the club after the labor unrest was settled. Shortly after joining the regulars, Kelvin was inserted into the starting lineup and became Dallas' primary deep threat. The opportunity to go through an entire Dallas training camp this year should benefit Kelvin tremendously. A former fourth-round draft pick of the Saints, the Cowboys and Edwards became interested in each other after his release from New Orleans last summer. During the strike, he was hailed by many as the league's best player. With Dallas, he could develop into the type of player who will be an offensive cornerstone for many years. Games/Starts: '86 (14/3—N.O.), '87 (13/9—Dallas). Total: 27–12.

Ht: 6-2, Wt: 205
Born: 7/19/64

Ron Francis   38

Cornerback ★ Baylor
2nd Year ★ D-2, 1987

The Cowboys invested a second-round pick on the former All-Southwest Conference star who led the league in interceptions his first two years. And they were not cheated, on the basis of his first-year performance. He was the only rookie to crack the starting lineup last year, and perhaps one reason Ron Fellows was traded to the Raiders last summer. Although Ron did have some typical rookie mishaps last year, he showed enough ability to give Dallas its most solid cornerback combination in years, opposite All-Pro Everson Walls. In his rookie year, Ron had 48 tackles, two interceptions and 12 passes defensed. He was also tied for the lead in two categories—fumbles forced and fumbles recovered, with two each. Games/Starts: '87 (11/11). Total: 11/11.

Ht: 5-9, Wt: 199
Born: 4/7/64

Kevin Gogan 66

Tackle ★ Washington
2nd Year ★ D-8, 1987

Another of the pleasant surprises from the '87 rookie class, Kevin was pushed into the starting lineup after the sudden retirement of Phil Pozderac. His play at right tackle was impressive, and his education as an NFL rookie a successful one. With excellent size, Gogan gives Dallas a fine pass-blocker and another player who fits the mold of beefy lineman the Cowboys now desire. Kevin was a former prep baseball standout before deciding to concentrate on football because he "liked contact sports." Attended Sacred Heart High School in Pacifica, Calif. Games/Starts: '87 (11/10). Total: 11/10.

Ht: 6-7, Wt: 310
Born: 11/2/64

Manny Hendrix 45

Cornerback ★ Utah
3rd Year ★ FA, 1986

Manny has indeed taken "the road less traveled" to life in the NFL. Before entering the Cowboys' camp in '86 as a free agent, Manny had not played a single down of football since high school. In college, Manny was a point guard, and a fine one at that for Utah. The quickness and excellent athletic skills that Manny displayed on the basketball court earned him the opportunity to try out with Dallas. Those same skills have aided his steady progress as a defensive back. Manny is used primarily as an extra defender in the team's 4−0 pass prevent defense, but he earned new respect when he started for injured Ron Francis in the season finale victory over the Cardinals, and earned a game ball. Games/Starts: '86 (13/0), '87 (12/1). Total: 25/1.

Ht: 5-10, Wt: 181
Born: 10/20/64

Tommy Haynes 27

Safety ★ Southern California
2nd Year ★ FA, 1987

In a sense, Tommy is a seasoned pro. He has spent a portion of the past three seasons with the Cowboys, in one form or another. Last year, he was one of the top players on the replacement team, with three interceptions, three traps and six passes defensed in three games. In 1986, he injured a thumb and was placed on injured reserve before being released midway through the campaign. Tommy also spent two weeks in the Dallas camp in 1985 after playing with the USFL's Portland Breakers. At Southern Cal, Tommy was a two-year starter who earned All-Pac 10 and honorable mention All-America honors in 1984.

Ht: 6-0, Wt: 190
Born: 2/6/63

Jeff Hurd 52

Linebacker ★ Kansas State
2nd Year ★ FA, 1987

After two seasons as a starting defensive lineman at Kansas State, Jeff was signed as a free agent last year and converted to linebacker—a position he played during his first two college campaigns. Jeff was released after the first preseason game in 1987, but rejoined the team during the replacement games. After injuries plagued the Dallas linebackers late last year, Hurd was re-signed and played in two games, primarily on special teams. While at Lincoln Academy High School, Jeff starred in football, baseball and basketball, and was the Kansas City prep athlete of the year in 1982.

Ht: 6-2, Wt: 245
Born: 5/25/64

Mike Hegman 58

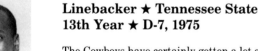

Linebacker ★ Tennessee State
13th Year ★ D-7, 1975

The Cowboys have certainly gotten a lot of mileage out of the former seventh-round draft pick. Mike has been one of the steadiest defenders since taking over the starting job in '79 following Thomas Henderson's release. "Mike's the type of player who doesn't make many mistakes and he's got great football instincts," says Dallas linebackers coach Jerry Tubbs. Always a tough defender against the run. Mike will always be remembered for his outstanding play in Super Bowl XIII, when he stripped Pittsburgh's Terry Bradshaw of the ball and raced 37 yards for a touchdown. Games/Starts: '76 (14/0), '77 (14/1), '78 (16/3), '79 (16/5), '80 (16/16), '81 (11/10), '82 (9/9), '83 (16/16), '84 (16/16), '85 (16/15), '86 (16/16), '87 (10/10). Total: 170/117.

Ht: 6-1, Wt: 226
Born: 1/17/53

Garth Jax 53

Linebacker ★ Florida State
3rd Year ★ FA, 1986

A broken hand limited Garth's contribution last season, allowing him to play in just three games. Since entering the Dallas camp in '86 as a longshot, Garth has been a player who has constantly overachieved. Coaches like his attitude, hustle and determination. Although he has been seldom-used at left linebacker, where he is third on the depth chart, Garth has been valuable on the special teams. Jax has worked hard to improve and has come a long way physically since a kidney and spleen injury his junior year in college put his football future in jeopardy. Garth is a native Texan, and attended Houston Jesuit High School. Games/Starts: '86 (16/0), '87 (3/0). Total: 19/0.

Ht: 6-2, Wt: 222
Born: 9/16/63

Jim Jeffcoat 77

Defensive End ★ Arizona State
6th Year ★ D-1, 1983

No one has ever questioned Jim's willingness to work. Coaches constantly praise him for his work habits, which have paid solid dividends. Jim's sack total slipped to five last year, after a career-high 14 the previous season. The pass rush he provides from the right end spot is crucial to the defense's success. Jeffcoat holds the club record for sacks in a game, with five in a 1985 game at Washington. Jim also has an impressive scoring streak of two, when he has intercepted a pass. One of four No. 1 draft picks on the Dallas defensive line, Jim has also played left end or left tackle in various sets on the Dallas defense. Jim is from Cliffwood, N.J., where he attended Matawan Regional High School. Games/Starts: '83 (16/0), '84 (16/16), '85 (16/16), '86 (16/16), '87 (12/12). Total: 76/60.

Ht: 6-5, Wt: 263
Born: 4/1/61

George Lilja 67

Center ★ Michigan
6th Year ★ FA, 1987

Signed by Dallas shortly after the regulars returned last fall, George emerged as a pleasant surprise, adding depth to the middle of the line and providing relief for longtime center Tom Rafferty. George was drafted by the Los Angeles Rams in 1981, but was released in 1983, and signed by the New York Jets. In 1984, he signed with the Cleveland Browns after a release by the Jets, and lasted until the final cut last summer. He has an excellent chance to solidify a position on the Dallas line. George was born and raised in the Chicago suburb of Orland Park, Ill. and attended Carl Sandburg High School. Dallas Games/Starts: '87 (5/0).

Ht: 6-4, Wt: 282
Born: 3/3/58

Ed Jones 72

Defensive End ★ Tennessee State
14th Year ★ D-1, 1974

Each year the question of how much longer Ed can play confronts him, and each season he seems to turn back the clock. At 37, "Too Tall" is the oldest Cowboy, but he is still a valued member of the defense. With 10 sacks last year, he led the team in that category for the second time in the past three years. He finished the 1987 season only two sacks short of 100 for his career. Last year Ed batted down seven passes, giving him a total of 68 the past eight campaigns. Ed was the first pick in the 1974 draft, the only time the Cowboys have had the lottery's first selection. Games/Starts: '74 (14/0), '75 (14/14), '76 (14/14), '77 (14/14), '78 (16/16), '79 (DNP), '80 (16/16), '81 (16/16), '82 (9/9), '83 (16/16), '84 (16/16), '85 (16/16), '86 (16/16), '87 (15/14). Total: 192/177.

Ht: 6-9, Wt: 275
Born: 2/23/51

Eugene Lockhart 56

Linebacker ★ Houston
5th Year ★ D-6A, 1984

Eugene is the latest in an exclusive group of players who have manned the Cowboys' middle linebacker position. It began with Jerry Tubbs, who was followed by Lee Roy Jordan, Bob Breunig and then Lockhart, who was the only one of the group to start as a rookie. Eugene, whose nickname is "The Hitting Machine," has certainly held up the solid tradition in the middle. Last year, Lockhart was third on the team with 80 tackles, and was the team's top tackler when he went down with a broken leg, which caused him to miss the final three games. Lockhart is also one of the team's hardest workers in the offseason conditioning program. Games/Starts: '84 (15/8), '85 (16/15), '86 (16/16), '87 (9/9). Total: 56/48.

Ht: 6-2, Wt: 230
Born: 3/8/61

Crawford Ker 68

Guard ★ Florida
4th Year ★ D-3, 1985

Since making the conversion from college tackle to professional guard, Crawford has been the most stable Dallas offensive lineman the past two years. Many predict future stardom for Ker, who took over the right guard spot in the early stages of the 1986 camp, when Kurt Petersen went down with a knee injury. The man who goes by the nickname, "Big Daddy," is an intense competitor on the field, and that trait has followed him to the weight room, where he has bench-pressed a Cowboys-record 540 pounds. Crawford also likes to condition himself in a variety of other ways, having experimented with karate and boxing. His father once served as a royal guard at London's Buckingham Palace. Games/Starts: '85 (5/0), '86 (16/16), '87 (12/12). Total: 33/28.

Ht: 6-3, Wt: 283
Born: 5/5/62

Paul McDonald 14

Quarterback ★ Southern Calif.
9th Year ★ FA, 1986

Signed by the Cowboys as insurance when Danny White was lost for the second half of the 1986 season with a broken wrist, Paul has continued to provide experienced backup support. The lefthander was praised by pass offense coordinator Paul Hackett for his ability to quickly pick up the Dallas offensive scheme. Paul played six seasons for the Cleveland Browns, and started all 16 games for them in 1984. At Southern Cal, Paul led the Trojans to two Rose Bowl victories. A native of Montebello, Calif., Paul attended Bishop Amat High School in La Puente, Calif. Games/Starts: '80 (16/0—Cleve.), '81 (12/0—Cleve.), '82 (9/3—Cleve.), '83 (16/2—Cleve.), '84 (16/16—Cleve.), '85 (16/0—Cleve.), '86 (1/0—Dallas), '87 (0/0). Total: 70/21.

Ht: 6-2, Wt: 182
Born: 2/23/58

Kelvin Martin — 83

Wide Receiver ★ Boston College
2nd Year ★ D-4, 1987

After battling injury problems early in his
rookie year, Kelvin began showing the talent
the Cowboys drafted him for in the second half
of the season. An excellent punt returner who
finished among the top 10 in the nation during
his final three seasons at Boston College, Kelvin
posted a 9.8 average return on 22 runbacks last
year. That mark ranked him seventh in the
NFC, and was the best mark for a Dallas player
since James Jones' 10.1 clip in 1980. He nearly
broke a couple of returns for scores, finishing
the year with a high punt return of 38 yards,
and matching that high on one of his 12 kickoff
returns. Kelvin was the Cowboys' special teams
player of the week for two straight games—
against Miami and Minnesota. Games/Starts:
'87 (7/0). Total: 7/0.

Ht: 5-9, Wt: 163
Born: 5/14/65

Danny Noonan — 73

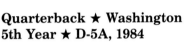

Defensive Tackle ★ Nebraska
2nd Year ★ D-1, 1987

An incredible physical specimen who spends
many hours working to improve, Danny showed
flashes of brilliance during his rookie season
last year. He is the heir apparent to Randy
White's right tackle position, after manning
the nose tackle spot his final two years at
Nebraska. Danny plays the run extremely
well, and is the type of player defensive lines
are built around. A training camp holdout
limited Danny's progress last season, but he was
still able to contribute later in the year. At
Nebraska, Noonan's dedication to his weight
training program was legendary, as he urged
the strength coach to leave the weight room
open longer and open up the facility on
weekends. Games/Starts: '87 (11/0). Total: 11/0.

Ht: 6-4, Wt: 270
Born: 7/14/65

Timmy Newsome — 30

Fullback ★ Winston-Salem
9th Year ★ D-6, 1980

One of the Cowboys' most underrated players,
Timmy plays a valuable but often unnoticed role
as a blocker in the running game. Newsome is
also a key to the Dallas passing game, as his
good hands and large frame give quarterbacks
an excellent target. Last year Timmy was
tied for fourth on the squad with 34 catches,
and finished the 1987 season with 182 career
receptions. He enters the 1988 campaign just
two receptions shy of passing Lance Rentzel for
10th place on the career receiving list. Only
Preston Pearson (189) Ron Springs (222) and
Tony Dorsett (382) have caught more passes as
Dallas running backs than Timmy. Games/
Starts: '80 (16/1), '81 (15/0), '82 (9/0), '83 (16/0),
'84 (15/4), '85 (14/14), '86 (16/12), '87 (11/8).
Total: 112/39.

Ht: 6-1, Wt: 235
Born: 5/17/58

Steve Pelluer — 16

Quarterback ★ Washington
5th Year ★ D-5A, 1984

Steve finished the '87 season as the starter in
two consecutive victories, and with a streak of
94 passes without an interception. It is the
eighth-longest streak in club history, and the
longest since Gary Hogeboom threw 96 straight
without an interception in 1984. Steve has put
himself in position to take over the starting
quarterback job on a permanent basis, and
entered training camp as the No. 1 candidate.
He saw his first extensive tour of duty during
the second half of the '86 season, taking over the
offense for seven games after Danny White's
wrist injury. Steve made his NFL debut in
dramatic style in the 1985 game against the
Giants for the NFC East crown. Games/Starts:
'84 (1/0), '85 (2/0), '86 (16/9), '87 (12/4). Total:
31/13.

Ht: 6-4, Wt: 208
Born: 7/29/62

Nate Newton — 61

Guard ★ Florida A&M
3rd Year ★ FA, 1986

This gigantic structure known as "The Kitchen"
moved into the starting lineup at left guard last
season, and according to offensive line coach
Jim Erkenbeck, has the potential to become
one of the finest players in the league at his
position. An exceptional athlete with extremely
quick feet, enough strength to bench-press 500
pounds and the ability to dunk a basketball,
Nate has the tools that it takes to become a top-
notch player. Newton has weighed as much as
360 pounds, well over his prescribed weight of
300 pounds. "At 297, he's got Pro Bowl
potential," said Erkenbeck. "At 320, he's just
another fat guy running around. At 360, he's
in the stands selling hot dogs . . . those he
doesn't eat." NFL Games/Starts: '86 (11/0), '87
(11/11). Total: 22/11.

Ht: 6-3, Wt: 315
Born: 12/20/61

Jesse Penn — 59

Linebacker ★ Virginia Tech
4th Year ★ D-2, 1985

At times, Jesse has shown signs he will become
the big-play linebacker the team has coveted
for years. The key now for Jesse is to become
more consistent, and crack the starting lineup.
When called on in the past three years to start,
Jesse has played well and produced big plays.
Last year, he was in the midst of a strong,
two-turnover performance against the Los
Angeles Rams when he broke bones in his
lower leg. A healthy return could trigger a push
for a starting job for Jesse at either outside
linebacker position. At Virginia Tech, Jesse
played standup defensive end. When the
Cowboys drafted him, he was the top-rated
outside linebacker on their board. Games/
Starts: '85 (16/1), '86 (15/0), '87 (11/1). Total:
42/2.

Ht: 6-3, Wt: 224
Born: 9/6/62

Tom Rafferty 64

Center ★ Penn State
13th Year ★ D-4, 1976

The senior member of the Cowboys' offensive line, Tom has been a constant to the unit and provides the leadership that a young developing line needs. Excluding the strike season, Tom has never missed a game in his caeer, starting 179 of 180 regular season and playoff games since 1977. Tom came to the Cowboys as a top college guard in 1976, and was the starter on the right side for four years before switching to center in 1981. Tom delivered a key block that paved the way for Tony Dorsett's NFL record 99-yard run against Minnesota in January '83. Games/Starts: '76 (14/0), '77 (14/14), '78 (16/16), '79 (16/16), '80 (16/16), '81 (16/16), '82 (9/9), '83 (16/15), '84 (16/16), '85 (16/16), '86 (16/16), '87 (12/12). Total: 177/162.

Ht: 6-3, Wt: 263
Born: 8/2/54

Roger Ruzek 9

Kicker ★ Weber State
2nd Year ★ FA, 1987

One of the truly amazing stories of the Cowboys' 1987 season, Roger has the distinction of being a player who had two tryouts with the Cowboys in the same summer. Released early in training camp, Roger was given a second chance in the search to replace Rafael Septien when he explained that he had altered his kicking style for his first stint at camp. Ruzek then went on to beat out his competitors. Roger had an outstanding first NFL season, leading the league with a club-record .880 field goal percentage. He connected on 22 of 25 field goal attempts, including a team-record five against the Rams. Roger was a USFL teammate of Herschel Walker, having played two seasons with the New Jersey Generals. NFL Games/Starts: '87 (12/0). Total: 12/0.

Ht: 6-1, Wt: 190
Born: 12/17/60

Mike Renfro 82

Wide Receiver ★ Texas Christian
11th Year ★ Trade, Houston, 1984

Dallas' most experienced receiver, Mike still has something to offer to the receiving corps. Always able to make the crucial catch under pressure, Mike led the Cowboys with four touchdown receptions last year and was second to Herschel Walker with 46 catches for 662 yards. Mike finished 1987 with 323 receptions. The son of former Cleveland All-Pro Ray Renfro, Mike surpassed the career catch total of his father (281) last year. He starts the 1988 season needing only 337 yards to reach the 5,000-yard plateau and 846 to surpass his dad's total for 5,508 receiving yards. Games/Starts: '78 (14/10—Hou.), '79 (15/2—Hou.), '80 (16/15—Hou.), '81 (12/12—Hou.), '82 (9/4—Hou.), '83 (7/7—Hou.), '84 (16/11—Dal.), '85 (16/16), '86 (12/6), '87 (14/11). Total: 131/94.

Ht: 6-0, Wt: 184
Born: 6/19/55

Mike Saxon 4

Punter ★ San Diego State
4th Year ★ FA, 1985

If Mike ever punts as consistently at the end of the season as he has at the beginning, he might be the best punter in the league. Inconsistency plagued Mike during his first three years with Dallas, but he has shown a vast amount of promise. Mike has also reduced his offseason duties a bit, in an attempt to save his leg for the latter stages of the season. Mike averaged 39.5 per kick last season, but more impressively, he led the NFL in punts downed inside the 20-yard line for the third straight season. Since he came into the league in 1985, Saxon has had 68 punts inside the 20, second only to the Rams' Dale Hatcher's 77. Mike's 41.9 average for the 1985 season was the best by a Dallas punter since Ron Widby's 43.3 mark in 1969. Games/Starts: '85 (16/0), '86 (16/0), '87 (12/0). Total: 44/0.

Ht: 6-3, Wt: 193
Born: 7/10/62

Jeff Rohrer 50

Linebacker ★ Yale
7th Year ★ D-2, 1982

Jeff has given the Cowboys solid play at the right outside position, since taking over the starting job in 1985 after Anthony Dickerson was traded. When the Cowboys selected him in the second round, Jeff was the highest NFL draft choice from Yale since Calvin Hill was chosen by the Cowboys in 1969. Jeff finished the 1987 campaign ranked fourth on the team's tackle chart, with 74 stops. In addition to providing fine play against the run, Jeff also contributed four sacks and two fumble recoveries last year as well. Intelligent and personable, Jeff once wore an earring for a month to win a bet with a friend. Games/Starts: '82 (8/0), '83 (16/0), '84 (16/0), '85 (15/12), '86 (16/16), '87 (12/12). Total: 83/40.

Ht: 6-2, Wt: 222
Born: 12/25/58

Victor Scott 22

Safety ★ Colorado
5th Year ★ D-2, 1984

Victor's unfortunate string of injuries has kept him from making a serious bid for a starting job the past two seasons, but he may be ready to make another run at the starting lineup. A fine tackler who has made a definite impact on the Dallas secondary in terms of aggressiveness, Victor has the talent to be a top player. He began his Dallas career as a cornerback, but was switched to safety after his second season. He has since found a home at free safety, playing a key role in the team's 4–0, pass-prevent defense. After earning four special teams game balls in 1985, Victor's teammates voted him special teams captain in 1986. Games/Starts: '84 (16/0), '85 (16/3), '86 (5/0), '87 (6/0). Total: 43/3.

Ht: 6-0, Wt: 203
Born: 6/1/62

Mike Sherrard — 86

Wide Receiver ★ UCLA
3rd year ★ D-1, 1986

A compound fracture to his right leg, suffered during training camp last summer, wiped out Mike's sophomore season, after an impressive rookie debut. He caught 41 passes for 744 yards and five touchdowns as a rookie, the best production by a Dallas rookie wideout since Bob Hayes' introduction to the league in 1965. Sherrard's injury forced Dallas coaches to restructure the passing game that had been built around his exceptional speed. Last March, while jogging on a California beach, Mike re-fractured his right leg. The second break was not as severe as the first, but it did set Mike's rehabilitation back several months and will cause him to miss at least the entire training camp. Games/Starts: '86 (16/4), '87 (0/0). Total: 16/4.

Ht: 6-2, Wt: 194
Born: 6/21/63

Kevin Sweeney — 19

Quarterback ★ Fresno State
2nd Year ★ D-7, 1987

After being released the final week of the preseason last fall, Kevin came back to start two replacement games, leading the Dallas strike team to victories on both occasions. Kevin stuck with the veteran squad after the strike ended, although he did not play. Kevin finished his brilliant career at Fresno State as the NCAA's most prolific passer, setting the career mark for passing yards, with 10,623. A four-year starter in college, Kevin was coached by his father, Jim Sweeney. As a youngster, Kevin was exposed to many up-and-coming quarterbacks. In 1973, while his father coached at the East–West Shrine Game, Kevin spent the entire week hanging around future teammate Danny White. Games/Starts: '87 (3/2). Total: 3/2.

Ht: 6-0, Wt: 193
Born: 11/16/63

Don Smerek — 60

Defensive Lineman ★ Nevada—Reno
8th year ★ FA, 1980

Throughout his pro career, Don has provided solid backup support at all four defensive line positions while occasionally challenging for a starting job. One reason he hasn't challenged more for a front line position is a variety of injury problems he's had to endure. In the past few seasons, he has fought off a knee injury, a shoulder setback, another knee injury and broken ribs. Says Cowboys defensive line coach Ernie Stautner, "Don's been a player who's had a black cloud hanging over his head." Born in Waterford, Mich., Don was raised outside of Las Vegas, in Henderson, Nev., where he attended Basic High School in Henderson. Games/Starts: '81 (2/0), '82 (7/0), '83 (15/0), '84 (16/0), '85 (10/1), '86 (11/0), '87 (8/3). Total: 69/4.

Ht: 6-7, Wt: 266
Born: 12/10/57

Glen Titensor — 63

Guard ★ Brigham Young
7th Year ★ D-3, 1981

A knee injury wiped out Glen's 1987 campaign, and he entered the current season hoping that all was well, allowing him to rebound from the setback. Before his injury, Glen had started every game at left guard since earning the job five games into the 1984 season. Glen played defensive line in college, and followed in the footsteps of Blaine Nye, John Fitzgerald, Pat Donovan and Kurt Petersen as converted defensive linemen. Glen spent two years at UCLA before transferring to BYU. A native of Westminster, Calif., Glen went to Bolsa Grande High School in Garden Grove, Calif. Games/Starts: '81 (16/0), '82 (3/0), '83 (15/1), '84 (15/12), '85 (16/16), '86 (16/16), '87 (0/0). Total: 81/45.

Ht: 6-4, Wt: 275
Born: 2/21/58

Daryle Smith — 79

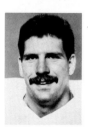

Tackle ★ Tennessee
2nd Year ★ FA, 1987

Daryle was one of the pleasant surprises last year, sticking after the replacement season ended, and then replacing an injured Mark Tuinei at left tackle for the final six weeks of the season. Smith even drew praise from several opponents for his fine play, as he did a tremendous job against opposing team's top pass rushers. Daryle was signed as a free agent by Seattle last year, but was released on the final cut. He is originally from Knoxville, Tenn., where he attended Powell High School. Games/Starts: '87 (9/7). Total: 9/7.

Ht: 6-5, Wt: 278
Born: 1/18/64

Mark Tuinei — 71

Tackle ★ Hawaii
6th Year ★ FA, 1983

Mark was making tremendous progress last year at left tackle before a knee injury cut his season short with six weeks to play. Having bounced around from the defensive line to center to guard and finally tackle, it was a long realized goal when he became a starter in October 1986. The week before he was named the starter, he led all Dallas defensive linemen with tackles against Denver. Indeed, the strong Tuinei is one of the team's most versatile players. Mark played two seasons at UCLA before transferring to Hawaii. Born in Oceanside, Calif., Mark was raised in Honolulu, where he was a star athlete at Punahou High School. Games/Starts: '83 (10/0), '84 (16/0), '85 (16/0), '86 (16/11), '87 (8–8). Total: 66/19.

Ht: 6-5, Wt: 282
Born: 3/31/60

Mark Walen 95

Defensive Tackle ★ UCLA
2nd year ★ D-3, 1986

Mark hopes to prove that he was worth the high draft pick the Cowboys used to claim him in 1986. His rookie season was wiped out after he suffered a broken right ankle prior to training camp. Mark played sparingly last season, and although he is a natural tackle, saw some duty at right end. At UCLA, Mark was the 1985 Pac-10 Player of the Year. Games/Starts: '86 (0/0), '87 (9/0). Total: 9/0.

Ht: 6-5, Wt: 262
Born: 3/10/63

Everson Walls 24

Cornerback ★ Grambling
8th Year ★ FA, 1981

Everson is one of the most successful free agents in club history, having blossomed into one of the league's premier cornerbacks. He is the only player in NFL history to lead the league in interceptions three times. Last year, Walls' five thefts led Dallas for the fourth time, tying Cornell Green's club record. Everson enters the 1988 season needing only 10 interceptions to tie Mel Renfro's career record of 52. He is third among active NFC players in interceptions, trailing only Green Bay's Dave Brown (53 in 13 seasons) and Minnesota's John Harris (47 in 10 seasons). Games/Starts: '81 (16/14), '82 (9/9), '83 (16/16), '84 (16/16), '85 (16/16), '86 (16/16), '87 (12/12). Total: 101/99.

Ht: 6-1, Wt: 192
Born: 12/28/59

Herschel Walker 34

Running Back ★ Georgia
3rd Year ★ D-5A, 1985

Since coming into the NFL in 1986, Herschel has gained 3,180 yards from scrimmage, a total that ranks second only to Indianapolis' Eric Dickerson. During his first two seasons, Walker gained 1,628 yards rushing and 1,552 yards receiving to become the first man in NFL history to gain over 700 yards rushing and receiving for two straight seasons. Last year, Herschel led the Cowboys with 891 rushing yards on 209 attempts, an impressive average of 4.3 per carry. He also caught a team-high 60 passes for another 715 yards. Herschel's 60-yard run that beat New England last year was the longest run in the history of NFL overtime play. NFL Games/Starts: '86 (16/9), '87 (12/11). Total: 28/20.

Ht: 6-1, Wt: 225
Born: 3/3/62

Randy Watts 94

Defensive End ★ Catawba
2nd Year ★ FA, 1986

Randy was signed by the Cowboys for the replacement games, and responded with three traps in a relief role. Coaches were impressed enough with his potential that he was one of the few players who remained with the team after the regulars returned. Randy spent several games on the inactive list after the strike, but did see action in two games with the regulars late in the season. The ninth-round pick of the Kansas City Chiefs in 1987, Randy was released on the final cutdown day after playing left tackle during the preseason. In 1986, Randy led Catawba's defensive line with 99 tackles and 7½ sacks.

Ht: 6-6, Wt: 305
Born: 6/22/63

Bob White — 65

Guard ★ Rhode Island
2nd Year ★ FA, 1987

A former New York Jets draft pick, the Cowboys signed Bob last year, but released him on the final cut. He rejoined the team during the strike, was able to stick with the Cowboys after the regulars returned, but remained inactive for the majority of the season. Bob was switched to center for the last two weeks of training camp last summer, and earned praise from the coaching staff for handling the transition well. He is listed as a backup at both guard spots and at center. A native of Lunenburg, Mass., Bob attended Lunenburg High School. Games/Starts: '87 (4/3). Total: 4/3.

Ht: 6-5, Wt: 267
Born: 4/9/63

Randy White — 54

Defensive Tackle ★ Maryland
14th Year ★ D-1A, 1975

Injuries have slowed Randy the past two seasons, and caused coaches to consider life without one of the Cowboys' greatest players. White will likely be used more as a standup defensive end this year. He finished the 1987 season with 112 1/2 career traps, just 12 1/2 away from Harvey Martin's club record of 125. White's illustrious career has included nine Pro Bowl appearances and a club-record eight All-Pro selections. He and Martin shared co-MVP honors at Super Bowl XII. Randy will tie a team mark this season, by playing in his 14th NFL campaign. Games/Starts: '75 (14/1), '76 (14/0), '77 (14/14), '78 (16/16), '79 (15/14), '80 (16/16), '81 (16/16), '82 (9/9), '83 (16/16), '84 (16/16), '85 (16/16), '86 (16/16), '87 (15/14). Total: 193/164.

Ht: 6-4, Wt: 263
Born: 1/15/53

Danny White — 11

Quarterback ★ Arizona State
13th Year ★ D-3A, 1974

Danny split duty at quarterback last year with Steve Pelluer, and is being pushed for the starting job he has held almost exclusively since Roger Staubach's retirement. The right wrist that was fractured midway through the 1986 campaign affected White's control last year, thus prompting the additional playing time for Pelluer. Last year, Danny set club records for career pass completions (1,832) and touchdown passes (154), surpassing old marks held by Staubach. He is in position to add two more career passing records to his resume—pass attempts and passing yards. Games/Starts: '76 (14/0), '77 (14/0), '78 (16/1), '79 (16/0), '80 (16/16), '81 (16/15), '82 (9/9), '83 (16/16), '84 (14/6), '85 (14/14), '86 (7/6), '87 (11/9). Total: 163/92.

Ht: 6-3, Wt: 198
Born: 2/9/52

Robert Williams — 23

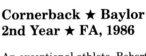

Cornerback ★ Baylor
2nd Year ★ FA, 1986

An exceptional athlete, Robert stuck with the Cowboys after the replacement season last year and was used primarily as an extra defensive back and on special teams. During the strike, he filled in at the right cornerback spot that belongs to Ron Francis, his former Baylor teammate. While in college, he and Francis also competed against each other at running back. Robert tried out with the Washington Redskins as a receiver in 1986, but was released. He tried out for the Cowboys last year, was released, but brought back during the replacement season. Games/Starts: '87 (11/3). Total: 11/3.

Ht: 5-10, Wt: 190
Born: 10/2/62

Gerald White — 37

Fullback ★ Michigan
2nd Year ★ FA, 1987

Gerald started all three contests at fullback during the replacement games last fall, with primary contributions as a blocker and receiver. He was released after the regulars returned, but re-signed during the off-season for another look. Gerald entered the Cowboys camp in 1987 as a free agent, but was released after the third preseason game. At Michigan, where he started his final 27 games, Gerald earned honorable mention All-Big 10 honors his senior year.

Ht: 5-11, Wt: 223
Born: 12/9/64

Jeff Zimmerman — 76

Guard ★ Florida
2nd Year ★ D-3, 1987

Another who fits the mold of the big linemen the Cowboys now favor, Jeff showed constant improvement as his rookie season progressed. He filled in for injured Nate Newton at left guard for his only start, but saw considerable spot duty throughout the year. Jeff was inserted into the starting lineup last spring when Newton arrived at the mini-camp overweight, but admitted that he thought the job would be won or lost in training camp. He gained to almost 350 pounds after his senior year at Florida, but lost more than 35 pounds in a two-month period before the draft. A college teammate of Crawford Ker, Zimmerman was one of four members of "The Great Wall" at Florida, who were all NFL draft picks. Games/Starts: '87 (11/1). Total: 11/1.

Ht: 6-3, Wt: 316
Born: 1/10/65

1988 Veterans Alphabetical Roster

NO.	NAME	POS.	HGT.	WGT.	BIRTHDATE	COLLEGE	NFL EXP.
36	Albritton, Vince	S	6-2	217	7/23/62	Washington	5
87	Banks, Gordon	WR	5-10	170	3/12/58	Stanford	6
80	Barksdale, Rod	WR	6-1	193	9/8/62	Arizona	3
40	Bates, Bill	S	6-1	199	6/6/61	Tennessee	6
99	Brooks, Kevin	DT	6-6	278	2/9/63	Michigan	4
15	Burbage, Cornell	WR	5-10	181	2/22/65	Kentucky	2
57	Burton, Ron	LB	6-1	245	5/2/64	North Carolina	2
89	Chandler, Thornton	TE	6-5	242	11/27/63	Alabama	3
70	Cisowski, Steve	OT	6-5	275	1/23/63	Santa Clara	2
42	Clack, Darryl	RB	5-10	220	10/29/63	Arizona State	3
84	Cosbie, Doug	TE	6-6	242	2/27/56	Santa Clara	10
55	DeOssie, Steve	LB	6-2	249	11/22/62	Boston College	5
26	Downs, Michael	S	6-3	212	6/9/59	Rice	8
81	Edwards, Kelvin	WR	6-2	205	7/19/64	Liberty Baptist	3
85	Folsom, Steve	TE	6-5	236	3/21/58	Utah	3
46	Fowler, Todd	FB	6-3	222	6/9/62	Stephen F. Austin	4
38	Francis, Ron	CB	5-9	199	4/7/64	Baylor	2
66	Gogan, Kevin	OT	6-7	310	11/2/64	Washington	2
27	Haynes, Tommy	S	6-0	190	2/6/63	Southern California	2
58	Hegman, Mike	LB	6-1	226	1/17/53	Tennessee State	13
45	Hendrix, Manny	CB	5-10	181	10/20/64	Utah	3
52	Hurd, Jeff	LB	6-2	245	5/25/64	Kansas State	2
53	Jax, Garth	LB	6-2	222	9/16/63	Florida State	3
77	Jeffcoat, Jim	DE	6-5	263	4/1/61	Arizona State	6
72	Jones, Ed	DE	6-9	275	2/23/51	Tennessee State	14
68	Ker, Crawford	OG	6-3	283	5/5/62	Florida	4
67	Lilja, George	C	6-4	282	3/3/58	Michigan	6
56	Lockhart, Eugene	LB	6-2	230	3/8/61	Houston	5
14	McDonald, Paul	QB	6-2	182	2/23/58	Southern California	9
83	Martin, Kelvin	WR	5-9	163	5/14/65	Boston College	2
30	Newsome, Timmy	FB	6-1	235	5/17/58	Winston-Salem	9
61	Newton, Nate	OG	6-3	315	12/20/61	Florida A&M	3
73	Noonan, Danny	DT	6-4	270	7/14/65	Nebraska	2
16	Pelluer, Steve	QB	6-4	208	7/29/62	Washington	5
59	Penn, Jesse	LB	6-3	224	9/6/62	Virginia Tech	4
64	Rafferty, Tom	C	6-3	263	8/2/54	Penn State	13
82	Renfro, Mike	WR	6-0	184	6/19/55	Texas Christian	11
50	Rohrer, Jeff	LB	6-2	222	12/25/58	Yale	7
9	Ruzek, Roger	K	6-1	190	12/17/60	Weber State	2
4	Saxon, Mike	P	6-3	193	7/10/62	San Diego State	4
22	Scott, Victor	S	6-0	203	6/1/62	Colorado	5
86	Sherrard, Mike	WR	6-2	194	6/21/63	UCLA	3
60	Smerek, Don	DL	6-7	266	12/10/57	Nevada—Reno	8
79	Smith, Daryle	OT	6-5	278	1/18/64	Tennessee	2
19	Sweeney, Kevin	QB	6-0	193	11/16/63	Fresno State	2
63	Titensor, Glen	OG	6-4	275	2/21/58	Brigham Young	7
71	Tuinei, Mark	OT	6-5	282	3/31/60	Hawaii	6
95	Walen, Mark	DT	6-5	262	3/10/63	UCLA	2
34	Walker, Herschel	RB	6-1	225	3/3/62	Georgia	3
24	Walls, Everson	CB	6-1	192	12/28/59	Grambling	8
94	Watts, Randy	DE	6-6	305	6/22/63	Catawba	2
65	White, Bob	OG	6-5	267	4/9/63	Rhode Island	2
11	White, Danny	QB	6-3	198	2/9/52	Arizona State	13
37	White, Gerald	FB	5-11	223	12/9/64	Michigan	2
54	White, Randy	DT	6-4	263	1/15/53	Maryland	14
23	Williams, Robert	CB	5-10	190	10/2/62	Baylor	2
76	Zimmerman, Jeff	OG	6-3	316	1/10/65	Florida	2

JUST WHAT THE COACHES ORDERED

For weeks leading up to April's NFL draft, the word from Cowboys Center seemed to reveal the obvious: the Dallas Cowboys were looking for a few good defensive men.

Naturally, that would be the case when considering the dependency on aging stars the Dallas defense has had in recent years. Players like Ed Jones, Randy White and Mike Hegman have worn the stars on their helmets well over the years, but aren't getting any younger. Also consider the lack of big plays from a linebacking crew and the lack of a consistent pass rush last season, and defense can be classified as an A-1 priority.

Offense puts people in the stands, the old saying goes, while defense wins championships. With that line of reasoning, and the Cowboys failing to make the playoffs for three of the past four years, the thought of infusing fresh blood to the Dallas defense makes even more sense.

The bottom-line result from the Cowboys' 1988 draft? Dallas selected just four defensive players with its 11 choices.

As we were saying, offense puts people in the stands.

"This just wasn't a defensive draft," said Cowboys president Tex Schramm. "It came at a time when we were primarily trying to build our defense. But as long as it wasn't that way, we thought we'd do a good job on our offense and we feel very, very pleased with that."

"Now, we'll have to solidify our

Michael Irvin of Miami was taken with the No. 11 pick in the draft.

offensive football team out of this draft," said head coach Tom Landry. "We will have to make it stronger at a lot of positions. We will have to

be strong enough to put us back in the winning column. We will have to work on the defense later."

The draftee expected to have the

most impact this season is first-round pick Michael Irvin, the former Miami receiver who was taken with the 11th pick in the draft. Irvin is a big play-type who finished his career as the most prolific receiver in Miami history. In just three seasons, Irvin set school marks with 143 catches, 2,433 yards and 26 touchdowns.

With the Cowboys, Irvin is being counted on to provide a consistent deep threat. The Cowboys hope he can fill a void created when the 1986 No. 1 pick, Mike Sherrard, broke his right leg. Landry says Irvin—who was the top-rated player on the Dallas board in the entire draft—should compete for a starting job in his first camp.

"We were a little bit nervous that he might not be there," Landry said on draft day. The 6-2, 202-pound Irvin was the third receiver taken in the draft. "But we felt very good when it happened. The guy has all the qualities. He's big and he can run a 4.5. That's really moving for a wide receiver. And he can catch all kinds of passes. He really doesn't have too many weaknesses."

Irvin has been compared to San Francisco's Jerry Rice and Washington's Art Monk because of his smooth running style and sure hands. A very intense competitor, Irvin will not hesitate from going over the middle, and was Miami's best blocking receiver. On top of the physical assets, Irvin has a confidence and enthusiasm that flows freely.

Said Irvin on draft day: "I told Vinny Testaverde that I'd go out and win the Heisman Trophy for him, and I did it. Danny White . . . All-Pro."

"You like to see a kid who has enthusiasm and is excited about the game," says Cowboys quarterback Danny White. "You know, Tony Hill's greatest quality was the confidence he had in himself. He didn't have the blazing speed and all of that, but the guy just believed that no matter how many guys they put on him, he could get open. Michael Irvin's got that same kind of confidence. It's obvious."

Another player who might be

Ken Norton, the second-round pick, also should help early.

able to contribute this season is second-round pick Ken Norton, Jr. The linebacker from UCLA and son of the former heavyweight champion will be tried at the left outside spot his rookie year, after playing the inside for the Bruins. Norton comes to Dallas with a reputation as a punishing tackler, and fits the profile of the active, aggressive defender the Cowboys have coveted for years.

The 6-2, 230-pound Norton is the latest in a string of outside linebackers the Cowboys have picked in the first two rounds of drafts in the 1980s. The others were Jeff Rohrer, Mike Walter, Billy Cannon, Jr. and Jesse Penn.

"He has a lot of experience for a top team," Landry says, speaking of Norton's role at UCLA. "He's a good tackler, a good competitor. I don't see any reason why he can't fit into our system very well."

Says Cowboys vice president for personnel development, Gil Brandt, "When you get Ken Norton, Jr., I think you're getting a player on the rise. He won't be 22 until September and he wasn't redshirted.

"What we're hoping is that he's enough of an athlete that he can make the move from the inside to the outside. He's a classy young guy. If he's as tough and has as much character as his dad does,

we've got a good player."

The Cowboys added a few more bodies for Jim Erkenbeck to work with on the offensive line, with their third-, fourth- and seventh-round picks. Dallas took Oklahoma's 6-3, 288-pound guard Mark Hutson in the third round, and Boston College's 6-6, 297-pound tackle Dave Widell in the fourth. Owen Hooven, a 6-9, 301-pounder from Oregon State was the seventh-round pick.

"Out of these offensive linemen, we should come up with a pretty solid future," Landry said. "If we don't have a future with this group of offensive linemen, we could be in trouble."

Scott Secules, a quarterback from Virginia, was selected in the sixth round. "The guy has an excellent delivery," said Landry. "It is amazing how he throws the ball. He probably has the quickest delivery that we have seen."

The eighth-round pick was Kentucky's 5-7, 195-pound running back Mark Higgs, while California receiver Brian Bedford was chosen in the ninth round. Billy Owens, a safety from Pitt, was the 10th rounder, while UCLA linebacker Ben Hummel was the 12th-round pick.

Dallas' 11th-round pick was another of those that could be considered a modern-day future pick, ala Roger Staubach. Chad Hennings, a 6-5, 260-pound defensive end from the Air Force was selected despite a five- to eight-year military commitment. Many projected Hennings—who won the Outland Trophy as the nation's outstanding lineman—as a first- or second-round pick, had it not been for the tour of duty. A first-team All-America, Hennings registered 24 sacks and 31 tackles for losses last year.

Of Hennings, Schramm says the Cowboys are "only interested if something were to happen when he gets done."

Of the entire draft class, Landry summed it up this way: "Our first pick is so good for what we need, that makes everything else look better."

COACHES

Tom Landry

Head Coach

As he begins his 29th season as head coach of the Dallas Cowboys, Tom Landry still has the type of enthusiasm toward his job that one would expect from a rookie assistant.

The dean of NFL head coaches, Landry has endured the pitfalls of his profession, as well as reaching the pinnacle of success. The third-winningest coach in NFL history, he has guided the Cowboys to 18 playoff berths and five Super Bowls.

"The amazing and significant thing about Tom is his ability, both from a football and a personal standpoint, to change with the times," says Cowboys president Tex Schramm. "The players coming out of college today are entirely different—in lifestyle and priorities—than they were when he started with the Cowboys. He has adapted to that and the changes in the game itself. He has been an innovator and that's hard to maintain over a 28-year period."

"He's one of the guys who other coaches in the league would like to be like," says Washington Redskins head coach Joe Gibbs. "The true test of a coach is if a guy has done it over a long period of time and done it with different teams and proven he has a formula. That's what he has done."

Landry's mission now is to rebuild the Cowboys into a playoff contender. Dallas has missed the playoffs in three of the past four seasons, and is in the midst of what Landry calls a "three-year rebuilding plan" aimed at returning the Cowboys to playoff contenders.

"I signed a three-year contract because I thought it would take three years to get things turned around," said Landry, who was an All-Pro defensive back with the New York Giants during his playing days in the early to mid-'50s. After retiring in 1955, Landry served as the Giants' defensive coach before joining the Cowboys.

"We are a very inexperienced football team," Landry, a native of Mission, Texas, and a former star at the University of Texas, added. "You don't gain experience overnight. We are in a rebuilding phase, no doubt about that, but given enough time we can get it done."

Perhaps New York Giants general manager George Young best summed up the respect that those around the league have for Landry and his ability to field a winner. "Sitting here and speaking for this franchise," Young said, "I can tell you I will be relieved when he retires. And I've been saying that for years."

Neill Armstrong

Research & Development

Neill studies and evaluates all players and teams in the NFL. His reports provide the basis for game plans. After four years as head coach of the Chicago Bears, Neill joined the Cowboys in 1982. He was the defensive coordinator for the Minnesota Vikings during their Super Bowl seasons. Armstrong also had a six-year tenure as head coach for the Canadian Football League's Edmonton Eskimos, and began his pro coaching career with the Houston Oilers. Neill also coached at Oklahoma State (then Oklahoma A&M), where he was an All-America receiver before playing on two NFL championship teams with the Philadelphia Eagles.

Al Lavan

Running Backs

In his ninth year as a Cowboys assistant, Al has helped the running game remain among the most respected in the NFL. Al coached running backs at Stanford for a year and backs and receivers at Georgia Tech for two years. Following his playing career at Colorado State, Al played three seasons as a defensive back for the Philadelphia Eagles and Atlanta Falcons. He began his coaching career at his alma mater, where he handled receivers. Al moved on to Louisville to coach defensive backs and then to Iowa State, where he coached receivers. In 1975 and '76, Al broke into the pro ranks, coaching defensive backs and special teams for the Falcons.

Jim Erkenbeck

Offensive Line

Jim is beginning his second season with the Cowboys after replacing the retired Jim Myers. He is faced with the task of rebuilding the Dallas line in the fashion that he helped the Saints make dramatic improvement from 1985 to 1986. New Orleans cut its sack total from 58 to 27 in one year under Erkenbeck. Jim also coached the offensive line for the USFL's Philadelphia/Baltimore Stars for three years, during which time the team advanced to the league title game three times. Jim began his pro coaching career with Winnipeg of the Canadian Football League.

Alan Lowry

Receivers

After directing the special teams for five years, Alan was promoted to receivers coach in 1987. He began his coaching career at Virginia Tech, before moving on to Wyoming. Prior to coaching defensive backs at his alma mater, the University of Texas, Alan worked in the Cowboys' scouting department. He is one of the few players in Southwest Conference history to earn All-Conference honors both as an offensive and defensive star. An All-SWC defensive back in 1971, Alan was switched to quarterback in '72 and led the Longhorns to a 10−1 season.

Paul Hackett

Pass Offense Coordinator

Paul is beginning his third year with the Cowboys, after three years as quarterbacks/receivers coach for the San Francisco 49ers. Paul has helped Tom Landry remodel the passing game since his arrival. He began his pro coaching career as director of quarterbacks with the Cleveland Browns in 1981. He also served as quarterbacks coach at Southern California and at the University of California, where he worked with Jim Erkenbeck. Paul was a quarterback at Cal-Davis, where he led the Far Western Conference in passing in 1969. He began his coaching career at his alma mater the year following his graduation.

Dick Nolan

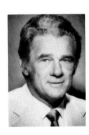

Defensive Backs

A member of the original "Doomsday Defense" coaching staff, Dick returned to the Cowboys in 1982. He is in his third season back at the position he handled from 1963–67, after four years as receivers coach. In 1962, Dick broke into coaching as a player-coach. He is a former head coach of the San Francisco 49ers and New Orleans Saints. His 49ers teams won three division titles in the early '70s. Dick was a teammate of Tom Landry's in the defensive backfield of the New York Giants. He played offensive and defensive halfback on Maryland's 1953 national championship team.

Mike Solari

Special Teams/
Assistant Offensive Line

Mike is in his second year in the pro ranks. He had a tremendous impact in his rookie season, helping the Cowboys special teams show dramatic improvement. Mike previously served as offensive coordinator and offensive line coach at Pittsburgh. He also coached offensive lines at Kansas, the University of Cincinnati, Boise State, U.S. International and Mira Vista Junior College. After an outstanding career at San Diego State, where he was honored for academic and athletic achievement, Mike began his coaching career at Mission Bay High School in California.

Jerry Tubbs

Linebackers

Jerry is the only original Cowboys player still with the club. He was the team's first middle linebacker, and has helped develop successors Lee Roy Jordan, Bob Breunig and Eugene Lockhart. During his eight-year playing career, Jerry became Dallas' first Pro Bowl and All-Pro linebacker. He also began his coaching career by serving as a player-coach. One of the greatest players in Oklahoma Sooners history, Jerry was the Walter Camp Award winner as the nation's most outstanding player in 1956. The native of Breckenridge has been inducted into the Texas High School Hall of Fame.

Ernie Stautner

Defensive Coordinator/
Defensive Line

Following a Hall of Fame career with the Pittsburgh Steelers, Ernie joined the Cowboys in 1966. He helped develop All-Pros Bob Lilly, George Andrie, Harvey Martin, Randy White, and Ed Jones. During his 15-year playing career, Ernie played in nine Pro Bowls. He was elected to the Hall of Fame in his first year of eligibility. Ernie is also a member of the Steelers' 50th anniversary team. Stautner was known as one of the most intense players during his era, and has continued to carry that trait throughout his coaching career.

Bob Ward

Conditioning

The director of the Cowboys' offseason program, Bob is noted as one of the leading innovators in his area of expertise. His programs include weightlifting, aerobic conditioning, martial arts, flexibility training and nutrition. Bob has a doctorate in physical science from Indiana University. A member of Delta Force, a U.S. Army think tank, Bob co-founded the National Association of Speed and Explosion. Bob was track coach at Fullerton College for 11 years before joining the Cowboys in 1975.

COWBOYS CLUB DIRECTORY

General Partner: H. R. "Bum" Bright
President and General Manager: Texas E. Schramm
Vice President-Personnel Development: Gil Brandt
Vice President-Treasurer: Don Wilson
Vice President-Administration: Joe Bailey
Vice President-Pro Personnel: Bob Ackles

Head Coach: Tom Landry
Coaching Staff: Neill Armstrong, *Research & Development;* Jim Erkenbeck, *Offensive Line;* Paul Hackett, *Pass Offense/Quarterbacks;* Al Lavan, *Running Backs;* Alan Lowry, *Receivers;* Dick Nolan, *Defensive Backs;* Mike Solari, *Special Teams/Offensive Line;* Ernie Stautner, *Defensive Coordinator/Defensive Line;* Jerry Tubbs, *Linebackers;* Bob Ward, *Conditioning.*
Coaching Secretaries: Marge Anderson (Coaching Staff), Barbara Goodman (Mr. Landry), Tula Johnapelus (Mr. Ackles/Coaching Staff)

Scouts: Bob Griffin, Walter Juliff, Charlie Mackey, Dick Mansperger, Ron Marciniak, Jeff Smith, John Wooten, Walt Yowarsky.
Scouting Secretaries: Wendy Bordinat (Mr. Brandt), Hazel Nichols (Scouting Staff)

Medical Staff: Don Cochren, *Trainer;* Ken Locker, *Assistant Trainer;* Jim Maurer, *Intern;* Dr. Robert D. Vandermeer, Dr. Marvin P. Knight, Dr. J. Pat Evens, Dr. J. R. Zamorano, *Consultant/Rehabilitation*

Counseling Services: Larry Wansley, *Director*

Photographic Services: Bob Friedman, *Director;* Robert Blackwell, *Assistant Director.*

Equipment: Buck Buchanan, *Manager;* Jerry Fowler, *Assistant Manager;* Otis Jackson, *Assistant.*

Public Relations: Doug Todd, *Director;* Greg Aiello, *Marketing Director;* David Pelletier, *Assistant.*
Public Relations Secretaries: Jerri Mote (Mr. Todd), Deana Patterson (Mr. Aiello)

Advertising: Peggie Bullock, *Director;* Holly Bell, *Assistant*

Building Services: Steve Forgey, *Maintenance Supervisor;* William Griffith, *Maintenance.*

Administration: Billy Hicks, *Director of Business Services;* Jim Lancaster, *Controller;* Debbie McBride, *Accounting;* Pat Miller, *Accounting;* Allan Cariker, *Computer Services;* Kathy Coleman, *Mail/Supplies;* Craig Glieber, *intern;* Bunker Hill, *Administrative Assistant;* Melissa Aucoin, *Receptionist;* Cherri Gamble, *Switchboard.*
Administrative Secretaries: Jill Buckley (Mr. Bailey), Dee Dee Ground (Mr. Wansley, Matticks), Connie Medina (Mr. Schramm).

Building Security: John Garza, Bill Petty, Bill Westfall.

Ticket Office: Steve Orsini, *Manager;* Ann Lloyd, *Assistant Manager/Alumni Coordinator;* Sandra Woods, *Assistant Manager;* Rebecca Nolte, *Assistant;* Mary Reed, *Assistant.*

Cheerleaders: Suzanne Mitchell, *Director;* Debbie Bond, *Assistant Director;* Shannon Werthmann, *Choreographer;* Judy Trammell, *Assistant Choreographer.*

Entertainment: Jim Skinner, *Halftime Director;* Bill Lively, *Band Director.*

Cowboys Weekly: Russ Russell, *Publisher;* Carlton Stowers, *Editor;* Jarrett Bell, *Assistant Editor;* Bobby Collier, *Production Manager;* Sharon Carnahan, *Circulation Manager;* Beth Egan, *Assistant;* Pam Peterson, *Assistant.*

Cowboys Travel: Dan Werner, *Director;* Cathy Boyd, *Manager;* Marti Carlson, *Manager;* Linda Creamer, *Manager;* Starla Lindsey, *Manager;* Lisa Baumann, Sara Benchoff, Jill Cleator, Barbara Cramer, Maria Frontario, Damon Green, Heather Green, Tammy Guthery, Karen Helms, Sandra Jacob, Terry Kalmi, Diane Manney, Dava Marquart, Dale Mills, Julianne Noblet, Cynthia Whorton.

Limited Partnership

H. R. Bright	Texas E. Schramm
J. L. Huffines, Jr.	Ed A. Smith, Jr.
Mrs. Amelia Hodges	Arthur Temple

The All-Time
DALLAS COWBOYS
Records & Statistics

The 1987 Season At A Glance

St. Louis 24, Cowboys 13

At St. Louis, Sept. 13, 1987

DALLAS	0	6	0	7—13
ST. LOUIS	3	0	0	21—24

Cardinals—FG Gallery 23
Cowboys—FG Ruzek 22
Cowboys—FG Ruzek 29
Cowboys—Banks 20 pass from D. White (Ruzek kick)
Cardinals—Green 16 pass from Lomax (Gallery kick)
Cardinals—Green 22 pass from Lomax (Gallery kick)
Cardinals—Ferrell 15 run (Gallery kick)
Attendance—47,241

	Cowboys	Cardinals
First Downs	19	20
Total Net Yards	322	360
Net Yards Rushing	125	108
Net Yards Passing	197	252
Passes	32–20	33–17
Passes Intercepted By	0	0
Punts-Average	8–46.0	8–45.6
Fumbles-Lost	1–1	1–0
Penalties-Yards	5–34	6–38

Rushing
Cowboys—Walker, 13 for 62; Dorsett, 18 for 60; D. White, 1 for 3.
Cardinals—Ferrell, 10 for 71, 1 touchdown; Mitchell, 14 for 41; Lomax, 3 for -4.

Passing
Cowboys—D. White, 20 of 32 for 256 yards, 1 touchdown.
Cardinals—Lomax, 17 of 33 for 270 yards, 2 touchdowns.

Receiving
Cowboys—Walker, 7 for 90; Cosbie, 4 for 44; Renfro, 4 for 42; Dorsett, 2 for 49; Banks, 1 for 20, 1 touchdown; Fowler, 1 for 6; Barksdale, 1 for 5.
Cardinals—J. T. Smith, 5 for 78; Green, 4 for 90, 2 touchdowns; Novacek, 4 for 43; Mitchell, 2 for 35; Holmes, 2 for 24.

Cowboys 16, N.Y. Giants 14

At New York, Sept. 20, 1987

DALLAS	3	7	3	3—16
N.Y. GIANTS	7	0	7	0—14

Giants—Robinson 5 pass from Simms (Allegre kick)
Cowboys—FG Ruzek 46
Cowboys—Chandler 1 pass from D. White (Ruzek kick)
Giants—Bavaro 1 pass from Simms (Allegre kick)
Cowboys—FG Ruzek 43
Cowboys—FG Ruzek 28
Attendance—73,426

	Cowboys	Giants
First Downs	21	14
Total Net Yards	356	265
Net Yards Rushing	114	60
Net Yards Passing	242	205
Passes	38–23	37–17
Passes Intercepted By	4	4
Punts-Average	4–41.8	4–40.3
Fumbles-Lost	1–0	1–1
Penalties-Yards	9–70	5–51

Rushing
Cowboys—Dorsett, 18 for 75; Walker, 17 for 27; Newsome, 2 for 14; D. White, 1 for -2.
Giants—Morris, 8 for 26; Rouson, 5 for 22; Anderson, 2 for 6; Carthon, 2 for 3; Simms, 1 for 2; Adams, 2 for 1.

Passing
Cowboys—D. White, 23 of 38 for 276 yards, 1 touchdown, 4 interceptions.
Giants—Simms, 17 of 36 for 219 yards, 2 touchdowns, 4 interceptions; Rutledge, 0 of 1.

Receiving
Cowboys—Banks, 6 for 96; Cosbie, 4 for 67; Dorsett, 4 for 12; Walker, 3 for 50; Newsome, 3 for 19; Barksdale, 1 for 20; Renfro, 1 for 11; Chandler, 1 for 1, 1 touchdown.
Giants—Galbreath, 5 for 59; Bavaro, 3 for 64, 1 touchdown; Robinson, 3 for 31; 1 touchdown; Manuel, 2 for 24; Ingram, 1 for 14; McConkey, 1 for 12; Rouson, 1 for 8; Anderson, 1 for 7.

Cowboys 38, N.Y. Jets 24

At New York, Oct. 4, 1987

DALLAS	7	17	14	0—38
N.Y. JETS	3	7	7	7—24

Jets—FG Ragusa 20
Cowboys—Burbage 13 pass from Sweeney (Zendejas kick)
Cowboys—FG Zendejas 33
Cowboys—Adams 27 run (Zendejas Kick)
Cowboys—Edwards 33 pass from Sweeney (Zendejas kick)
Jets—Kurisko 41 pass from Norrie (Ragusa kick)
Jets—Chirico 3 run (Ragusa kick)
Cowboys—Blount 1 run (Zendejas kick)
Cowboys—Edwards 35 pass from Sweeney (Zendejas kick)
Jets—Harper 78 punt return (Ragusa kick)
Attendance—12,370

	Cowboys	Jets
First Downs	14	22
Total Net Yards	246	241
Net Yards Rushing	114	82
Net Yards Passing	132	159
Passes	15-6	35-18
Passes Intercepted By	2	1
Punts-Average	6-42.5	4-25.8
Fumbles-Lost	4-3	4-3
Penalties-Yards	16-131	10-150

Rushing
Cowboys—Blount, 28 for 72, 1 touchdown; Adams, 5 for 43, 1 touchdown; Sweeney, 3 for 3; G. White, 1 for -4.
Jets—Hunter, 15 for 48; Chirico, 9 for 16, 1 touchdown; Foster, 1 for 9; Norrie, 4 for 5; Briggs, 1 for 4.

Passing
Cowboys—Sweeney, 6 of 14 for 139 yards, 3 touchdowns, 1 interception; Snyder, 0 of 1.
Broncos—Norrie, 18 of 33 for 213 yards, 1 touchdown, 1 interception; Briggs, 0 of 2, 1 interception.

Receiving
Cowboys—Burbage, 3 for 46, 1 touchdown; Edwards, 2 for 68, 2 touchdowns; Spivey, 1 for 25.
Jets—Harper, 6 for 89; Holman, 4 for 40; Chirico, 4 for 18; Kurisko, 1 for 41, 1 touchdown; Gaffney, 1 for 10; Foster, 1 for 9; Hunter, 1 for 6.

Cowboys 41, Philadelphia 22

At Dallas, Oct. 11, 1987

PHILADELPHIA	3	7	6	6—22
DALLAS	21	6	14	0—41

Cowboys—Edwards 62 run (Zendejas kick)
Cowboys—Blount 8 run (Zendejas kick)
Cowboys—Burbage 77 pass from Sweeney (Zendejas kick)
Eagles—FG Jacobs 40
Eagles—Bowman 62 pass from Tinsley (Jacobs kick)
Cowboys—FG Zendejas 44
Cowboys—FG Zendejas 50
Cowboys—Dorsett 10 run (Zendejas kick)
Cowboys—Blount 1 run (Zendejas kick)
Eagles—Siano 13 pass from Tinsley (kick failed)
Eagles—Clemons 13 pass from Tinsley (kick blocked)
Attendance—40,622

	Eagles	Cowboys
First Downs	24	19
Total Net Yards	434	400
Net Yards Rushing	72	160
Net Yards Passing	362	240
Passes	45-29	25-15
Passes Intercepted By	0	0
Punts-Average	6-30.1	5-42.2
Fumbles-Lost	4-3	3-2
Penalties-Yards	9-68	10-71

Rushing

Eagles—R. Brown, 17 for 43; Ross, 7 for 24; Robinson, 2 for 6; Clemons, 1 for 0; Horn, 1 for 0; Tinsley, 2 for -1.
Cowboys—Edwards, 1 for 62, 1 touchdown; Blount, 18 for 53, 2 touchdowns; Dorsett, 4 for 27, 1 touchdown; E. J. Jones, 2 for 7; Adams, 2 for 6; Sweeney, 2 for 5; Snyder, 2 for 0.

Passing

Eagles—Tinsley, 24 of 34 for 338 yards, 3 touchdowns; Horn, 5 of 11 for 68 yards.
Cowboys—Sweeney, 8 of 14 for 152 yards, 1 touchdown; D. White, 3 of 3 for 59 yards; Snyder, 4 of 8 for 44 yards.

Receiving

Eagles—Siano, 6 for 83, 1 touchdown; Bowman, 5 for 123, 1 touchdown; Grant, 5 for 97; Ross, 5 for 41; R. Brown, 4 for 20; Bailey, 2 for 17; Clemons, 1 for 13, 1 touchdown; Repko, 1 for 12.
Cowboys—Edwards, 6 for 100; Burbage, 3 for 110, 1 touchdown; G. White, 1 for 11; Scott, 1 for 11; Spivey, 1 for 9; Lavette, 1 for 6; Blount, 1 for 5; E. J. Jones, 1 for 3.

Washington 13, Dallas 7

At Dallas, Oct. 19, 1987

WASHINGTON	3	0	7	3—13
DALLAS	0	0	7	0— 7

Redskins—FG Ariri 19
Redskins—T. Wilson 16 run (Ariri kick)
Cowboys—Edwards 38 pass from D. White (Brady kick)
Redskins—FG Ariri 39
Attendance—60,612

	Redskins	Cowboys
First Downs	19	18
Total Net Yards	339	316
Net Yards Rushing	186	93
Net Yards Passing	153	223
Passes	20-12	36-21
Passes Intercepted By	1	2
Punts-Average	3-40.0	5-34.6
Fumbles-Lost	1-1	2-2
Penalties-Yards	8-55	5-31

Rushing

Redskins—Vital, 26 for 136; T. Wilson, 2 for 28, 1 touchdown; Jessie, 9 for 23; Robinson, 2 for 0; W. Wilson, 3 for -1.
Cowboys—Dorsett, 19 for 81; D. White, 3 for 12.

Passing

Redskins—Robinson, 11 of 18 for 152 yards, 2 interceptions; Rubbert, 1 of 2 for 22 yards.
Cowboys—D. White, 21 of 36 for 262 yards, 1 touchdown, 1 interception.

Receiving

Redskins—McEwen, 7 for 108; Allen, 2 for 31; T. Wilson, 2 for 13; Caravello, 1 for 22.
Cowboys—Edwards, 6 for 104, 1 touchdown; Renfro, 5 for 79; G. White, 4 for 35; E. J. Jones, 2 for 13; Dorsett, 2 for 11; Burbage, 1 for 12; Adams, 1 for 8.

Philadelphia 37, Cowboys 20

At Philadelphia, Oct. 25, 1987

DALLAS	3	7	3	7—20
PHILADELPHIA	3	10	7	17—37

Cowboys—FG Ruzek 23
Eagles—FG McFadden 46
Eagles—FG McFadden 45
Eagles—Spagnola 10 pass from Cunningham (McFadden kick)
Cowboys—Walker 1 run (Ruzek kick)
Cowboys—FG Ruzek 25
Eagles—Toney 1 run (McFadden kick)
Eagles—FG McFadden 21
Eagles—Spagnola 5 pass from Cunningham (McFadden kick)
Cowboys—Dorsett 19 pass from D. White (Ruzek kick)
Eagles—Byars 1 run (McFadden kick)
Attendance—61,630

	Cowboys	Eagles
First Downs	18	18
Total Net Yards	294	237
Net Yards Rushing	97	141
Net Yards Passing	197	96
Passes	36-22	24-10
Passes Intercepted By	0	0
Punts-Average	4-39.5	4-36.8
Fumbles-Lost	5-3	2-1
Penalties-Yards	10-113	6-27

Rushing

Cowboys—Walker, 12 for 54, 1 touchdown; Dorsett, 11 for 32; Newsome, 2 for 10; Pelluer, 1 for 1.
Eagles—Byars, 20 for 94, 1 touchdown; Cunningham, 8 for 39; Toney, 6 for 8, 1 touchdown.

Passing

Cowboys—D. White, 22 of 36 for 257 yards, 1 touchdown.
Eagles—Cunningham, 10 of 24 for 127 yards, 2 touchdowns.

Receiving

Cowboys—Cosbie, 6 for 31; Banks, 4 for 59; Dorsett, 3 for 40, 1 touchdown; Edwards, 3 for 38; Renfro, 2 for 41; Walker, 2 for 14; Newsome, 1 for 30; Barksdale, 1 for 4.
Eagles—Quick, 3 for 61; Toney, 3 for 43; Spagnola, 2 for 15, 2 touchdowns; Tautalatasi, 2 for 8.

Cowboys 33, N.Y. Giants 24

At Dallas, Nov. 2, 1987

N.Y. GIANTS	0	10	7	7—24
DALLAS	7	7	0	19—33

Cowboys—Walker 1 run (Ruzek kick)
Giants—Morris 5 run (Allegre kick)
Giants—FG Allegre 35
Cowboys—Cosbie 2 pass from D. White (Ruzek kick)
Giants—Manuel 50 pass from Simms (Allegre kick)
Giants—Manuel 33 pass from Simms (Allegre kick)
Cowboys—FG Ruzek 34
Cowboys—Jeffcoat 26 interception return (Ruzek kick)
Cowboys—FG Ruzek 49
Cowboys—FG Ruzek 40
Cowboys—FG Ruzek 35
Attendance—55,730

	Giants	Cowboys
First Downs	16	15
Total Net Yards	287	240
Net Yards Rushing	55	26
Net Yards Passing	242	214
Passes	27-20	33-24
Passes Intercepted By	1	2
Punts-Average	5-49.4	6-38.1
Fumbles-Lost	3-3	2-1
Penalties-Yards	12-95	9-63

Rushing

Giants—Morris, 17 for 26, 1 touchdown; Simms, 3 for 15; Adams, 3 for 9; Galbreath, 1 for 5.
Cowboys—Walker, 9 for 28, 1 touchdown; Dorsett, 14 for 3; Cosbie, 1 for -5.

Passing

Giants—Simms, 15 of 21 for 230 yards, 2 touchdowns, 2 interceptions; Rutledge, 5 of 6 for 50 yards.
Cowboys—D. White, 24 of 33 for 245 yards, 1 touchdown, 1 interception.

Receiving

Giants—Manuel, 7 for 151, 2 touchdowns; Galbreath, 4 for 32; Bavaro, 3 for 43; Adams, 3 for 40; Morris, 1 for 9; Baker, 1 for 8; Rouson, 1 for 7.
Cowboys—Cosbie, 6 for 72, 1 touchdown; Walker, 6 for 62; Banks, 4 for 56; Newsome, 3 for 9; Renfro, 2 for 32; Edwards, 1 for 7; Chandler, 1 for 5; Dorsett, 1 for 2.

Detroit 27, Cowboys 17

At Detroit, Nov. 8, 1987

DALLAS	0	10	7	0	—17
DETROIT	10	0	7	10	—27

Lions—FG Murray 30
Lions—Rubick 20 pass from Long (Murray kick)
Cowboys—Newsome 1 run (Ruzek kick)
Cowboys—FG Ruzek 38
Lions—James 2 run (Murray kick)
Cowboys—Newsome 24 run (Ruzek kick)
Lions—James 4 run (Murray kick)
Lions—FG Murray 19
Attendance—45,325

	Cowboys	Lions
First Downs	20	20
Total Net Yards	290	293
Net Yards Rushing	123	76
Net Yards Passing	167	217
Passes	38-17	28-15
Passes Intercepted By	2	4
Punts-Average	6-41.8	5-46.4
Fumbles-Lost	2-1	2-2
Penalties-Yards	11-94	6-38

Rushing

Cowboys—Walker, 13 for 65; Newsome, 4 for 29, 2 touchdowns; Dorsett, 11 for 29; D. White, 1 for 0.
Lions—Jones, 9 for 46; James, 18 for 32, 2 touchdowns; Long, 3 for -2.

Passing

Cowboys—D. White, 17 of 38 for 193 yards, 4 interceptions.
Lions—Long, 15 of 28 for 217 yards, 1 touchdown, 2 interceptions.

Receiving

Cowboys—Walker, 5 for 55; Renfro, 4 for 67; Cosbie, 3 for 26; Newsome, 2 for 20; Edwards, 2 for 20; Dorsett, 1 for 5.
Lions—Mandley, 8 for 97; Chadwick, 3 for 72; Rubick, 2 for 41, 1 touchdown; Jones, 1 for 4; James, 1 for 3.

Cowboys 23, New England 17

At New England, Nov. 15, 1987

DALLAS	7	7	0	3	6—23
NEW ENGLAND	0	7	0	10	0—17

Cowboys—Francis 18 interception return (Ruzek kick)
Patriots—Grogan 2 run (Franklin kick)
Cowboys—Cosbie 3 pass from D. White (Ruzek kick)
Patriots—FG Franklin 41
Patriots—Morgan 5 pass from Ramsey (Franklin kick)
Cowboys—FG Ruzek 20
Cowboys—Walker 60 run (Ruzek kick)
Attendance—60,567

	Cowboys	Patriots
First Downs	24	15
Total Net Yards	438	265
Net Yards Rushing	181	88
Net Yards Passing	257	177
Passes	44-25	28-14
Passes Intercepted By	1	2
Punts-Average	7-40.3	6-35.2
Fumbles-Lost	1-1	4-1
Penalties-Yards	15-112	5-35

Rushing

Cowboys—Walker, 28 for 173, 1 touchdown; Dorsett, 1 for 5; Newsome, 1 for 3.
Patriots—Collins, 14 for 40; Ramsey, 3 for 17; Tatupu, 6 for 14; Perryman, 4 for 9; Dupard, 3 for 7; Grogan, 3 for 1, 1 touchdown.

Passing

Cowboys—D. White, 25 of 44 for 286 yards, 1 touchdown, 2 interceptions.
Patriots—Ramsey, 8 of 16 for 136 yards, 1 touchdown; Grogan, 6 of 12 for 73 yards, 1 interception.

Receiving

Cowboys—Newsome, 6 for 49; Walker, 5 for 59; Renfro, 4 for 79; Barksdale, 3 for 40; Cosbie, 3 for 26, 1 touchdown; Dorsett, 2 for 19; Edwards, 1 for 11; Chandler, 1 for 3.
Patriots—Morgan, 5 for 56; 1 touchdown; Fryar, 2 for 59; Starring, 2 for 42; Dawson, 2 for 18; Tatupu, 1 for 23; Perryman, 1 for 7; Collins, 1 for 4.

Miami 20, Cowboys, 14

At Dallas, Nov. 22, 1987

MIAMI	7	3	3	7	—20
DALLAS	7	0	0	7	—14

Cowboys—Newsome 8 pass from Pelluer (Ruzek kick)
Dolphins—Stradford 19 run (Reveiz kick)
Dolphins—FG Reveiz 26
Dolphins—FG Reveiz 33
Dolphins—Pruitt 2 pass from Marino (Reveiz kick)
Cowboys—Newsomr 18 pass from Pelluer (Ruzek kick)
Attendance—56,519

	Dolphins	Cowboys
First Downs	21	16
Total Net Yards	440	319
Net Yards Rushing	182	185
Net Yards Passing	258	134
Passes	39-22	18-12
Passes Intercepted By	2	1
Punts-Average	4-46.7	5-41.6
Fumbles-Lost	0-0	1-1
Penalties-Yards	7-55	6-80

Rushing

Dolphins—Stradford, 17 for 169, 1

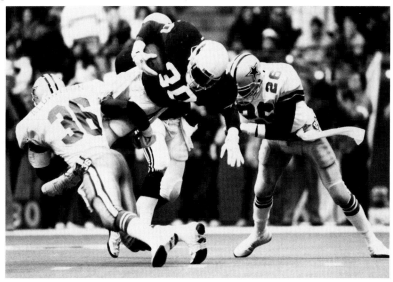

touchdown; Hampton, 4 for 9; Davenport, 2 for 5; Nathan, 1 for 3; Marino, 1 for -2.
Cowboys—Walker, 19 for 82; Pelluer, 11 for 79; Newsome, 4 for 24.

Passing

Dolphins—Marino, 22 of 39 for 265 yards, 1 touchdown, 1 interception.
Cowboys—Pelluer, 12 of 18 for 134 yards, 2 touchdowns, 2 interceptions.

Receiving

Dolphins—Stradford, 6 for 83; Clayton, 4 for 95; Davenport, 3 for 27; Nathan, 2 for 23; Hampton, 2 for 7; Jensen, 1 for 11; Johnson, 1 for 7; Hardy, 1 for 6; Duper, 1 for 4; Pruitt, 1 for 2, 1 touchdown.
Cowboys—Newsome, 7 for 53, 2 touchdowns; Walker, 4 for 74; Cosbie, 1 for 7.

Minnesota 44, Cowboys 38

At Dallas, Nov. 26, 1987

MINNESOTA	14	7	7	10	6—44
DALLAS	0	14	10	14	0—38

Vikings—Carter 11 pass from Kramer (C. Nelson kick)
Vikings—Kramer 1 run (C. Nelson kick)
Cowboys—D. White 1 run (Ruzek kick)
Cowboys—Walker 3 pass from D. White (Ruzek kick)
Vikings—Carter 37 pass from Kramer (C. Nelson kick)
Vikings—D. Nelson 52 run (C. Nelson kick)
Cowboys—FG Ruzek 38
Cowboys—Renfro 8 pass from D. White (Ruzek kick)
Vikings—FG C. Nelson 33
Vikings—Fenney 1 run (C. Nelson kick)
Cowboys—Renfro 14 pass from D. White (Ruzek kick)
Cowboys—Renfro 18 pass from D. White (Ruzek kick)
Vikings—D. Nelson 24 run
Attendance—54,229

	Vikings	Cowboys
First Downs	27	23
Total Net Yards	476	403
Net Yards Rushing	188	112
Net Yards Passing	288	291
Passes	36-18	41-25
Passes Intercepted By	3	2
Punts-Average	6-39.3	5-38.2
Fumbles-Lost	1-0	3-2
Penalties-Yards	5-53	8-64

Rushing

Vikings—D. Nelson, 16 for 118, 2 touchdowns; Anderson, 10 for 38; Fenney, 10 for 31, 1 touchdown; Kramer, 1 for 1, 1 touchdown; Rice, 3 for 0.
Cowboys—Walker, 21 for 76, Dorsett, 7 for 19; Newsome, 3 for 18; D. White, 3 for -1, 1 touchdown.

Passing

Vikings—Wilson, 9 of 18 for 189 yards, 1 interception; Kramer, 9 of 18 for 123 yards, 2 touchdowns, 1 interception.
Cowboys—D. White, 25 of 41 for 341 yards, 4 touchdowns, 3 interceptions.

Receiving

Vikings—Carter, 8 for 184, 2 touchdowns; D. Nelson, 5 for 43; Jordan, 3 for 41; Lewis, 2 for 44.
Cowboys—Renfro, 7 for 100, 3 touchdowns; Walker, 7 for 91, 1 touchdown; Newsome, 5 for 34; Barksdale, 3 for 60; Edwards, 2 for 26; Cosbie, 1 for 30.

Atlanta 21, Cowboys 10

At Dallas, Dec. 6, 1987

ATLANTA	14	0	7	0—21
DALLAS	3	7	0	0—10

Falcons—Dixon 28 pass from Campbell (Luckhurst kick)
Falcons—R. Moore 20 fumble return

(Luckhurst kick)
Cowboys—FG Ruzek 44
Cowboys—Walker 1 run (Ruzek kick)
Falcons—Campbell 1 run (Luckhurst kick)
Attendance—40,103

	Falcons	Cowboys
First Downs	18	24
Total Net Yards	364	354
Net Yards Rushing	111	91
Net Yards Passing	253	263
Passes	30-17	43-26
Passes Intercepted By	1	2
Punts-Average	5-42.6	5-40.0
Fumbles-Lost	2-2	2-2
Penalties-Yards	5-68	3-42

Rushing

Falcons—Riggs, 30 for 119; Campbell, 1 for 1, 1 touchdown; Dixon, 1 for -9.
Cowboys—Walker, 15 for 35, 1 touchdown; Dorsett, 7 for 33; Newsome, 3 for 13; Pelluer, 1 for 11; Edwards, 1 for -1.

Passing

Falcons—Campbell, 17 of 30 for 253 yards, 1 touchdown, 2 interceptions.
Cowboys—Pelluer, 18 of 31 for 203 yards; D. White, 8 of 12 for 83 yards, 1 interception.

Receiving

Falcons—Dixon, 7 for 80, 1 touchdown; Matthews, 3 for 45; Settle, 2 for 62; C. Brown, 2 for 43; Emery, 2 for 18; Riggs, 1 for 5.
Cowboys—Edwards, 7 for 88; Walker, 7 for 62; Renfro, 6 for 68; Newsome, 4 for 35; Martin, 1 for 17; Barksdale, 1 for 16.

Washington 24, Cowboys 20

At Washington, Dec. 13, 1987

DALLAS	3	0	10	7—20
WASHINGTON	7	10	7	0—24

Redskins—Rogers 1 run (Haji-Sheikh kick)
Cowboys—FG Ruzek 22
Redskins—FG Haji Sheikh 31
Redskins—Clark 56 pass from Schroeder (Haji-Sheikh kick)
Redskins—Rogers 1 run (Haji-Sheikh kick)
Cowboys—FG Ruzek 37
Cowboys—Renfro 25 pass from D. White (Ruzek kick)
Cowboys—Barksdale 5 pass from D. White (Ruzek kick)
Attendance—55,882

	Cowboys	Redskins
First Downs	25	15
Total Net Yards	428	317
Net Yards Rushing	87	68
Net Yards Passing	341	249
Passes	49-27	26-13
Passes Intercepted By	1	1
Punts-Average	5-35.8	6-43.1
Fumbles-Lost	1-1	1-1
Penalties-Yards	7-75	6-35

Rushing

Cowboys—Walker, 14 for 44; Dorsett, 8 for 40; D. White, 1 for 2; Newsome, 2 for 1.
Redskins—Rogers, 27 for 64, 2 touchdowns; Bryant, 1 for 8; Schroeder, 3 for -4.

Passing

Cowboys—D. White, 27 of 49 for 359 yards,

2 touchdowns, 1 interception.
Redskins—Schroeder, 13 of 26 for 250 yards, 1 touchdown, 1 interception.

Receiving

Cowboys—Renfro, 6 for 97, 1 touchdown; Cosbie, 5 for 79; Walker, 5 for 54; Martin, 2 for 55; Newsome, 2 for 20; Barksdale, 2 for 20, 1 touchdown; Edwards, 2 for 18; Dorsett, 2 for 9; Chandler, 1 for 7.
Redskins—Clark, 9 for 187, 1 touchdown; Sanders, 2 for 55; Warren, 1 for 6; Didier, 1 for 2.

Cowboys 29, L.A. Rams 21

At Los Angeles, Dec. 21, 1987

DALLAS	10	6	10	3—29
L.A. RAMS	7	0	7	7—21

Cowboys—Walker 1 run (Ruzek kick)
Rams—White 8 run (Lansford kick)
Cowboys—FG Ruzek 24
Cowboys—FG Ruzek 42
Cowboys—FG Ruzek 44
Cowboys—FG Ruzek 47
Cowboys—Cosbie 27 pass from Pelluer (Ruzek kick)
Rams—Everett 1 run (Lansford kick)
Cowboys—FG Ruzek 37
Rams—House 15 pass from Dils (Lansford kick)
Attendance—60,700

	Cowboys	Rams
First Downs	20	19
Total Net Yards	365	311
Net Yards Rushing	194	74
Net Yards Passing	171	237
Passes	30-15	39-19
Passes Intercepted By	3	0
Punts-Average	6-34.0	5-41.4
Fumbles-Lost	1-0	2-1
Penalties-Yards	8-56	3-18

Rushing

Cowboys—Walker, 23 for 108, 1 touchdown; Dorsett, 12 for 52; Pelluer, 5 for 29; Newsome, 2 for 5.
Rams—White, 26 for 66, 1 touchdown; Everett, 3 for 8, 1 touchdown; Dils, 1 for 0.

Passing

Cowboys—Pelluer, 15 of 30 for 183 yards, 1 touchdown.
Rams—Everett, 12 of 24 for 189 yards, 2 interceptions; Dils, 7 of 15 for 73 yards, 1 touchdown, 1 interception.

Receiving

Cowboys—Walker, 6 for 54; Renfro, 3 for 33; Cosbie, 2 for 35, 1 touchdown; Martin, 2 for 31; Dorsett, 2 for 30.
Rams—Ellard, 5 for 75; Guman, 5 for 73; Ron Brown, 3 for 52; Johnson, 2 for 35; White, 2 for 3; House, 1 for 15, 1 touchdown; Tyrrell, 1 for 9.

Cowboys 21, St. Louis 16

At Dallas, Dec. 27, 1987

ST. LOUIS	3	7	0	6—16
DALLAS	0	14	0	7—21

Cardinals—FG Del Greco 32
Cowboys—Walker 11 run (Ruzek kick)
Cowboys—Walker 11 run (Ruzek kick)
Cardinals—J. T. Smith 2 pass from Lomax (Del Greco kick)
Cardinals—FG Del Greco 28
Cowboys—Pelluer 5 run (Ruzek kick)
Cardinals—FG Del Greco 37
Attendance—36,788

	Cardinals	Cowboys
First Downs	26	17
Total Net Yards	422	285
Net Yards Rushing	126	163
Net Yards Passing	296	122
Passes	55-28	22-10
Passes Intercepted By	0	1
Punts-Average	4-39.5	7-35.4
Fumbles-Lost	1-1	0-0
Penalties-Yards	7-65	9-55

Rushing

Cardinals—Mitchell, 22 for 91; Lomax, 2 for 14; McAdoo, 3 for 11; Wolfley, 3 for 10.
Cowboys—Walker, 25 for 137, 2 touchdowns; Pelluer, 7 for 22, 1 touchdown; Newsome, 2 for 4.

Passing

Cardinals—Lomax, 28 of 54 for 314 yards, 1 touchdown, 1 interception; Mitchell, 0 of 1.
Cowboys—Pelluer, 10 of 22 for 122 yards.

Receiving

Cardinals—J. T. Smith, 11 for 102, 1 touchdown; Green, 7 for 112; Novacek, 4 for 42; Wolfley, 3 for 14; Mitchell, 2 for 30; T. Johnson, 1 for 14.
Cowboys—Walker, 3 for 50; Edwards, 2 for 41; Renfro, 2 for 13; Chandler, 1 for 9; Newsome, 1 for 5; Cosbie, 1 for 4.

Dallas Cowboys 1987 Statistics

RESULTS AND ATTENDANCE (7-8)

(L)	13	@ St. Louis	47,241	24
(W)	16	@ N.Y. Giants	73,426	14 (SO)
		SUN SEP 27 BUFFALO—cancelled		
(W)	38	@ N.Y. Jets	12,370	24
(W)	41	PHILADELPHIA	40,622	22
(L)	7	WASHINGTON	60,415	13
(L)	20	@ Philadelphia	61,630	37 (SO)
(W)	33	N.Y. GIANTS	55,730	24
(L)	17	@ Detroit	45,325	27
(W) OT	23	@ New England	60,567	17 (SO)
(L)	14	MIAMI	56,519	20 (SO)
(L) OT	38	MINNESOTA	54,229	44
(L)	10	ATLANTA	40,103	21
(L)	20	@ Washington	54,882	24 (SO)
(W)	29	@ L.A. Rams	60,700	21 (SO)
(W)	21	ST. LOUIS	36,788	16

TEAM STATISTICS

	DALLAS	OPP
FIRST DOWNS	293	294
Rushing	93	85
Passing	176	175
Penalty	24	34
Third Down-Made/Att	86/222	96/223
Third Down Efficiency	38.3	43.1
Fourth Down-Made/Att	3/9	6/14
TOTAL NET YARDS	5056	5061
Avg. Per Game	337.1	337.4
Total Plays	1017	1012
Avg. Per Play	5.0	5.0
NET YARDS RUSHING	1865	1617
Avg. Per Game	124.3	107.8
Total Rushes	465	459
Avg. Per Rush	4.0	3.5
NET YARDS PASSING	3191	3444
Avg. Per Game	212.7	229.6
Tackled/Yards Lost	52/403	51/337
Gross Yards	3594	3781
Attempts/Completions	500/288	502/269
Pct. of Completions	57.6	53.6
Had Intercepted	20	23
PUNTS/AVERAGE	84/39.6	75/40.6
Net Punting Average	33.7	34.0
PUNT RETURNS/ AVERAGE	41/8.6	45/8.4
KICKOFF RETURNS/ AVERAGE	64/20.4	65/19.7
INTERCEPTIONS/ AVG. RET.	23/9.0	20/14.0
PENALTIES/YARDS	131/1091	100/851
FUMBLES/BALL LOST	30/20	29/20
TOUCHDOWNS	38	42
Rushing	17	19
Passing	19	21
Returns	2	2
EXTRA POINTS/ ATTEMPTS	37/37	39/41
FIELD GOALS/ ATTEMPTS	25/29	19/29
TOTAL POINTS	340	348
AVG. TIME OF POSSESSION	31:01	29:28

SCORING

	TDR	TDP	TDRt	FG	PAT	TP
Ruzek	0	0	0	22/25	26/26	92
Walker	7	1	0	0	0	48
Edwards	1	3	0	0	0	24
Newsome	2	2	0	0	0	24
Renfro	0	4	0	0	0	24
Zendejas	0	0	0	3/4	10/10	19
Blount	3	0	0	0	0	18
Cosbie	0	3	0	0	0	18
Burbage	0	2	0	0	0	12
Dorsett	1	1	0	0	0	12
Adams	1	0	0	0	0	6
Banks	0	1	0	0	0	6
Barksdale	0	1	0	0	0	6
Chandler	0	1	0	0	0	6
Francis	0	0	1	0	0	6
Jeffcoat	0	0	1	0	0	6
Pelluer	1	0	0	0	0	6
D. White	1	0	0	0	0	6
Brady	0	0	0	0/0	1/1	1
TOTALS	17	19	2	25/29	37/37	340
Opp. Totals	19	21	2	19/29	39/41	348

RUSHING

	ATT	YDS	AVG	LG	TD
Walker	209	891	4.3	60t	7
Dorsett	130	456	3.5	24	1
Pelluer	25	142	5.7	21	1
Blount	46	125	2.7	15	3
Newsome	25	121	4.8	24t	2
Edwards	2	61	30.5	62t	1
Adams	7	49	7.0	27t	1
D. White	10	14	1.4	8	1
Sweeney	5	8	1.6	5	0
E. J. Jones	2	7	3.5	5	0
Snyder	2	0	0.0	0	0
G. White	1	−4	−4.0	−4	0
Cosbie	1	−5	−5.0	−5	0
TOTALS	465	1865	4.0	62t	17
Opp. Totals	459	1617	3.5	52t	19

RECEIVING

	NO	YDS	AVG	LG	TD
Walker	60	715	11.9	44	1
Renfro	46	662	14.4	43	4
Cosbie	36	421	11.7	30	3
Edwards	34	521	15.3	38t	3
Newsome	34	274	8.1	30	2
Dorsett	19	177	9.3	33	1
Banks	15	231	15.4	34	1
Barksdale	12	165	13.8	22	1
Burbage	7	168	24.0	77t	2
Martin	5	103	20.6	33	0
G. White	5	46	9.2	14	0
Chandler	5	25	5.0	9	1
E. J. Jones	3	16	5.3	10	0
Spivey	2	34	17.0	25	0
C. Scott	1	11	11.0	11	0
Adams	1	8	8.0	8	0
Fowler	1	6	6.0	6	0
Lavette	1	6	6.0	6	0
Blount	1	5	5.0	5	0
TOTALS	288	3594	12.5	77t	19
Opp. Totals	269	3781	14.1	62t	21

INTERCEPTIONS

	NO	YDS	AVG	LG	TD
Walls	5	38	7.6	30	0
Downs	4	56	14.0	27	0
Bates	3	28	9.3	28	0
Haynes	3	7	2.3	7	0
Francis	2	18	9.0	18t	1
Jeffcoat	1	26	26.0	26t	1
Penn	1	21	21.0	21	0
Lockhart	1	13	13.0	13	0
Scott	1	1	1.0	1	0
Green	1	0	0.0	0	0
R. White	1	0	0.0	0	0
TOTALS	23	208	9.0	30	2
Opp. Totals	20	279	14.0	69	0

PUNTING

	NO	YDS	AVG	TB	IN20	LG	BL	NET
Saxon	68	2685	39.5	5	20	63	0	34.2
Sawyer	16	639	39.9	1	3	54	0	31.4
TOTALS	84	3324	39.6	6	23	63	0	33.7
Opp. Totals	75	3042	40.6	7	14	64	1	34.0

KICKOFF RETURNS

	NO	YDS	AVG	LG	TD
Clack	29	635	21.9	48	0
Spivey	2	49	24.5	29	0
Edwards	7	155	22.1	32	0
Martin	12	237	19.8	38	0
Adams	6	113	18.8	27	0
Lavette	4	72	18.0	22	0
Newsome	2	22	11.0	12	0
Chandler	1	7	7.0	7	0
Borresen	1	5	5.0	5	0
TOTALS	64	1295	20.2	48	0
Opp. Totals	65	1281	19.7	45	0

PUNT RETURNS

	NO	FC	YDS	AVG	LG	TD
Martin	22	2	216	9.8	38	0
Edwards	8	1	75	9.4	13	0
Banks	5	1	33	6.6	12	0
Burbage	5	1	29	5.8	13	0
Livingston	1	0	0	0.0	0	0
TOTALS	41	5	353	8.6	38	0
Opp. Totals	45	17	376	8.4	78t	1

SCORE BY QUARTERS

	1	2	3	4	OT	T
COWBOYS	71	108	78	77	6	340
Opponents	84	68	79	111	6	348

FIELD GOALS

	11-19	20-29	30-39	40-49	50+
COWBOYS	0-0	8-8	7-8	9-12	1-1
Opponents	2-2	5-6	8-10	4-11	0-0

Ruzek: (22, 29); (46, 43, 28); (–); (–); (–); (23, 49B, 25); (34, 49, 40, 35); (38, 36M); (20); (–); (38); (44); (22, 43M, 37); (24, 42, 44, 47, 37); (–)

Zendejas: (–); (–); (33); (49M, 44, 50); (–)

PASSING

PASSING	ATT	COMP	YDS	PCT	AVG ATT	TD	PCT TD	INT	PCT INT	LG	TRAPS/ YDS	RATING
D. White	362	215	2617	59.4	7.23	12	3.3	17	4.7	43	44/353	73.2
Sweeney	28	14	291	50.0	10.39	4	14.3	1	3.6	77t	3/15	111.8
Pelluer	101	55	642	54.5	6.36	3	3.0	2	2.0	44	5/35	75.6
Snyder	9	4	44	4.89	44.4	0	0.0	0	0.0	22	0/0	59.5
TOTALS	500	288	3594	57.6	7.19	19	3.8	20	4.0	77t	52/403	76.0
Opp. Totals	502	269	3781	53.6	7.53	21	4.2	23	4.6	62t	51/337	73.0

Cowboys 1987 Defensive Statistics

Fifteen Games
Tackles (Primary-Assists—Combined)

1.	Downs	58-28—86	13.	Burton	18-11—29	25.	Penn	8- 7—15
2.	Bates	46-35—81	14.	Swan	15-14—29	26.	Smerek	8- 6—14
3.	Lockhart	52-28—80	15.	Noonan	19- 8—27	27.	D. Jones	4- 5— 9
4.	Rohrer	41-33—74	16.	Williams	21- 5—26		Hill	6- 2— 8
5.	Brooks	46-21—67	17.	DeOssie	15-11—26	29.	Perkins	3- 5— 8
6.	R. White	39-25—64	18.	Haynes	18- 5—23	30.	Watts	4- 3— 7
7.	E. Jones	41-20—61	19.	M. Hendrix	18- 4—22	31.	Hurd	2- 2— 4
8.	Walls	42-14—56	20.	Dwyer	13- 9—22	32.	Coleman	3- 0— 3
9.	Francis	40- 8—48	21.	Green	12- 8—20	33.	Walen	2- 0— 2
10.	Hegman	29-18—47	22.	Duliban	11- 9—20	34.	Simmons	1- 1— 2
11.	Jeffcoat	30-14—44	23.	Armstrong	16- 1—17	35.	Johnson	1- 0— 1
12.	Albritton	23-12—35	24.	V. Scott	14- 1—15	36.	Livingston	1- 0— 1

Special Teams Tackles

1.	Burton	15- 4—19	8.	Rohrer	5- 2— 7		V. Scott	2- 3— 5
2.	Albritton	13- 5—18	9.	Francis	3- 3— 6	16.	Clack	2- 1— 3
3.	Bates	9- 5—14		Williams	3- 3— 6	17.	Swan	1- 1— 2
4.	DeOssie	6- 7—13	11.	Ruzek	5- 0— 5	18.	Lockhart	1- 0— 1
5.	Penn	7- 3—10	12.	Jax	3- 2— 5		Pelluer	1- 0— 1
6.	Walls	5- 3— 8	13.	Downs	2- 3— 5	20.	Hurd	0- 1— 1
7.	Fowler	3- 5— 8		Hendrix	2- 3— 5		Rafferty	0- 1— 1

QB Traps (51)—E. Jones 10, R. White 6, Jeffcoat 5, Brooks 4, Rohrer 4, Bates 3, Haynes 3, Hegman 3, Watts 3, Duliban 2, Lockhart 2, Perkins 2, Dwyer 1, Johnson 1, Noonan 1, Walen 1.

Interceptions (23)—Walls 5, Downs 4, Bates 3, Haynes 3, Francis 2, Green 1, Jeffcoat 1, Lockhart 1, Penn 1, Scott 1, R. White 1.

Passes Defensed (100)—Walls 19, Francis 12, Downs 8, E. Jones 7, Haynes 6, Hill 5, Lockhart 5, Scott 5, Bates 4, Burton 4, M. Hendrix 4, Green 3, Jeffcoat 3, Albritton 2, DeOssie 2, R. White 2, Williams 2, Armstrong 1, Brooks 1, Duliban 1, Hegman 1, Penn 1, Rohrer 1, Swan 1.

Fumbles Recovered (20)—Dwyer 2, Francis 2, Jeffcoat 2, D. Jones 2, Rohrer 2, Brooks 1, Burton 1, Downs 1, Hegman 1, E. Jones 1, Lockhart 1, Penn 1, V. Scott 1, Watts 1, Williams 1.

Forced Fumbles (15)—Burton 2, Francis 2, Swan 2, Albritton 1, Bates 1, Brooks 1, Jeffcoat 1, E. Jones 1, Penn 1, Walls 1, Watts 1, R. White 1.

1987 Awards

Herschel Walker . . . . . All-Pro (AP—2nd Team, NEA—
2nd Team)
All-NFC (Pro Football Weekly, UPI—
2nd Team)
Pro Bowl

Roger Ruzek . . . . All-NFC (UPI—2nd Team)
All-Rookie (UPI, Pro Football Weekly)

1987 Final Standings

NATIONAL FOOTBALL CONFERENCE

Eastern Division

	W	L	T	Pct.	Pts.	OP
*Washington	11	4	0	.733	379	285
Dallas	7	8	0	.467	340	348
St. Louis	7	8	0	.467	362	368
Philadelphia	7	8	0	.467	337	380
N.Y. Giants	6	9	0	.400	280	312

Central Division

	W	L	T	Pct.	Pts.	OP
*Chicago	11	4	0	.733	356	282
**Minnesota	8	7	0	.533	336	335
Green Bay	5	9	1	.367	255	300
Tampa Bay	4	11	0	.267	286	360
Detroit	4	11	0	.267	269	384

Western Division

	W	L	T	Pct.	Pts.	OP
*San Francisco	13	2	0	.867	459	253
**New Orleans	12	3	0	.800	422	283
L.A. Rams	6	9	0	.400	317	361
Atlanta	3	12	0	.200	205	436

*Division Champion
**Wild Card for Playoffs

AMERICAN FOOTBALL CONFERENCE

Eastern Division

	W	L	T	Pct.	Pts.	OP
*Indianapolis	9	6	0	.600	300	238
New England	8	7	0	.533	320	293
Miami	8	7	0	.533	362	335
Buffalo	7	8	0	.467	270	305
N.Y. Jets	6	9	0	.400	334	360

Central Division

	W	L	T	Pct.	Pts.	OP
*Cleveland	10	5	0	.667	390	239
**Houston	9	6	0	.600	345	349
Pittsburgh	8	7	0	.533	285	299
Cincinnati	4	11	0	.267	285	370

Western Division

	W	L	T	Pct.	Pts.	OP
*Denver	10	4	1	.700	379	288
**Seattle	9	6	0	.600	371	314
San Diego	8	7	0	.533	253	317
L.A. Raiders	5	10	0	.333	301	289
Kansas City	4	11	0	.267	273	388

PLAYOFFS

AFC Wild Card Game:
@ Houston 23, Seattle 20 (OT)

NFC Wild Card Game:
Minnesota 44, @ New Orleans 10

AFC Divisional Playoffs:
@ Cleveland 38, Indianapolis 21
@ Denver 34, Houston 10

NFC Divisional Playoffs:
Washington 21, @ Chicago 17
Minnesota 36, @ San Francisco 24

AFC Championship Game:
@ Denver 38, Cleveland 33

NFC Championship Game:
@ Washington 17, Minnesota 10

Super Bowl XXII:
(@ San Diego, Ca.)
Washington 42, Denver 10

Pro Bowl:
AFC 15   NFC 6

How the Cowboys Were Built

There were 57 veteran players on the Cowboys roster at the end of the 1987 season. Here's a look at how they came to Dallas:

FROM THE DRAFT
1974—Ed Jones (1st, Tennessee State); Danny White (3rd, Arizona State).
1975—Randy White (1st, Maryland); Mike Hegman (7th, Tennessee State).
1976—Tom Rafferty (4th, Penn State).
1977—Tony Dorsett (1st, Pittsburgh).
1979—Doug Cosbie (3rd, Santa Clara).
1980—Timmy Newsom (6th, Winston-Salem).
1981—Glen Titensor (3rd, Brigham Young).
1982—Jeff Rohrer (2nd, Yale).
1983—Jim Jeffcoat (1st, Arizona State).
1984—Victor Scott (2nd, Colorado); Steve DeOssie (4th, Boston College); Steve Pelluer (5th, Washington); Eugene Lockhart (6th, Houston).
1985—Kevin Brooks (1st, Michigan); Jesse Penn (2nd, Virginia Tech); Crawford Ker (3rd, Florida); Herschel Walker (5th, Georgia, USFL).
1986—Mike Sherrard (1st, UCLA); Darryl Clack (2nd, Arizona State); Mark Walen (3rd, UCLA); Thornton Chandler (6th, Alabama); Garth Jax (11th, Florida State).
1987—Danny Noonan (1st, Nebraska); Ron Francis (2nd, Baylor); Jeff Zimmerman (3rd, Florida); Kelvin Martin (4th, Boston College); Kevin Sweeney (7th, Fresno State); Kevin Gogan (8th, Washington).

SUPPLEMENTAL DRAFT:
1984—Todd Fowler (1st, Stephen F. Austin, USFL).

SIGNED AS FREE AGENTS:
1980—Don Smerek (Nevada-Reno).
1981—Michael Downs (Rice); Everson Walls (Grambling).
1982—Brian Baldinger (Duke).
1983—Bill Bates (Tennessee); Mark Tuinei (Hawaii).
1984—Vince Albritton (Washington).
1985—Gordon Banks (Stanford, USFL); Mike Saxon (San Diego State).
1986—Manny Hendrix (Utah); Paul McDonald (Southern California); Nate Newton (Florida A&M, USFL).
1987—Ron Burton (North Carolina); Steve Cisowski (Santa Clara); Kelvin Edwards (Liberty); Steve Folsom (Utah); Jeff Hurd (Kansas State); George Lilja (Michigan); Roger Ruzek (Weber State); Daryle Smith (Tennessee); Robert Smith (Grambling); Russ Swan (Virginia); Bob White (Rhode Island); Robert Williams (Baylor).

OBTAINED IN TRADES:
1984—Mike Renfro (TCU, from Houston along with 5th round choice in 1985 for Butch Johnson. Also switched 5th round choices in 1984).
1987—Rod Barksdale (Arizona, from L.A. Raiders for Ron Fellows).

Historical Highlights

1960

NFL FRANCHISE—Clint Murchison, Jr., and Bedford Wynne were awarded an expansion franchise in the NFL at the annual league meeting in Miami Beach, Fla. The Cowboys were to play as a "swing" team, playing every other team one time during the first season, although listed in the Western Conference standings (January 28).

COWBOYS STOCKED—A player pool was set up in a league meeting at L.A., with each of 12 NFL teams freezing 25 names on its roster and the Cowboys allowed to pick three from each team for a total of 36 veterans. Dallas, once given the list, had to select its 36 players within 24 hours (March 13).

TRAINING STARTS—Rookies report to first Cowboys camp at Patific U., in Forest Grove, Oregon (July 9).

FIRST PRE-SEASON GAME—The Cowboys, less than six months in existence, get their first test and drop a 10-16 pre-season game to San Francisco in Seattle (August 6).

FIRST HOME GAME—In their Dallas debut, in the Salesmanship Club pre-season game, the Cowboys led the World Champion Baltimore Colts into the final minute before a 62-yard pass from Johnny Unitas to Lenny Moore gave the Colts a 14-10 victory (August 19).

FIRST VICTORY—In a pre-season game at Louisville, Ky., the Cowboys beat New York's Giants, 14-3, with Frank Clarke catching touchdown passes of 73 yards (Eddie LeBaron) and 74 yards (Don Meredith) (August 27).

FIRST LEAGUE GAME—In their first league game, Dallas fell to Pittsburgh, 35-28, with Bobby Layne leading a fourth period Steeler rally (Sept. 24, Saturday night).

STREAK SNAPPED—Dallas snaps a 10-game loss streak by tying New York, 31-31, at Yankee Stadium (Dec. 4).

1961

TRAINING STARTS—Rookies launch training at new campsite—St. Olaf College in Northfield, Minn. (July 9).

FIRST LEAGUE WIN—Scoring ten points in the final 56 seconds, the Cowboys score their first NFL victory, 27-24, over Pittsburgh in the '61 league opener in the Cotton Bowl. Allen Green's 27-yard field goal on the game's final play won it before 23,500 (Sept. 17).

1962

TRAINING STARTS—Team begins training at new campsite—Northern Michigan College in Marquette, Mich. (July 13).

PENALTY HISTORY—For the first time in anyone's memory in an NFL game, points were awarded for a penalty. The Cowboys were detected holding in the end zone on a 99-yard TD pass from LeBaron to Clarke, and Pittsburgh was awarded a safety. The Steelers eventually won, 30-28 (Sept. 23).

100-YARD FIRSTS—Cowboys Amos Marsh returned a kickoff 101 yards and Mike Gaechter returned a pass interception 100 yards, both plays for fourth quarter TDs in a 41-19 win over Philadelphia in Dallas. It was the first time in NFL history that two 100-yard runs had been made in the same game, much less by the same team in the same quarter (Oct. 14).

1963

SHIFT TO KANSAS CITY—The rival Dallas Texans of the AFL announce they are moving the franchise to Kansas City (Feb. 8).

CALIFORNIA TRAINING SITE—The Cowboys open training at California Lutheran College in Thousand Oaks, Calif. (July 12).

HOWTON SETS RECORD—Bill Howton broke Don Hutson's all-time receiving mark with a 14-yard catch against Washington (there). Hutson's record was 7,991 yards and the catch gave Howton an even 8,000 yards (Sept. 29).

1964

LANDRY CONTRACT—With one year to go on his original contract, Tom Landry is signed to a ten-year extension, in effect giving him an 11-year pact, possibly the longest in major pro sports history (Feb. 5).

1965

FIRST SELLOUT—An overflow crowd of 76,251 jams the Cotton Bowl for the Cleveland game, notching the team's first home sellout. Cleveland won, 24-17. (Nov. 21).

1966

PLAYOFF BOWL—After defeating New York, 38-20, in the season finale (and winning five of their last seven games) to get into the Playoff Bowl at Miami, the Cowboys fall to Baltimore, 35-3 (Jan. 15).

MERGER—Peace comes to pro football with Cowboys GM Tex Schramm completing two months of negotiations with AFL's Lamar Hunt, merging the two leagues under the NFL banner (June 8).

SCHRAMM ELEVATED—Texas E. Schramm, Vice-President and General Manager of the Cowboys from the beginning, was named President of the club by owner Clint Murchison, Jr., who retained the title of Chairman of the Board.

NEELY CASE SOLVED—Dallas and Houston reached agreement in the Ralph Neely case. Neely remained with Dallas with Houston receiving the Cowboys' Nos. 1, 2 and two fifth place picks in the 1967 draft (Nov. 17).

THE CHAMPIONSHIP—The Cowboys won their first championship, capturing the Eastern Conference title with a 10-3-1 record, but lost the NFL Championship Game to Green Bay, 34-27.

1967

TEXAS STADIUM—On Dec. 23, owner Clint Murchison, Jr., formally announced plans to build Texas Stadium in suburban Irving. The stadium, to be financed through a bond-option plan, would be ready for the 1970 season. The stadium would seat a maximum of 58,000.

SECOND CHAMPIONSHIP—Under the NFL's new format, the Cowboys easily won the Capitol Division and defeated Cleveland, Century Division winner, 52-14, in the Cotton Bowl for the Eastern conference championship. However, on Dec. 31 in Green Bay, the Cowboys lost their second bid for an NFL title, falling to the Packers, 21-17, in the 13 degree below weather.

1968

WIN CAPITOL—For the second straight year the Cowboys won the Capitol Division, but for the first time in three years the Cowboys did not win the Eastern Championship, being upset at Cleveland, 31-20, on December 21st. Dallas won the Runner-Up Bowl over Minnesota, 17-13.

1969

TEXAS STADIUM—Ground was broken for Texas Stadium in suburban Irving on January 25, and on June 29 Bert Rose was named general manager of the stadium.

ORIGINALS RETIRE—An era ended for the Cowboys in July. On July 5th at a press conference in Dallas, quarterback Don Meredith, the last of the original Cowboys, announced his retirement. Then, on July 18th, the day the veterans were to report to training camp, all-time rushing great Don Perkins officially retired.

REPEAT CAPITOL WINS—Once again the Cowboys rolled to the Capitol Division Championship with an 11-2-1 season. However, the Cowboys failed to win the Eastern Championship when on Dec. 28, the Cowboys lost to Cleveland, 38-14, in the Cotton Bowl.

1970

FIVE STRAIGHT PLAYOFFS—The Cowboys won their last five games to finish 10-4, claim the Eastern Division championship and make the playoffs, for the fifth year in a row. They defeated Detroit, 5-0, in the opening round to get a shot at the National Conference championship.

FIRST NFC TITLE—The Cowboys captured the biggest prize of their 11-year history on Jan. 3 when they downed San Francisco, 17-10, for the NFC crown. A 16-13 loss to Baltimore in the Super Bowl Jan. 17 left Dallas with one major goal still unrealized.

1971

TEXAS STADIUM—The Cowboys opened a new era in their sparkling Irving, Tex., home with a 44-21 victory over the New England Patriots on October 24. Duane Thomas scored the first touchdown in the new stadium, a 56-yard run just two minutes and 16 seconds after the opening kickoff. Attendance was 65,708.

SIX STRAIGHT PLAYOFFS—The Cowboys won their last seven games to finish 11-3, claim the Eastern Division championship and make the playoffs for the sixth year in a row. They defeated Minnesota 20-12 in the opening round.

SECOND NFC TITLE—For the second consecutive year, the Cowboys met the San Francisco 49ers in the National Conference showdown. This time Dallas won, 14-3, to qualify for its second straight Super Bowl.

FIRST WORLD CHAMPIONSHIP—The Cowboys downed the Miami Dolphins, 24-3, to win Super Bowl VI in New Orleans on Jan. 16. It was the 10th victory in a row for Dallas as Roger Staubach passed for two touchdowns and was named the game's Most Valuable Player.

1972

FIRST 1,000-YARD BACK—Calvin Hill became the first Dallas player to rush for 1,000 yards when he gained 111 on Dec. 9 against the Washington Redskins in Texas Stadium. Hill wound up with 1,036 yards for the season on a record 245 carries.

SEVEN STRAIGHT PLAYOFFS—The Cowboys qualified for the NFL playoffs a record seventh consecutive year, their 10-4 record earning them the National Conference Wild Card berth. Roger Staubach passed for two touchdowns in the last 1½ minutes to give the Cowboys a 30-28 victory at San Francisco in the first round. Then, at Washington on New Year's Eve, Dallas was foiled in its bid for a third straight NFL title when the Redskins won 26-3.

1973

100 VICTORIES—The Cowboys and Coach Tom Landry recorded their 100th victory with a 40-3 Texas Stadium win over the New Orleans Saints on Sept. 24. Landry,

the only head coach the Cowboys have had, ended the season with a career mark of 108-80-6 to rank ninth on the list of the NFL's all-time winningest coaches.

EIGHT STRAIGHT PLAYOFFS—The Cowboys regained the NFC Eastern Division title with a 10-4 record and broke their own NFL record by reaching the playoffs for the eighth year in a row. Dallas defeated Western Division champion Los Angeles in the first round, 27-16, but fell to Central Division winner Minnesota in the NFC Championship Game, 27-10.

1974

FIRST TOP DRAFT CHOICE—For the first time in their history, the Cowboys had the very first choice in the NFL college draft. The No. 1 pick came to Dallas from Houston in exchange for Tody Smith and Billy Parks. The Cowboys selected Ed "Too Tall" Jones, a 6-9, 260-pound defensive end from Tennessee State.

PLAYOFFS MISSED—The Cowboys record-breaking string of eight straight years in the NFL playoffs was broken when the club's 8-6 record failed to qualify.

1975

LILLY HONORED—"Mr. Cowboy" was honored on Bob Lilly Day at Texas Stadium at halftime of the Philadelphia game on Nov. 23. It was the first such recognition ever given to a Dallas player. Lilly never missed a game in 14 years with the Cowboys, earning All-Pro honors seven times at defensive tackle before retiring prior to the '75 season.

TEN STRAIGHT WINNING SEASONS—The Cowboys' 10-4 record earned them the NFC Wild Card berth in the playoffs. The composite record over 10 straight winning seasons was 101-37-2.

THIRD NFC TITLE—After shocking Minnesota in the first round, 17-14 on Roger Staubach's 50-yard "Hail Mary" pass to Drew Pearson, the Cowboys traveled to Los Angeles for the NFC showdown. Staubach threw four touchdown passes, three to Preston Pearson, and Dallas won, 37-7. Pittsburgh won Super Bowl X on Jan. 18 in Miami, 21-17.

1976

ELEVEN STRAIGNT WINNING SEASONS—The Cowboys won the NFC Eastern Division title after their 11-3 record, giving them their 11th straight winning season and 10th playoff berth in that period. A 14-12 first round loss to Los Angeles—the first time Dallas had lost in the first round under the current playoff setup—ended the season.

MEREDITH, PERKINS HONORED—Former Cowboys greats Don Meredith and Don Perkins joined Bob Lilly in the "Ring of Honor" at Texas Stadium during halftime ceremonies at the New York Giants Game on Nov. 7.

1977

HOWLEY HONORED—Former All-Pro linebacker Chuck Howley, a Cowboy from 1961 through 1973, became the fourth member of the Ring of Honor. Howley was honored during ceremonies at halftime of the Detroit Lions game on Oct. 30.

TWELVE STRAIGHT WINNING SEASONS—Getting off to an 8-0 start, their best ever, the Cowboys rolled to a 12-2 record, the championship of the NFC East, and their 12th consecutive winning season. They opened their 11th visit to the playoffs in those 12 years with a 37-7 first-round victory over the Chicago Bears at Texas Stadium.

FOURTH NFC TITLE—Dallas crushed the Minnesota Vikings at Texas Stadium, 23-6, for National Conference crown No. 4 and the right to meet the Denver Broncos in Super Bowl XII.

SECOND WORLD CHAMPIONSHIP—The Cowboys stopped the Denver Broncos, 27-10, to win Super Bowl XII in New Orleans on January 15, 1978. In the process, Dallas tied Minnesota for most Super Bowl appearances (four) and Green Bay, Miami and Pittsburgh for most Super Bowl victories (two). Defensive linemen Harvey Martin and Randy White were name co-Most Valuable Players in the game.

1978

THIRTEEN STRAIGHT WINNING SEASONS—After a mediocre 6-4 start, the Cowboys won six straight games to finish the expanded regular season with a 12-4 record and their 10th Division crown. It marked the Cowboys' 13th consecutive winning season and 12th trip to the playoffs in that span. Dallas rallied to beat Atlanta 27-20 in a divisional playoff at Texas Stadium, sending the Cowboys to their seventh NFC championship game in the last nine years.

FIFTH NFC TITLE—Dallas shut out the Rams in Los Angeles 28-0 in the National Conference title game to advance to the Super Bowl a record fifth time, including three of the last four. In the first Super Bowl rematch, Pittsburgh edged the Cowboys 35-31 for the NFL championship on Jan. 21 in Miami's Orange Bowl.

1979

TWENTIETH ANNIVERSARY—The Cowboys celebrated their 20th anniversary season at halftime of the St. Louis Cardinals game at Texas Stadium on Oct. 21. Stars from each of those 20 seasons plus Coach Tom Landry were introduced during the halftime ceremonies.

FOURTH STRAIGHT NFC EAST TITLE—Rallying from a mid-season slump, the Cowboys won their final three games to finish with an 11-5 record, their 11th

division championship, including the past four NFC East titles, and 14th consecutive winning season. The Cowboys made their 13th trip to the playoffs in those 14 years, but were eliminated by Los Angeles 21-19 in a divisional playoff at Texas Stadium.

1980

LILLY ENTERS HALL OF FAME—Bob Lilly, a seven-time all-pro defensive tackle in his 14-year career with the Cowboys from 1961–74, became the first Cowboys-only player to be inducted into the Pro Football Hall of Fame. Enshrined along with Lilly on Aug. 2 at Canton, Ohio, were Herb Adderley, who played for the Cowboys from 1970–72, Jim Otto and Deacon Jones.

STAUBACH RETIRES—At a press conference at Texas Stadium on March 31, Roger Staubach announced his retirement after 11 record-breaking years as the Cowboys' quarterback. Staubach held all major Cowboys passing records and was the all-time leading NFL passer.

FIFTEEN STRAIGHT WINNING SEASONS—Behind new starting quarterback Danny White, the Cowboys rolled to their 15th consecutive winning season with a surprising 12-4 record, tied for best in the league with Philadelphia and Atlanta. The Cowboys lost the NFC East title to Philadelphia on a tie-breaker, but entered the playoffs for the 14th time in 15 years, this time as a wild card team. The Cowboys beat Los Angeles 34-13 at Texas Stadium in the NFC wild card playoff and rallied past the Falcons at Atlanta 30-27 to advance to the NFC Championship Game at Philadelphia. But the Cowboys lost 20-7 in their bid for a sixth Super Bowl appearance.

LANDRY's 200th VICTORY—Tom Landry joined George Halas and Curly Lambeau as the only coaches with 200 NFL victories when the Cowboys beat Los Angeles 34-13 on Dec. 28 at Texas Stadium in the NFC wild card playoff, raising Landry's record to 200-119-6, counting regular-season and playoff games.

1981

RENFRO HONORED—Former All-Pro defensive back Mel Renfro, the Cowboys all-time leading pass interceptor, became the fifth member of the Cowboys' Ring of Honor. Renfro, who played for Dallas from 1964 through 1977, was honored during halftime ceremonies of the Cowboys-Miami Dolphins game at Texas Stadium Oct. 25.

TWELFTH DIVISION CHAMPIONSHIP—The Cowboys regained the NFC Eastern Division Championship, their 12th division title since 1966, with a 12-4 record and tied Oakland's NFL mark of 16 consecutive winning seasons. Entering the playoffs for the 15th time in that span, the Cowboys advanced to the NFC Championship Game for the ninth time in 12 years by routing Tampa Bay 38-0 at Texas Stadium. But for the second year in a row Dallas lost the conference title game. San Francisco scored a last minute touchdown at Candlestick Park to edge the Cowboys 28-27 for a berth in Super Bowl XVI.

1982

200th REGULAR-SEASON VICTORY—The Cowboys beat Washington 24-10 at RFK Stadium on Dec. 5 for the club's and Coach Tom Landry's 200th regular-season victory.

SEVENTEEN STRAIGHT WINNING SEASONS—The Cowboys finish the strike-shortened regular season with a 6-3 record to establish an NFL record of 17 consecutive

winning seasons. Entering the playoffs for a record-tying eighth straight year and for the 16th time in 17 years, the Cowboys beat Tampa Bay 30-17 and Green Bay 37-26, both at Texas Stadium, to advance to the NFC Championship Game for the third year in a row. But again the Cowboys come up short, losing 31-17 at Washington.

1983

STAUBACH HONORED—Former quarterback Roger Staubach, who led the Cowboys to four Super Bowls, became the sixth member of the club's Ring of Honor during halftime ceremonies of the Cowboys' 27-24 overtime victory over Tampa Bay at Texas Stadium Oct. 9.

VALLEY RANCH AND COWBOYS CENTER—Formal ground-breaking ceremonies took place on Nov. 29 for the Cowboys' new headquarters and training facility at Valley Ranch in northwest Dallas County. On March 27, 1984 the Cowboys and Triland International announced plans for Cowboys Center, an innovative joint venture that will develop business opportunities in a conference center, visitors center, athletic club and retail and restaurant outlets at Valley Ranch.

COWBOYS SOLD—During halftime of the Cowboys-San Diego Chargers game at San Diego, Cowboys President and General Manager Tex Schramm confirms that the club is for sale. On March 19, 1984 the NFL approved the sale of the Cowboys by Clint Murchison, Jr., and the estate of John Murchison to a group headed by Dallas businessman H. R. "Bum" Bright at the annual NFL meeting in Honolulu.

LANDRY TIES LAMBEAU—At the Kingdome in Seattle, the Cowboys defeated the Seahawks 36-10 to give coach Tom Landry his 234th career victory, including playoffs, tying him for second place on the NFL's career list with Curly Lambeau (234-135-23). Landry's record is 234-134-6.

EIGHTEEN STRAIGHT WINNING SEASONS—The Cowboys' 12-4 regular-season record extended their NFL record of 18 consecutive winning seasons. The Los Angeles Rams cut short the Cowboys' NFL record ninth straight playoff appearance by defeating Dallas 24-17 at Texas Stadium in the NFC Wild Card Game.

1984

RETIREMENTS—The Cowboys were hit hard offensively and defensively with the retirements of former Pro Bowlers Billy Joe DuPree, Pat Donovan, Harvey Martin,

Drew Pearson and veteran fullback Robert Newhouse. DuPree never missed playing in a Cowboys game during his 11 years, a streak of 160 games. Donovan earned four consecutive trips to the Pro Bowl at left tackle. Martin led the club in quarterback traps 10 of the 11 years he was with the team. Pearson, retiring because of injuries sustained in an auto accident, left as the Cowboys all-time leading receiver.

25th ANNIVERSARY TEAM—The Cowboys introduced their 25th anniversary, all-time team at halftime of their game against the New York Giants at Texas Stadium on Nov. 4. The team was selected by fans in voting sponsored by The Southland Corporation and KRLD Radio.

NINETEEN STRAIGHT WINNING SEASONS—At Veterans Stadium in Philadelphia, the Cowboys defeat the Eagles 26-10 to extend their NFL record to 19 consecutive winning seasons. However, Dallas failed to make the playoffs for the first time since 1974 ending the Cowboys' NFL record string of nine straight years in postseason play.

1985

STAUBACH ENTERS HALL OF FAME—Former quarterback Roger Staubach, who led the Cowboys to four Super Bowls during his 11-year career, is named to the Pro Football Hall of Fame on Jan. 22. Staubach joins Bob Lilly as the only two players who spent their entire careers with the Cowboys to be elected to the Hall of Fame.

TWENTY STRAIGHT WINNING SEASONS—With a 37-17 triumph over St. Louis at Texas Stadium the Cowboys clinch their 20th consecutive winning season, the longest active streak in professional team sports. In the traditional Thanksgiving Day game, Danny White throws four TD's, including two to Tony Hill to key the Dallas win.

THIRTEENTH DIVISION CHAMPIONSHIP—The Cowboys win the NFC Eastern Division title with a 28-21 triumph over the New York Giants. The victory gives Dallas 13 division championships in 20 seasons and a playoff berth for the 18th time in the past 20 years. With his nine-yard reception on the Cowboys' first series, Tony Hill breaks Cowboys records for catches in a season (74) and consecutive games with a reception (59). The Cowboys scored two touchdowns late in the first half, including a 65-yard interception return by Jim Jeffcoat, to erase a 14-7 deficit. Second-year quarterback Steve Pelluer comes off the bench to lead Dallas to the winning TD with 4:06 remaining.

1986

NEW HEADQUARTERS—The Cowboys moved into their new headquarters at Valley Ranch. For the first time in club history the administrative offices will be housed under the same roof as the locker room and training areas. The 80,000 square-foot building will also include the ticket office, a travel agency, retail merchandise, Cowboys Cheerleaders rehearsal studio and the *Dallas Cowboys Weekly* offices.

100th WIN AT TEXAS STADIUM—Dallas defeats St. Louis 37-6 on Oct. 26 for the club's 100th victory at Texas Stadium. Since the Stadium opened in 1971 the Cowboys have compiled a 100-25 (.800) record, including playoffs.

1987

MURCHISON DIES—Cowboys founder Clint Murchison, Jr. dies on Mar. 31 after a long illness. Murchison, who owned the club until 1984, acquired the expansion Dallas franchise in the NFL in 1960. He hired Tex Schramm as general manager, gave Tom Landry a 10-year contract when his coaching career was in doubt in 1964 and was instrumental in the building of Texas Stadium.

Cowboys All-Time Roster

ASSISTANT COACHES
Allen, Ermal, 1962-83
Armstrong, Neill, 1982-87
Berry, Raymond, 1968
Dahms, Tom, 1960-62
Dimancheff, Babe, 1960-62
Ditka, Mike, 1973-81
Ecklund, Brad, 1960-63
Erkenbeck, Jim, 1987
Franklin, Bobby, 1968-72

Gillman, Sid, 1972
Hackett, Paul, 1986-87
Hickey, Red, 1964
Hughes, Ed, 1973-76
Lavan, Al, 1980-87
Lowry, Alan, 1982-87
Mackovic, John, 1981-82
Myers, Jim, 1962-86
Nolan, Dick, 1962-67, 1982-87

Reeves, Dan, 1970-80
Renfro, Ray, 1968-72
Roy, Alvin, 1973-75
Shofner, Jim, 1983-85
Solari, Mike, 1987
Stallings, Gene, 1972-85
Stautner, Ernie, 1966-87
Tubbs, Jerry, 1966-87
Ward, Bob, 1976-87

PLAYERS
Adams, David, RB, Arizona, 1987
Adderley, Herb, CB, Mich. St., 1970-72
Adkins, Margene, WR, Henderson J.C., 1970-71
Albritton, Vince, S, Washington, 1984-87
Allen, Fary, RB, Hawaii, 1983-84
Alworth, Lance, WR, Arkansas, 1971-72
Andrie, George, DE, Marquette, 1962-72
Armstrong, Jimmy DB, Appalachian State, 1987
Arneson, Jim, G-C, Arizona, 1973-74
Asher, Bob, T, Vanderbilt, 1970
Aughtman, Dowe, OL, Auburn, 1984
Babb, Gene, LB-RB, Austin College, 1960-61
Babinecz, John, LB, Villanova, 1972-73
Baker, Jesse, DE, Jacksonville State, 1986
Baker, Sam, P-K, Oregon State, 1962-63
Baldinger, Brian, C, Duke 1982-84, 1986-87
Banks, Gordon, WR, Stanford, 1985-87
Barnes, Benny, CB, Stanford, 1972-82
Barnes, Gary, WR, Clemson, 1963
Barnes, Rodrigo, LB, Rice, 1973-74
Bateman, Marv, P, Utah, 1972-74
Bates, Bill, S, Tennessee, 1983-87
Baynham, Craig, RB, Georgia Tech, 1967-69
Belden, Bob, QB, Notre Dame, 1969-70
Bercich, Bob, S, Michigan State, 1960-61
Bethea, Larry, DE, Michigan St., 1978-83
Bielski, Dick, TE, Maryland, 1960-61
Bishop, Don, CB, CCLA, 1960-65
Blackwell, Alois, RB, Houston, 1978-79
Blount, Alvin, RB, Maryland, 1987
Boeke, Jim, T, Heidelberg, 1964-67
Borden, Nate, DE, Indiana, 1960-61
Borresen, Rich, TE, Northwestern, 1987
Braatz, Tom, LB, Marquette, 1960
Bradfute, Byron, T, So. Miss., 1960-61
Brady, Kerry, K, Hawaii, 1987
Breunig, Bob, LB, Arizona State, 1975-84
Brinson, Larry, RB, Florida, 1977-79
Brock, Clyde, DT, Utah State, 1962-63
Brooks, Kevin, DL, Michigan, 1985-87
Brown, Guy, LB, Houston, 1977-82
Brown, Otto, CB-S, Prairie View, 1969
Bullocks, Amos, RB, So. Ill., 1962-64
Burbage, Cornell, WR, Kentucky, 1987
Burkett, Jackie, LB, Auburn, 1968-69
Burnette, Dave, T, Central Arkansas, 1987
Butler, Bill, S. Chattanooga, 1960
Caffey, Lee Roy, LB, Texas A&M, 1971
Cannon, Billy, LB, Texas A&M, 1984
Capone, Warren, LB, Louisiana State, 1975
Carano, Glenn, QB, Nevada-Las Vegas, 1977-83
Carmichael, Harold, WR, Southern, 1984
Carroll, Duane, P, Florida State, 1974
Chandler, Thornton, TE, Alabama, 1986-87
Clack, Darryl, RB, Arizona State, 1986-87
Clark, Mike, K, Texas A&M, 1968-71, 1973
Clark, Monte, T, Southern California, 1962
Clark, Phil, CB-S, Northwestern, 1967-69
Clarke, Frank, TE-WR, Colorado, 1960-67
Clinkscale, Dextor, S, South Carolina St., 1980, 1982-85
Cole, Larry, DE-DT, Hawaii, 1968-80
Coleman, Anthony, DB, Baylor, 1987
Coleman, Ralph, LB, N. Car., A&T, 1972
Collier, Reggie, QB, So. Mississippi, 1986
Colvin, Jim, DT, Houston, 1964-66
Cone, Fred, K, Clemson, 1960

Connelly, Mike, C, Utah State, 1960-67
Conrad, Bobby Joe, WR, Texas A&M, 1969
Cooper, Jim, C-G, Temple, 1977-86
Cornwell, Fred, TE, Southern Cal., 1984-85
Cosbie, Doug, TE, Santa Clara, 1979-87
Courville, Vince, WR, Rice, 1987
Cronin, Gene, DE, Pacific, 1960
Cvercko, Andy, G, Northwestern, 1961-62
Daniels, Dick, S, Pacific (Ore.), 1966-68
Davis, Donnie, WR, Southern, 1962
Davis, Kyle, C, Oklahoma, 1975
Davis, Sonny, LB, Baylor, 1961
DeOssie, Steve, LB, Boston College, 1984-86
Dennison, Doug, RB, Kutztown State, 1974-78
Deters, Harold, K, North Carolina St., 1967
Dial, Buddy, WR, Rice, 1964-66
Dickerson, Anthony, LB, SMU, 1980-84
Dickson, Paul, T, Baylor, 1960
Diehl, John, DT, Virginia, 1965
Ditka, Mike, TE, Pittsburgh, 1969-72
Doelling, Fred, S, Pennsylvania, 1960
Donley, Doug, WR, Ohio State, 1981-84
Donohue, Leon, G, San Jose State, 1965-67
Donovan, Pat, T, Stanford, 1975-83
Doran, Jim, WR, Iowa State, 1960-61
Dorsett, Tony, RB, Pittsburgh, 1977-87
Douglas, Merrill, RB, Utah, 1961
Dowdle, Mike, RB-LB, Texas, 1960-62
Downs, Michael, S, Rice, 1981-87
Duckett, Kenny, WR, Wake Forest, 1985
Dugan, Fred, WR, Dayton, 1960
Duliban, Chris, LB, Texas, 1987
Dunn, Perry Lee, RB, Mississippi, 1964-65
Dupre, L.G., RB, Baylor, 1960-61
DuPree, Billy Joe, TE, Michigan St., 1973-83
Dutton, John, DE, Nebraska, 1979-87
Dwyer, Mike, DT, Massachusetts, 1987
Easmon, Ricky, DB, Florida, 1985
East, Ron, DT, Montana State, 1967-70
Edwards, Dave, LB, Auburn, 1963-75
Edwards, Kelvin, WR, Liberty, 1987
Eidson, Jim, G-C, Miss. State, 1976
Falls, Mike, G, Minnesota, 1960-61
Fellows, Ron, CB, Missouri, 1981-86
Fisher, Ray, T, Eastern Illinois, 1960
Fitzgerald, John, G-C, Bost. Coll., 1971-80
Flaherty, Harry, LB, Holy Cross, 1987
Flowers, Richmond, S, Tennessee, 1969-71
Folkins, Lee, TE, Washington, 1962-64
Folsom, Steve, TE, Utah, 1987
Fowler, Todd, FB, Stephen F. Austin, 1985-86
Francis, Ron, CB, Baylor, 1987
Franckhauser, Tom, CB, Purdue, 1960-61
Frank, Bill, T, Colorado, 1964
Frederick, Andy, T, New Mexico, 1977-81
Fritsch, Toni, K, Vienna, Austria, 1971-73, 1975
Frost, Ken, DT, Tennessee, 1961-62
Fry, Bob, T, Kentucky, 1960-64
Fugett, Jean, TE, Amherst, 1972-75
Gaechter, Mike, S, Oregon, 1962-69
Garrison, Walt, RB, Okla. St., 1966-74
Gent, Pete, WR-TE, Mich. St., 1964-68
Gibbs, Sonny, QB, Texas Christian, 1963
Gogan, Kevin, T, Washington, 1987
Gonzaga, John, DE, no college, 1960
Gonzalez, Leon, WR, Bethune-Cookman, 1985

Gowdy, Cornell, CB, Morgan St., 1986
Granger, Charlie, T, Southern, 1961
Granger, Norm, RB, Iowa, 1984
Green, Alex, DB, Indiana, 1987
Green, Allen, P-K, Mississippi, 1961
Green, Cornell, CB-S, Utah State, 1962-74
Gregg, Forrest, G-T, SMU, 1971
Gregory, Bill, DT-DE, Wisconsin, 1971-77
Gregory, Glynn, WR-CB-S, SMU, 1961-62
Grottkau, Bob, G, Oregon, 1961
Guy, Buzz, G, Duke, 1960

Hagen, Halvor, C-G, Webster State, 1969-70
Hansen, Wayne, LB, Texas Western, 1960
Harris, Cliff, S, Ouachita, 1970-79
Harris, Duriel, WR, New Mexico State, 1984
Harris, Jim, S. Oklahoma, 1961
Hayes, Bob, WR, Florida A&M, 1965-74
Hayes, Wendell, RB, Humboldt State, 1963
Haynes, Tommy, DB, Southern California, 1987
Hays, Harold, LB, So. Miss., 1963-67
Healy, Don, DT, Maryland, 1960-61
Hegman, Mike, LB, Tennessee State, 1976-86
Heinrich, Don, QB, Washington, 1960
Henderson, Thomas, LB, Langston, 1975-79
Hendrix, Manny, CB, Utah, 1986-87
Hendrix, Tim, TE, Tennessee, 1987
Herchman, Bill, DT, Texas Tech, 1960-61
Herrera, Efren, K, UCLA, 1974, 1976-77
Hill, Bill, DB, Rutgers, 1987
Hill, Calvin, RB, Yale, 1969-74
Hill, Rod, CB, Kentucky State, 1982-83
Hill, Tony, WR, Stanford, 1977-86
Hogeboom, Gary, QB, Central Michigan, 1980-85
Holloway, Johnny, CB, Kansas, 1986
Homan, Dennis, WR, Alabama, 1968-70
Hoopes, Mitch, P, Arizona, 1975
Houser, John, C-G, Redlands, 1960-61
Houston, Bill, WR, Jackson State, 1974
Howard, Carl, DB, Rutgers, 1984
Howard, Percy, WR, Austin Peay, 1975
Howard, Ron, TE, Seattle, 1974-75
Howe, Glen, T, Southern Mississippi, 1987
Howley, Chuck, LB, West Virginia, 1961-73
Howton, Bill, WR, Rice, 1960-63
Hoyem, Lynn, C-G, Long Beach, 1962-63
Hughes, Randy, S, Oklahoma, 1975-80
Humphrey, Buddy, QB, Baylor, 1961
Hunt, John, OL, Florida, 1984
Hunter, Monty, S, Salem, 1982
Hurd, Jeff, LB, Kansas State, 1987
Hurt, Eric, CB, San Jose St., 1980
Husmann, Ed, DT, Nebraska, 1960
Hutcherson, Ken, LB, Livingston State, 1974
Huther, Bruce, LB, New Hampshire, 1977-80, 1983

Isbell, Joe Bob, G, Houston, 1962-65
Jax, Garth, LB, Florida State, 1986-87
Jeffcoat, Jim, DE, Arizona State, 1983-87
Jensen, Jim, RB, Iowa, 1976
Johnson, Butch, WR, Cal-Riverside, 1976-83
Johnson, Mike, CB, Kansas, 1966-69
Johnson, Mitch, G, UCLA, 1965
Johnson, Walter, DT, Pittsburgh, 1987
Jones, Dale, LB, Tennessee, 1987
Jones, E. J., RB, Kansas, 1987
Jones, Ed, DE, Tennessee State, 1974-78, 1980-86
Jones, James, RB, Miss. State, 1980-82, 1984-85
Jordan, Lee Roy, LB, Alabama, 1963-76
Keller, Mike, LB, Michigan, 1972
Ker, Crawford, G, Florida, 1985-87
Killian, Gene, G, Tennessee, 1974
Kiner, Steve, LB, Tennessee, 1970
King, Angelo, LB, South Carolina St., 1981-83
Kitson, Syd, OL, Wake Forest, 1984
Klein, Dick, T, Iowa, 1960
Kowalczyk, Walt, RB, Michigan State, 1960
Kupp, Jake, G, Washington, 1964-65
Kyle, Aaron, CB, Wyoming, 1976-79
Laidlaw, Scott, RB, Stanford, 1975-79
Lavette, Robert, RB, Georgia Tech, 1985-87
Lawless, Burton, G, Florida, 1975-79
LeBaron, Eddie, QB, Pacific, 1960-63
Lewis, D. D., LB, Miss. State, 1968-81
Lewis, Woodley, WR, Oregon, 1960
Lilja, George, C, Michigan, 1987
Lilly, Bob, DE-DT, Texas Christian, 1961-74
Liscio, Tony, T, Tulsa, 1963-64, 1966-71
Livingston, Bruce, DB, Arkansas Tech, 1987
Livingston, Warren, CB, Arizona, 1961-66
Lockett, J. W., RB, Central Okla., 1961-62
Lockhart, Eugene, LB, Houston, 1984-87
Logan, Obert, S, Trinity (Tex.), 1965-66
Long, Bob, LB, UCLA, 1962
Longley, Clint, QB, Abilene Christian, 1974-75
Lothridge, Billy, P-QB, Georgia Tech, 1964
Maegle, Dick, S, Rice, 1961
Manders, Dave, C, Mich. State, 1964-66, 1968-74
Manning, Wade, CB, Ohio State, 1979
Marsh, Amos, RB, Oregon State, 1961-64
Martin, Harvey, DE, East Texas St., 1973-83
Martin, Kelvin, WR, Boston College, 1987
Mathews, Ray, WR, Clemson, 1960
McCreary, Bob, T, Wake Forest, 1961
McDaniels, David, WR, Miss. Val., 1968
McDonald, Paul, QB, USC, 1986-87
McDonald, Tommy, WR, Oklahoma, 1964
McIlhenny, Don, RB, SMU, 1960-61
McLean, Scott, LB, Florida State, 1983

McSwain, Chuck, RB, Clemson, 1983-84
Memmelaar, Dale, G, Wyoming, 1962-63
Meredith, Don, QB, SMU, 1960-68
Meyers, John, DT, Washington, 1962-63
Miller, Jim, P, Mississippi, 1983-84
Mitchell, Aaron, CB, Nevada-Las Vegas, 1979-80
Montgomery, Mike, RB-WR, Kans. St., 1972-73
Mooty, Jim, CB, Arkansas, 1960
Morgan, Dennis, RB, Western Illinois, 1974
Morton, Craig, QB, California, 1965-74
Murchison, Ola Lee, WR, Pacific, 1961
Neely, Ralph, G-T, Oklahoma, 1965-77
Newhouse, Robert, RB, Houston, 1972-83
Newsome, Timmy, RB, Winston-Salem, 1980-87
Newton, Nate, G, Florida A&M, 1986-87
Niland, John, G, Iowa, 1966-74
Nolan, Dick, S, Maryland, 1962
Noonan, Danny, DT, Nebraska, 1987
Norman, Pettis, TE, J. C. Smith, 1962-70
Norton, Jerry, S, SMU, 1962
Nutting, Ed, T, Georgia Tech, 1963
Nye, Blaine, G, Stanford, 1968-76
Otto, Bob, DE, Idaho State, 1986
Overton, Jerry, S, Utah, 1963
Parks, Billy, WR, Long Beach State, 1972
Patera, Jack, LB, Oregon, 1960-61
Pearson, Drew, WR, Tulsa, 1973-83
Pearson, Preston, RB, Illinois, 1975-80
Pelleur, Steve, QB, Washington, 1984-87
Penn, Jesse, LB, Virginia Tech, 1985-87
Peoples, George, RB, Auburn, 1982
Percival, Mac, K, Texas Tech, 1974
Perkins, Don, RB, New Mexico, 1961-68
Perkins, Ray, DE, Virginia, 1987
Petersen, Kurt, G, Missouri, 1980-85
Peterson, Calvin, LB, UCLA, 1974-75
Phillips, Kirk, WR, Tulsa, 1984
Pinder, Cyril, RB, Illinois, 1973
Ploeger, Kurt, DE, Gustavus Adolphus, 1986
Poimboeul, Lance, K, SW La., 1963
Ponder, David, DT, Florida State, 1985
Porterfield, Garry, DE, Tulsa, 1965
Powe, Karl, WR, Alabama State, 1985-86
Pozderac, Phil, T, Notre Dame, 1982-87
Pugh, Jethro, DT, Eliz. City St., 1965-78
Putnam, Duane, G, Pacific, 1960
Rafferty, Tom, G-C, Penn State, 1976-86
Randall, Tom, DG, Iowa State, 1978
Randle, Sonny, WR, Virginia, 1968
Reece, Beasley, CB-WR, N. Texas St., 1976
Reese, Guy, DT, SMU, 1962-63
Reeves, Dan, RB-QB, S. Car., 1965-72
Renfro, Mel, CB-RB-S, Oregon, 1964-77
Renfro, Mike, WR, TCU, 1984-87
Rentzel, Lance, WR, Oklahoma, 1967-70
Rhome, Jerry, QB, Tulsa, 1965-68
Richards, Golden, WR, Hawaii, 1973-78
Richards, Howard, T, Missouri, 1981-86
Richardson, Gloster, WR, Jack. St., 1971
Ridgway, Colin, P-K, Lamar Tech, 1965
Ridlon, Jim, S, Syracuse, 1963-64
Roach, John, QB, SMU, 1964
Robinson, Larry, RB, Tennessee, 1973
Roe, Bill, LB, Colorado, 1980
Rohrer, Jeff, LB, Yale, 1982-87
Rucker, Reggie, WR, Boston U., 1970-71
Ruzek, Roger, K, Weber State, 1987
Saldi, Jay, TE, South Carolina, 1976-82
Salonen, Brian, TE/LB, Montana, 1984-85
Sandeman, Bill, DT, Pacific, 1966
Sawyer, Buzz, P, Baylor, 1987
Saxon, Mike, P, San Diego State, 1985-87
Schaum, Greg, DE, Michigan State, 1976
Schoenke, Ray, T, SMU, 1963-64
Schultz, Chris, T, Arizona, 1983, 1985
Scott, Chuck, WR, Vanderbilt, 1987
Scott, Herbert, G, Virginia Union, 1975-84
Scott, Victor, DB, Colorado, 1984-87
Sellers, Ron, WR, Florida State, 1972
Septien, Rafael, K, SW Louisiana, 1978-86
Shaw, Robert, G, Tennessee, 1979-81
Shearin, Joe, C, Texas, 1987
Sherer, Dave, P, SMU, 1960
Sherrard, Mike, WR, UCLA, 1986
Shields, Jon, OL, Portland State, 1987
Shy, Les, RB, Long Beach State, 1966-69
Simmons, Cleo, TE, Jackson State, 1983
Simmons, Dave, LB, Georgia Tech, 1968
Simmons, Victor, LB, Central State

(OH), 1987
Smerek, Don, DL, Nevada-Reno, 1981-87
Smith, Daryle, T, Tennessee, 1987
Smith, J. D., RB, N. Car. A&T, 1965-66
Smith, Jackie, TE, NW Louisiana, 1978
Smith, Jim Ray, G-T, Baylor, 1963-64
Smith, Tody, DE-DT, USC, 1971-72
Smith, Waddell, WR, Kansas, 1984
Snyder, Loren, QB, Northern Colorado, 1987
Solomon, Roland, S. Utah, 1980
Spivey, Sebron, WR, Southern Illinois, 1987
Spradlin, Danny, LB, Tennessee, 1981-82
Springs, Ron, RB, Ohio State, 1979-84
Stalls, Dave, DE, Northern Colorado, 1977-79
Staubach, Roger, QB, Navy, 1969-79
Steele, Robert, WR, N. Alabama, 1978
Stephens, Larry, DE, Texas, 1963-67
Stiger, Jim, RB, Washington, 1963-65
Stincic, Tom, LB, Michigan, 1969-71
Stokes, Sim, WR, Northern Arizona, 1967
Stowe, Otto, WR, Iowa State, 1973
Strayhorn, Les, RB, East Carolina, 1973-74
Stynchula, Andy, DE, Penn State, 1968
Swan, Russ, LB, Virginia, 1987
Sweeney, Kevin, QB, Cal State—Fresno, 1987
Talbert, Don, DE-T, Texas, 1962, 1965, 1971
Thomas, Bill, RB, Boston College, 1972
Thomas, Duane, RB, W. Texas St., 1970-71
Thomas, Ike, CB, Bishop, 1971
Thompson, Broderick, G, Kansas, 1985
Thornton, Bruce, DE-DT, Illinois, 1979-81
Thurman, Dennis, CB, USC, 1978-85
Timmer, Kirk, LB, Montana State, 1987
Titensor, Glen, G, Brigham Young, 1981-86
Toomay, Pat, DE, Vanderbilt, 1970-74
Townes, Willie, DE, Tulsa, 1966-68
Truax, Billy, TE, Louisiana State, 1971-73
Tubbs, Jerry, LB, Oklahoma, 1960-67
Tuinei, Mark, DT/OL, Hawaii, 1983-87
Turner, Jimmie, LB, Presbyterian, 1984
Van Raaphorst, Dick, K, Ohio State, 1964
Villanueva, Danny, P-K, New Mex. St., 1965-67
Walen, Mark, DE, UCLA, 1987
Walker, Gary, OL, Boston University, 1987
Walker, Herschel, RB, Georgia, 1986-87
Walker, Louie, LB, Colorado State, 1974
Walker, Malcolm, C, Rice, 1966-69
Wallace, Rodney, G-T, New Mex., 1971-73
Walls, Everson, CB, Grambling, 1981-87
Walter, Mike, LB, Oregon, 1983
Walton, Bruce, G, UCLA, 1973-75
Warren, John, P, Tennessee, 1983-84
Washington, Mark, CB, Morgan St., 1970-78
Waters, Charlie, S-CB, Clemson, 1970-78, 1980-81
Watts, Randy, DE, Catawba, 1987
Wayt, Russell, LB, Rice, 1965
Welch, Claxton, RB, Oregon, 1969-71
Wells, Norm, G, Northwestern, 1980
Westberry, Gary, C, Hampton, 1987
White, Bob, OL, Rhode Island, 1987
White, Danny, QB-P, Arizona State, 1976-87
White, Gerald, RB, Michigan, 1987
White, Randy, LB-DE, Maryland, 1975-87
Whitfield, A. D., RB, N. Texas St., 1965
Whittingham, Fred, LB, Cal. Poly, 1969
Widby, Ron, P, Tennessee, 1968-71
Wilbur, John, T, Stanford, 1966-69
Williams, Joe, RB, Wyoming, 1971
Williams, John, RB, Wisconsin, 1985
Williams, Robert, DB, Baylor, 1987
Wilson, Steve, WR, Howard, 1979-81
Wisener, Gary, DB, Baylor, 1960
Woolsey, Rolly, CB-S, Boise State, 1975
Wright, Brad, QB, New Mexico, 1982
Wright, Rayfield, TE-T, Ft. Valley St., 1967-79
Wright, Steve, T, Northern Iowa, 1981-82
Youmans, Maury, DE, Syracuse, 1964-65
Young, Charles, RB, N.C. State, 1974-76
Zendejas, Luis, K, Arizona State, 1987
Zentic, Mike, C, Oklahoma State, 1987
Zimmerman, Jeff, G, Florida, 1987

Cowboys All-Time Draft

1961
(Drafted 2nd)
1. (A) **NO CHOICE**
Choice traded along with sixth choice to Washington for EDDIE LeBARON.
1. (B) **BOB LILLY**
T, Texas Christian University, 6-5, 242—Choice from Cleveland for first round pick in 1962.
2. **E. J. HOLUB**
LB, Texas Tech, 6-4, 218 (went to AFL).
3. **STEW BARBER**
G, Penn State, 6-3, 230 (went to AFL).
4. **SONNY DAVIS**
E, Baylor, 6-2, 210.
5. **NO CHOICE**
Choice traded to San Francisco for GENE BABB.
6. **NO CHOICE**
Choice traded, along with first choice, to Washington for LeBARON.
7. **ART GILMORE**
HB, Oregon State, 6-0, 200.
8. **DON TALBERT**
T, Texas, 6-5, 220.
9. **GLENN GREGORY**
HB, SMU, 6-2, 195.
10. **NO CHOICE**
Choice traded to Green Bay for FRED CONE.
11. **NORRIS STEVENSON**
HB, Missouri, 6-1, 205.
12. **LOWNDES SHINGLER**
QB, Clemson, 6-1, 205.
13. **DON GOODMAN**
HB, Florida, 6-0, 200.
14. **BILL SHAW**
T, Georgia Tech, 6-3, 222 (went to AFL).
15. **JULIUS VARNADO**
T, San Francisco State, 6-4, 220 (went to AFL).
16. **JERRY STEFFEN**
HB, Colorado, 6-10, 190.
17. **EVERETT CLOUD**
HB, Maryland, 6-0, 190.
18. **RANDY WILLIAMS**
HB, Indiana, 6-3, 208.
19. **LYNN HOYEM**
C, Long Beach State, 6-4, 225.
20. **JERRY MORGAN**
QB, Iowa State, 6-3, 195.

1962
(Drafted 4th)
1. **NO CHOICE**
Choice traded to Cleveland for first round pick in 1961 when Cowboys picked BOB LILLY.
2. **SONNY GIBBS***
QB, TCU, 6-7, 225.
3. (A) **NO CHOICE**
Choice to Chicago for DON MEREDITH.
3. (B) **BOBBY PLUMMER**
G, TCU, 6-2, 235—Choice from Cleveland for DUANE PUTNAM.
4. **NO CHOICE**
Choice to San Francisco for BILL HERCHMAN.
5. **NO CHOICE**
Choice to Los Angeles for JIMMY HARRIS.
6. (A) **DONNIE DAVIS**
E, Southern University, 6-2, 235.
6. (B) **GEORGE ANDRIE**
E, Marquette, 6-7, 247—Choice and ALLEN GREEN from New York for FRED DUGAN.
7. **NO CHOICE**
Choice to Los Angeles for JOHN HOUSER.
8. **KEN TUREAUD**
B, Michigan, 6-1, 198.
9. **NO CHOICE**
Choice to Baltimore for DON PERKINS.
10. **JOHN M. LONGMEYER**
G, Southern Illinois, 6-3, 230.
11. **LARRY HUDAS**
E, Michigan State, 6-4, 208.
12. **NO CHOICE**
Choice to Green Bay for STEVE MEILINGER.
13. **ROBERT MOSES**
E, Texas, 6-3, 211.
14. **HAROLD HAYS***
G, Southern Mississippi, 6-3, 218.
15. **GUY REESE**
T, SMU, 6-5, 238.
16. **ROBERT JOHNSTON**
T, Rice, 6-4, 215.
17. **RAY JACOBS**
T, Howard Payne, 6-3, 265 (went to AFL).
18. **DAVE CLOUTIER***
B, Maine, 6-0, 195 (went to AFL).

19. **PAUL HOLMES**
T, Georgia, 6-5, 220.
20. **AMOS BULLOCKS**
B, Southern Illinois, 6-1, 197.

1963
(Drafted 6th)
1. **LEE ROY JORDAN**
LB, Alabama, 6-2, 210.
2. **NO CHOICE**
Choice traded, along with ninth choice, to Chicago for CHUCK HOWLEY.
3. **JIM PRICE**
LB, Auburn, 6-3, 225.
4. **WHALEY HALL***
G, Mississippi, 6-3, 230.
5. **NO CHOICE**
Choice traded to New York for DICK NOLAN.
6. **NO CHOICE**
Choice traded to Green Bay for JOHN SUTRO.
7. **MARV CLOTHIER**
G, Kansas, 6-4, 220.
8. **NO CHOICE**
Choice traded to Green Bay for LEE FOLKINS.
9. **NO CHOICE**
Choice traded to Chicago.
10. **ROD SCHEYER**
T, Washington, 6-2, 220.
11. **RAY SCHOENKE**
C, SMU, 6-3, 225.
12. **BILL PERKINS**
B, Iowa, 6-2, 218.
13. **PAUL WICKER***
T, Fresno State, 6-5, 248.
14. **LOU CIOCI**
LB, Boston College, 6-2, 225.
15. **JERRY OVERTON**
B, Utah, 6-2, 192.
16. **DENNIS GOLDEN**
T, Holy Cross, 6-4, 235.
17. **ERNEST PARKS***
G, McMurry, 6-4, 230 (went to AFL).
18. **BILL FRANK**
T, Colorado, 6-4, 250.
19. **JIM STIGER**
B, Washington, 5-11, 195.
20. **TOMMY LUCAS**
E, Texas, 6-3, 218.

1964
(Drafted 4th)
1. **NO CHOICE**
Choice traded to Pittsburgh for BUDDY DIAL.
2. **MEL RENFRO**
B, Oregon, 6-0, 195.
3. **NO CHOICE**
Choice traded to Los Angeles for BOB LONG and JOHN MEYERS.
4. **PERRY LEE DUNN**
B, Mississippi, 6-2, 205.
5. **NO CHOICE**
Choice traded to Green Bay for GARY BARNES.
6. (A) **BILLY LOTHRIDGE**
QB, Georgia Tech, 6-1, 188.
6. (B) **JIM CURRY**

E, Cincinnati, 6-4, 215—Choice from Cleveland for ANDY CVERCKO.
6. (C) **JIMMY EVANS**
E, Texas Western, 6-1, 194—Choice from Green Bay for JERRY NORTON.
7. **BOB HAYES***
WR, Florida A&M, 5-11, 189.
8. **AL GEVERINK**
B, UCLA, 6-2, 190.
9. **JAKE KUPP**
E, Washington, 6-3, 215.
10. **ROGER STAUBACH***
QB, Navy, 6-2, 190.
11. **BOBBY CRENSHAW**
G, Baylor, 6-3, 230 (went to AFL).
12. **JOHNNY NORMAN**
E, Northwestern Louisiana, 6-1, 185.
13. **JERRY RHOME**
QB, Tulsa, 6-0, 185.
14. **JIM WORDEN**
LB, Wittenberg, 6-1, 230.
15. **BILL VAN BURKLEO**
B, Tulsa, 5-11, 185.
16. **PAUL CERCEL**
C, Pittsburgh, 6-2, 222.
17. **HARRY ABELL**
E, Missouri, 6-3, 212 (went to AFL).
18. **NO SELECTION**
Player chosen not eligible.
19. **H. D. MURPHY**
B, Oregon, 6-0, 190.
20. **JOHN HUGHES**
LB, SMU, 6-2, 220.

1965
(Drafted 5th)
1. **CRAIG MORTON**
QB, California, 6-4, 215.
2. **MALCOLM WALKER**
LB, Rice, 6-4, 245.
3. **NO CHOICE**
Choice traded to Green Bay (who traded it to New York) for JOHN ROACH.
4. (A) **JIM SIDLE**
B, Auburn, 6-2, 215.
4. (B) **BOB SVIHUS**
T, USC, 6-4, 240 (went to AFL)—Choice from Detroit for SONNY GIBBS.
5. **ROGER PETTEE**
LB, Florida, 6-4, 230.
6. **SONNY UTZ**
RB, VPI, 5-11, 215.
7. **BRIG OWENS**
B, Cincinnati, 5-11, 183.
8. **RUSSELL WAYT**
LB, Rice, 6-4, 235.
9. **JIM ZANIOS**
FB, Texas Tech, 6-0, 215.
10. **GAYLON McCOLLOUGH**
C, Alabama, 6-2, 215.
11. **JETHRO PUGH**
T, Elizabeth City State, 6-6, 255.
12. **ERNIE KELLERMAN**
QB, Miami (Ohio), 6-0, 175.
13. **JACK SCHRAUB**
E, California, 6-6, 210.
14. **GARRY PORTERFIELD**
E, Tulsa, 6-3, 235.
15. **GENE FOSTER**
B, Arizona State, 6-0, 195 (went to AFL).

---

16. **DOUG McDOUGAL**
E, Oregon State, 6-4, 228.
17. **MITCH JOHNSON**
T, UCLA, 6-4, 245.
18. **MARTIN AMSLER**
T, Evansville, 6-5, 250.
19. **MERV RETTENMUND**
HB, Ball State, 5-10, 195.
20. **RON BARLOW***
T, Kansas State, 6-2, 230.

1966
(Drafted 5th)
1. **JOHN NILAND**
G, Iowa, 6-3, 245.
2. **WILLIE TOWNES***
DE, Tulsa, 6-5, 265.
3. **NO CHOICE**
Choice to San Francisco for LEON DONOHUE.
4. **NO CHOICE**
Choice to Baltimore for RALPH NEELY.
5. (A) **NO CHOICE**
Choice to San Francisco for J. D. SMITH.
5. (B) **WALT GARRISON**
RB, Oklahoma State, 6-0, 209—Choice from Baltimore thru Detroit for AMOS MARSH.
6. **BOB DUNLEVY**
E, West Virginia, 6-4, 195.
7. **ART ROBINSON**
E, Florida A&M, 6-0, 208.
8. **DON KUNIT**
RB, Penn State, 6-2, 200.
9. **DARRELL ELAM**
FL, West Virginia Tech, 6-2, 189.
10. **MASON MITCHELL**
RB, Washington, 6-1, 170.
11. **AUSTIN DENNEY***
E, Tennessee, 6-2, 225.
12. (A) **LES SHY**
RB, Long Beach State, 6-1, 200—Choice from Pittsburgh for LEE FOLKINS.
12. (B) **CRAIG BAYNHAM***
RB, Georgia Tech, 6-1, 200.
13. **RONNIE LAMB**
B, South Carolina, 6-2, 216.
14. **LEWIS TURNER**
RB, Norfolk State, 6-2, 183.
15. **MARK GARTUNG**
DT, Oregon State, 6-4, 255.
16. **TOM PIGGEE**
RB, San Francisco State, 5-11, 200.
17. **GEORGE ALLEN**
T, West Texas State, 6-7, 245 (went to AFL).
18. **STEVE ORR**
DT, Washington, 6-4, 230.
19. **BYRON JOHNSON**
E, Central Washington State, 6-5, 255.
20. **LOU HUDSON**
FL, Minnesota, 6-5, 220.

1967
(Drafted 23rd)
1. **NO CHOICE**
Choice given, along with second and two fifths, to Houston for RALPH NEELY.
2. **NO CHOICE**
NEELY trade.
3. **PHIL CLARK**
DB, Northwestern, 6-2, 207.
4. **CURTIS MARKER**
G, Northern Michigan, 6-2, 253.
5. (A) **NO CHOICE**
Choice and JIM STEFFEN from Washington for BRIG OWENS, MITCH JOHNSON and JAKE KUPP; NEELY trade.
5. (B) **NO CHOICE**
Choice from Cleveland for JOE BOB ISBELL; NEELY trade.
5. (C) **NO CHOICE**
Choice to Green Bay for HENRY GREMMINGER.
6. **SIMS STOKES**
E, Northern Arizona, 6-1, 198.
7. **RAYFIELD WRIGHT**
T, Ft. Valley State, 6-7, 235.
8. **STEVE LAUB**
QB, Illinois Wesleyan, 6-1, 190.
9. **BYRON MORGAN**
DB, Findlay (Ohio), 6-3, 212.
10. **EUGENE BOWEN**
RB, Tennessee A&I, 5-8, 210.
11. **PAT RILEY**
E, Kentucky, 6-2, 205.
12. **HAROLD DETERS**
K, North Carolina State, 6-0, 200.
13. **AL KERKIAN**
DE, Akron, 6-6, 235.
14. **TOM BOYD**
G, Tarleton State, 6-3, 250.
15. **LEAVIE DAVIS**

DB, Edward Waters College (Florida), 6-4, 210.
16. **PAUL BROTHERS**
HB, Oregon State, 6-1, 195.
17. **GEORGE ADAMS**
LB, Morehead State (Kentucky), 6-2, 218.

1968
(Drafted Alternately 20th, 19th, 21st)
1. **DENNIS HOMAN**
FL, Alabama, 6-1, 181.
2. **DAVID McDANIELS**
E, Mississippi Valley, 6-4, 200.
3. (A) **NO CHOICE**
Choice to Minnesota for LANCE RENTZEL.
3. (B) **ED HARMON**
LB, Louisville, 6-4, 246—Choice from Chicago for AUSTIN DENNEY and MAC PERCIVAL.
4. (A) **NO CHOICE**
Choice to New Orleans for LARRY STEPHENS.
4. (B) **JOHN DOUGLAS**
LB, Missouri, 6-2, 215—Choice from New York for JIM COLVIN.
5. **BLAINE NYE**
G, Stanford, 6-4, 255.
6. **D. D. LEWIS**
LB, Mississippi State, 6-1, 210.
7. **BOB TAUCHER**
T, Nebraska, 6-4, 251.
8. **FRANK BROWN**
DE, Albany (Ga.) State, 6-3, 249.
9. **KEN KMIEC**
DB, Illinois, 6-2, 187.
10. **BEN OLISON**
FL, Kansas, 6-1, 170.
11. **RON SHOTTS**
RB, Oklahoma, 6-0, 206.
12. **WILSON WHITTY**
LB, Boston University, 6-3, 224.
13. **CARTER LORD**
TE, Harvard, 6-2, 214.
14. **RON WILLIAMS**
DB, West Virginia, 6-2, 190.
15. **TOMMY LUNCEFORD**
P, Auburn, 6-2, 202.
16. **LARRY COLE**
DE, Hawaii, 6-5, 250.
17. **GEORGE NORDGREN**
RB, Houston, 6-0, 200.

1969
(Drafted Alternately 24th, 23rd, 22nd)
1. **CALVIN HILL**
RB, Yale, 6-3, 230.
2. **RICHMOND FLOWERS**
WR, Tennessee, 6-0, 183.
3. (A) **TOM STINCIC**
LB, Michigan, 6-2, 226.
3. (B) **HALVOR HAGEN**
DE, Weber State, 6-5, 250—Choice from San Francisco for HAROLD HAYS.
4. **NO CHOICE**
Choice to New Orleans for DAVE SIMMONS.
5. (A) **NO CHOICE**
Choice to Baltimore for ANDY STYNCHULA.
5. (B) **CHUCK KYLE**
LB, Purdue, 6-1, 220—Choice from Los Angeles for COY BACON.
6. **RICH SHAW**
FL, Arizona State, 6-4, 205.
7. **LARRY BALES**
WR, Emory & Henry, 5-11, 185.
8. **ELMER BENHARDT**
LB, Missouri, 6-2, 200.
9. **CLAXTON WELCH**
RB, Oregon, 5-11, 200.
10. **STUART GOTTLIEB**
G, Weber State, 6-5, 250.
11. **CLARENCE WILLIAMS**
DT, Prairie View A & M, 6-5, 250.
12. **BOB BELDEN**
QB, Notre Dame, 6-2, 210.
13. **RENE MATISON**
WR, New Mexico, 6-0, 185.
14. **GERALD LUTRI**
T, Northern Michigan, 6-4, 256.
15. **BILL JUSTUS**
DB, Tennessee, 6-1, 180.
16. **FLOYD KERR**
DB, Colorado State, 6-3, 195.
17. **BILL BAILEY**
DT, Lewis & Clark, 6-4, 260.

1970
(Drafted 23rd)
1. **DUANE THOMAS**
RB, West Texas, 6-1, 220.
2. (A) **BOB ASHER**
T, Vanderbilt, 6-5, 250—Choice from Chicago for CRAIG BAYNHAM and PHIL CLARK.
2. (B) **MARGENE ADKINS**
WR, Henderson, J.C., 5-10, 183.
3. (A) **CHARLIE WATERS**
CB, Clemson, 6-1, 193—Choice from

Houston through Cleveland for JERRY RHOME.
3. (B) **STEVE KINER**
LB, Tennessee, 6-1, 220—Choice from Cleveland for JERRY RHOME.
3. (C) **DENTON FOX**
S, Texas Tech, 6-2, 205.
4. **JOHN FITZGERALD**
T, Boston College, 6-4, 265.
5. **NO CHOICE**
Choice to St. Louis for BOBBY JOE CONRAD.
6. **PAT TOOMAY**
DE, Vanderbilt, 6-5, 230.
7. **DON ABBEY**
LB, Penn State, 6-2, 252.
8. **JERRY DOSSEY**
G, Arkansas, 6-4, 244.
9. **ZENON ANDRUSYSHYN**
K, UCLA, 6-2, 212.
10. **PETE ATHAS**
S, Dade J.C., 6-0, 186.
11. **IVAN SOUTHERLAND**
DT, Clemson, 6-4, 246.
12. **JOE WILLIAMS**
RB, Wyoming, 6-1, 193.
13. **MARK WASHINGTON**
CB, Morgan State, 5-11, 183.
14. **JULIAN MARTIN**
WR, North Carolina Central, 6-3, 190.
15. **KEN DeLONG**
TE, Tennessee, 6-2, 223.
16. **SEABERN HILL**
CB, Arizona State, 6-2, 195.
17. **GLENN PATTERSON**
C, Nebraska, 6-3, 220.

1971
(Drafted 25th)
1. **TOBY SMITH**
DE, Southern California, 6-5, 250.
2. **ISAAC THOMAS**
CB, Bishop, 6-2, 190.
3. (A) **SAM SCARBER**
RB, New Mexico, 6-2, 235—Choice from St. Louis for JOHN WILBUR.
3. (B) **BILL GREGORY**
DE, Wisconsin, 6-5, 240.
4. (A) **JOE CARTER**
TE, Grambling, 6-3, 219—Choice from New Orleans for WILLIE TOWNES.
4. (B) **BUDDY MITCHELL**
T, Mississippi, 6-5, 232.
5. **RON KADZIEL**
LB, Stanford, 6-3, 215.
6. **STEVE MAIER**
WR, Northern Arizona, 6-3, 192.
7. **BILL GRIFFIN**
T-G, Catawba, 6-5, 250.
8. **RON JESSIE**
WR, Kansas, 6-0, 183.
9. **HONOR JACKSON**
WR, Pacific, 6-2, 190.
10. **RODNEY WALLACE**
DT, New Mexico, 6-5, 260.
11. **ERNEST BONWELL**
LB, Lane College, 6-4, 225.
12. **STEVE GOEPEL**
QB, Colgate, 6-1½, 200.
13. **JAMES FORD**
RB, Texas Southern, 6-0, 200.
14. **TYRONE JESSIE**
DB, Utah State, 6-1½, 194.
15. **BOB YOUNG**
TE, Delaware, 6-5, 250.
16. **JOHN BRENNAN**
T, Boston College, 6-2½, 260.
17. **JOHN BOMER**
C, Memphis State, 6-3, 230.

1972
(Drafted 26th)
1. **BILL THOMAS**
RB, Boston College, 6-2, 225.
2. (A) **ROBERT NEWHOUSE**
RB, Houston, 5-10, 202—Choice from New England for HALVOR HAGEN and HONOR JACKSON.
2. (B) **JOHN BABINECZ**
LB, Villanova, 6-2, 222—Choice from New Orleans for MARGENE ADKINS.
2. (C) **CHARLES McKEE**
WR, Arizona, 6-2, 199.
3. (A) **MIKE KELLER**
LB, Michigan, 6-4, 221—Choice from New England for HALVOR HAGEN and HONOR JACKSON.
3. (B) **MARV BATEMAN**
P-K, Utah, 6-4, 213.
4. (A) **TIM KEARNEY**
LB, Northern Michigan, 6-2, 225—Choice from New Orleans for JOE WILLIAMS.
4. (B) **ROBERT WEST**
WR, San Diego State, 6-4, 218—Choice from New England for STEVE KINER.
4. (C) **CHARLES ZAPIEC**
LB, Penn State, 6-2, 222—Choice from Detroit for RON JESSIE.
4. (D) **NO CHOICE**
Choice to New Orleans for DON TALBERT.

5. **NO CHOICE**
Choice to San Diego for TONY LISCIO.
6. **CHARLES BOLDEN**
DB, Iowa, 6-3, 195.
7. **NO CHOICE**
Choice to Chicago for LEE ROY CAFFEY.
8. **RALPH COLEMAN**
LB, North Carolina A & T, 6-4, 216.
9. **ROY BELL**
RB, Oklahoma, 5-10, 208.
10. **RICHARD AMMAN**
DE, Florida State, 6-5, 234.
11. **LONNIE LEONARD**
T-G, North Carolina A & T, 6-4, 244.
12. **JIMMY HARRIS**
WR, Ohio State, 5-10, 180.
13. **JEAN FUGETT**
TE, Amherst, 6-3, 219.
14. **ALAN THOMPSON**
RB, Wisconsin, 6-0, 225.
15. **CARLOS ALVAREZ**
WR, Florida, 5-10, 184.
16. **GORDON LONGMIRE**
QB, Utah, 6-1, 205.
17. **ALFONSO CAIN**
DT, Bethune-Cookman, 6-3, 271.

1973
(Drafted Alternately 20th, 22nd and 21st)
1. **BILLY JOE DuPREE**
TE, Michigan State, 6-4, 225.
2. (A) **GOLDEN RICHARDS**
WR, Hawaii, 6-0, 172—Choice from Green Bay for RON WIDBY and IKE THOMAS.
2. (B) **NO CHOICE**
Choice to Chicago as compensation for signing JACK CONCANNON.
3. (A) **HARVEY MARTIN**
DT, East Texas State, 6-5, 262—Choice from Houston through New Orleans for TOM STINCIC.
3. (B) **NO CHOICE**
Choice to New England for RON SELLERS.
4. **DRANE SCRIVENER**
DB, Tulsa, 6-0, 176.
5. **BRUCE WALTON**
T, UCLA, 6-6, 251.
6. **BOB LEYEN**
G, Yale, 6-4, 256.
7. **RODRIGO BARNES**
LA, Rice, 6-1, 215.
8. **DAN WERNER**
QB, Michigan State, 6-4, 195.
9. **MIKE WHITE**
CB, Minnesota, 6-0, 196.
10. **CARL JOHNSON**
LB, Tennessee, 6-1, 225.
11. **GERALD CASWELL**
G, Colorado State, 6-4, 250.
12. **JIM ARNESON**
G, Arizona, 6-3, 236.
13. **JOHN SMITH**
WR, UCLA, 6-1, 187.
14. **BOB THORNTON**
G-C, North Carolina, 6-3, 234.
15. **WALT BAISY**
LB, Grambling, 6-2, 222.
16. **JOHN CONLEY**
TE, Hawaii, 6-2, 228.
17. **LES STRAYHORN**
RB, East Carolina, 5-10, 205.

1974
(Drafted Alternately 22nd, 21st, 20th and 23rd)
1. (A) **ED JONES**
DE, Tennessee State, 6-8, 260—Choice from Houston for TODY SMITH and BILLY PARKS.
1. (B) **CHARLES YOUNG**
RB, North Carolina State, 6-1, 215.
2. **NO CHOICE**
Choice and RON SELLERS to Miami for OTTO STOWE.
3. (A) **DANNY WHITE**
QB, Arizona State, 6-2, 180—Choice from Houston for TODY SMITH and BILLY PARKS.
3. (B) **CALVIN PETERSON**
LB, UCLA, 6-3, 218.
4. (A) **KEN HUTCHERSON**
LB, Livingston State, 6-1, 214—Choice from Oakland for GLOSTER RICHARDSON.
4. (B) **ANDY ANDRADE**
RB-DB, Northern Michigan, 5-11, 193.
5. **JOHN KELSEY**
T, Missouri, 6-6, 226.
6. **JIM BRIGHT**
DB, UCLA, 6-1, 210.
7. **RAYMOND NESTER**
LB, Michigan State, 6-2, 224.
8. **MIKE HOLT**
DB, Michigan State, 5-11, 176.
9. **BILL DULIN**
T, Johnson C. Smith, 6-6, 244.
10. **DENNIS MORGAN**
DB, Western Illinois, 5-11, 203.
11. **HARVEY McGEE**
WR, Southern Mississippi, 6-2, 209.

12. **KEITH BOBO**
QB, Southern Methodist, 6-3, 196.
13. **FRED LIMA**
K, Colorado, 5-9, 202.
14. **DOUG RICHARDS**
DB, Brigham Young, 6-4, 185.
15. **BRUCE CRAFT**
DT, Geneva, Pa., 6-4, 232.
16. **GENE KILLIAN**
T, Tennessee, 6-4, 225.
17. **LAWRIE SKOLROOD**
T, North Dakota, 6-5, 230.

1975
(Drafted 18th)
1. (A) **RANDY WHITE**
DE, Maryland, 6-4, 250—Choice from N.Y. Giants for CRAIG MORTON.
1. (B) **THOMAS HENDERSON**
LB, Langston, 6-2, 214.
2. **BURTON LAWLESS**
G, Florida, 6-4, 253.
3. **BOB BREUNIG**
LB, Arizona State, 6-2, 236.
4. (A) **PAT DONOVAN**
DE, Stanford, 6-5, 240—Choice from Houston for MIKE MONTGOMERY.
4. (B) **RANDY HUGHES**
DB, Oklahoma, 6-4, 209.
5. (A) **KYLE DAVIS**
C, Oklahoma, 6-3, 240—Choice from Green Bay for JACK CONCANNON.
5. (B) **NO CHOICE**
Choice to Cincinnati for CLINT LONGLEY.
6. **ROLLY WOOLSEY**
DB, Boise State, 6-1, 175.
7. **MICHAEL HEGMAN**
LB, Tennessee State, 6-4, 220.
8. **MITCH HOOPES**
P, Arizona, 6-0, 210.
9. **ED JONES**
DB, Rutgers, 6-0, 193.
10. **DENNIS BOOKER**
RB, Millersville State, 6-1, 235.
11. **GREG KRPALEK**
C, Oregon State, 6-5, 242.
12. **CHUCK BLAND**
DB, Cincinnati, 5-11, 188.
13. **HERBERT SCOTT**
G, Virginia Union, 6-2, 248.
14. **SCOTT LAIDLAW**
RB, Stanford, 6-0, 206.
15. **WILLIE HAMILTON**
RB, Arizona, 5-11, 182.
16. **PETE CLARK**
TE, Colorado State, 6-4, 234.
17. **JIM TESTERMAN**
TE, Dayton, 6-5, 225.

1976
(Drafted 27th)
1. **AARON KYLE**
DB, Wyoming, 5-11, 183.
2. (A) **JIM JENSEN**
RB, Iowa, 6-4, 226—Choice from N.Y. Giants for CRAIG MORTON.
2. (B) **JIM EIDSON**
G, Mississippi St., 6-4, 253.
3. (A) **DUKE FERGUSON**
WR, San Diego St., 6-1, 186—Choice from San Francisco for BOB HAYES.
3. (B) **JOHN SMITH**
RB, Boise State, 6-0, 191—Choice from Denver for OTTO STOWE.
3. (B) **BUTCH JOHNSON**
WR, UC-Riverside, 6-1, 175.
4. **TOM RAFFERTY**
G, Penn State, 6-3, 248.
5. **WALLY PESUIT**
T, Kentucky, 6-4, 260.
6. **GREG McGUIRE**
T, Indiana, 6-3, 265.
7. (A) **GREG SCHAUM**
DT, Michigan State, 6-4, 246—Choice from San Diego for KEN HUTCHERSON.
7. (B) **DAVID WILLIAMS**
RB, Colorado, 6-2, 210.
8. **HENRY LAWS**
DB, South Carolina, 5-10, 171.
9. **BEASLEY REECE**
DB, North Texas, 6-1, 193.
10. **LEROY COOK**
DE, Alabama, 6-4, 212.
11. **CORNELIUS GREEN**
QB, Ohio, 5-11, 170.
12. **CHARLES McSHANE**
LB, Cal Lutheran, 6-2, 211.
13. **MARK DRISCOLL**
QB, Colorado St., 6-1, 184.
14. **LARRY MUSHINSKIE**
TE, Nebraska, 6-3, 217.
15. **DALE CURRY**
LB, UCLA, 6-2, 222.
16. **RICH COSTANZO**
T, Nebraska, 6-4, 260.
17. **STAN WOODFILL**
K, Oregon, 6-0, 190.

1977
(Drafted Alternately 24th, 25th and 26th)
1. **TONY DORSETT**

RB, Pittsburgh, 5-11, 192—Choice from Seattle for Cowboys' first-round choice and three second-round choices.
2. **GLENN CARANO**
QB, Nevada-Las Vegas, 6-3, 195—Choice from Seattle for DUKE FERGERSON.
3. (A) **TONY HILL**
WR, Stanford, 6-2, 196—Choice from Philadelphia for JOHN NILAND.
3. (B) **VAL BELCHER**
G, Houston, 6-3, 250.
4. **GUY BROWN**
LB, Houston, 6-4, 215.
5. **ANDY FREDERICK**
OL, New Mexico, 6-6, 241.
6. **JIM COOPER**
T, Temple, 6-5, 252.
7. **DAVID STALLS**
DT, Northern Colorado, 6-4, 236.
8. (A) **AL CLEVELAND**
DL, Pacific, 6-4, 246—Choice from San Diego for MITCH HOOPES.
8. (B) **FRED WILLIAMS**
RB, Arizona State, 5-10, 189.
9. **MARK CANTRELL**
C, North Carolina, 6-3, 252.
10. **STEVE DeBERG**
QB, San Jose State, 6-2, 205.
11. **DON WARDLOW**
TE, Washington, 6-6, 230.
12. **GREG PETERS**
OL, California, 6-5, 257.

1978
(Drafted 28th)
1. **LARRY BETHEA**
DL, Michigan State, 6-5, 258.
2. **TODD CHRISTENSEN**
RB-TE, Brigham Young, 6-3, 224.
3. **DAVID HUDGENS**
OL, Oklahoma, 6-5, 245.
4. **ALOIS BLACKWELL**
RB, Houston, 5-11, 194.
5. **RICH ROSEN**
G, Syracuse, 6-3, 242.
6. **HAROLD RANDOLPH**
LB, East Carolina, 6-1, 191.
7. **TOM RANDALL**
DT, Iowa State, 6-5, 248.
8. **HOMER BUTLER**
WR, UCLA, 6-1, 184.
9. **RUSS WILLIAMS**
DB, Tennessee, 6-1, 197.
10. **BARRY TOMASETTI**
OL, Iowa, 6-3, 249.
11. **DENNIS THURMAN**
S. Southern Cal., 5-11, 172.
12. **LEE WASHBURN**
OL, Montana State, 6-6, 253.

1979
(Drafted 27th)
1. **ROBERT SHAW**
C, Tennessee, 6-4, 252.
2. **AARON MITCHELL**
CB, Nevada-Las Vegas, 6-1, 196.
3. **DOUG COSBIE**
TE, Santa Clara, 6-6, 230. Swapped choices with Seattle in BILL GREGORY trade.
4. **RALPH DeLOACH**
DE, California, 6-5, 254.
5. (A) **BOB HUKILL**
OL, North Carolina, 6-5, 250. Choice from Chicago for GOLDEN RICHARDS.
5. (B) **CURTIS ANDERSON**
DE, Central State (0), 6-6, 240. Choice from Seattle for EFREN HERRERA.
5. (C) **RON SPRINGS**
RB, Ohio State, 6-0, 197.
6. (A) **TIM LAVENDER**
CB, So. California, 6-3, 187. Choice from Seattle for BILL GREGORY.
6. (B) **MIKE SALZANO**
OL, North Carolina, 6-3, 242. Choice from Denver for JIM JENSEN.
6. (C) **CHRIS DeFRANCE**
WR, Arizona St., 6-1, 205.
7. **GREG FITZPATRICK**
LB, Youngstown, 6-2, 227.
8. **BRUCE THORNTON**
DT, Illinois, 6-5, 266.
9. **GARRY COBB**
LB, So. California, 6-2, 209.
10. **MIKE CALHOUN**
DT, Notre Dame, 6-4, 228.
12. **QUENTIN LOWRY**
LB, Youngstown, 6-2, 225.

1980
(Drafted Alternately 23rd, 24th, and 25th)
1. **NO CHOICE**
Choice given along with second-round choice to Baltimore for JOHN DUTTON.
2. **NO CHOICE**
Choice given along with first-round choice to Baltimore for JOHN DUTTON.
3. (A) **BILL ROE**
LB, Colorado, 6-3, 220—Choice from Chicago for GOLDEN RICHARDS.
3. (B) **JAMES JONES**
RB, Mississippi State, 5-10, 200.
4. **KURT PETERSEN**
DL, Missouri, 6-5, 255.
5. **GARY HOGEBOOM**
QB, Central Michigan, 6-4, 195.
6. **TIMMY NEWSOME**
RB, Winston-Salem St., 6-1, 228.
7. **LESTER BROWN**
CB, Clemson, 5-11, 176.
8. **LARRY SAVAGE**
LB, Michigan State, 6-3, 225.
9. **JACKIE FLOWERS**
WR, Florida State, 6-0, 194.
10. **MATTHEW TEAGUE**
DE, Prairie View A&M, 6-4, 238.
11. **GARY PADJEN**
LB, Arizona State, 6-1, 238.
12. **NORM WELLS**
DT, Northwestern, 6-5, 249.

1981
(Drafted Alternately 25th, 26th)
1. **HOWARD RICHARDS**
OT, Missouri, 6-5, 255.
2. **DOUG DONLEY**
WR, Ohio St., 6-0, 180.
3. **GLEN TITENSOR**
DL, Brigham Young, 6-4, 250.
4. (A) **SCOTT PELLUER**
LB, Wash. St., 6-1, 213—Choice from San Francisco for THOMAS HENDERSON.
4. (B) **DERRIE NELSON**
LB, Nebraska, 6-2, 217.
5. **DANNY SPRADLIN**
LB, Tennessee, 6-1, 229.
6. **VINCE SKILLINGS**
DB, Ohio St., 5-11, 176.
7. (A) **RON FELLOWS**
DB, Missouri, 5-11, 165—Choice from Tampa Bay for DAVE STALLS.
7. (B) **KEN MILLER**
DB, East. Michigan, 5-11, 180.
8. **PAUL PIUROWSKI**
LB, Florida St., 6-2, 219.
9. **MIKE WILSON**
WR, Wash. St., 6-3, 202.
10. **PAT GRAHAM**
DT, California, 6-3, 257.
11. **TIM MORRISON**
OG, Georgia, 6-3, 258.
12. **NATE LUNDY**
WR, Indiana, 6-0, 169.

1982
(Drafted 26th)
1. **ROD HILL**
CB, Kentucky State, 6-0, 182.
2. **JEFF ROHRER**
LB, Yale, 6-3, 228.
3. **JIM ELIOPULOS**
LB, Wyoming, 6-2, 224.
4. (A) **BRIAN CARPENTER**
CB, Michigan, 5-11, 166—Choice from Tampa Bay for DAVE STALLS.
4. (B) **MONTY HUNTER**
S, Salem College, 6-0, 201.
5. **PHIL POZDERAC**
T, Notre Dame, 6-8, 264.
6. (A) **KEN HAMMOND**
G, Vanderbilt, 6-3, 270—Choice from Cleveland for BRUCE HUTHER.
6. (B) **CHARLES DAUM**
DL, Cal Poly-SLO, 6-6, 229.
7. **BILL PURIFOY**
DL, Tulsa, 6-8, 248.
8. (A) **GEORGE PEOPLES**
RB, Auburn, 6-0, 202—Choice from Denver through Buffalo for WADE MANNING.
8. (B) **DWIGHT SULLIVAN**
RB, North Carolina State, 5-9, 204.
9. **JOE GARY**
DL, UCLA, 6-4, 262.
10. **TODD ECKERSON**
T, North Carolina State, 6-4, 268.
11. (A) **GEORGE THOMPSON**
WR, Albany State (Ga.), 6-3, 211—Choice from Tampa Bay for AARON MITCHELL.
11. (B) **MICHAEL WHITING**
RB, Florida State, 6-0, 214.
12. **RICH BURTNESS**
G, Montana, 6-4, 235.

1983
(Drafted 23rd)
1. **JIM JEFFCOAT**
DE, Arizona State, 6-5, 260.
2. **MIKE WALTER**
LB, Oregon, 6-3, 230.
3. **BRYAN CALDWELL**
DE, Arizona State, 6-4, 248.
4. **CHRIS FAULKNER**
TE, Florida, 6-4, 257.
5. **CHUCK McSWAIN**
RB, Clemson, 6-0, 190.
6. **REGGIE COLLIER**
QB, Southern Mississippi, 6-3, 207.

7. **CHRIS SCHULTZ**
T, Arizona, 6-8, 259.
8. **LAWRENCE RICKS**
RB, Michigan, 5-9, 194.
9. **AL GROSS**
S, Arizona, 6-3, 186.
10. **ERIC MORAN**
T, Washington, 6-5, 282.
11. **DAN TAYLOR**
T, Idaho State, 6-3, 258.
12. **LORENZO BOUIER**

1984
(Drafted 25th)
1. **BILLY CANNON**
LB, Texas A&M, 6-4, 235.
2. **VICTOR SCOTT**
DB, Colorado, 5-10, 182—Choice from Minnesota through Houston for BUTCH JOHNSON.
3. **FRED CORNWELL**
TE, Southern Cal, 6-5, 236.
4. **STEVE DeOSSIE**
LB, Boston College, 6-2, 250.
5. (A) **STEVE PELLUER**
QB, Washington, 6-4, 204—Choice from Tampa Bay for DANNY SPRADLIN.
5. (B) **NORM GRANGER**
RB, Iowa, 5-9, 217.
6. (A) **EUGENE LOCKHART**
LB, Houston, 6-2, 228—Choice from Chicago for JAY SALDI.
6. (B) **JOE LEVELIS**
OG, Iowa, 6-3, 270.
7. **ED MARTIN**
LB, Indiana State, 6-3, 218.
8. **MIKE REVELL**
RB, Bethune Cookman, 5-11, 197.
9. (A) **JOHN HUNT**
OL, Florida, 6-4, 262—Choice from Indianapolis for RAUL ALLEGRE.
9. (B) **NEAL MAUNE**
OL, Notre Dame, 6-4, 249.
10. **BRIAN SALONEN**
TE, Montana, 6-2, 227.
11. **DOWE AUGHTMAN**
DL, Auburn, 6-2, 272.
12. **CARL LEWIS**
WR, Houston, 6-3, 187.

*Drafted as Future

1985
(Drafted Alternately 17th, 16th, 20th, 19th, 18th)
1. **KEVIN BROOKS**
DE, Michigan, 6-7, 265.
2. **JESSE PENN**
LB, Virginia Tech, 6-3, 255.
3. **CRAWFORD KER**
G, Florida, 6-4, 290.
4. **ROBERT LAVETTE**
RB, Georgia Tech, 5-11, 195.
5. (A) **HERSCHEL WALKER**
RB, Georgia, 6-1, 224—Choice from Houston for BUTCH JOHNSON.
5. (B) **MATT DARWIN**
C/G, Texas A&M, 6-4, 265—Choice from Cleveland through Buffalo for ROD HILL.
6. (A) **KURT PLOEGER**
DT, Gustavus Adolphus, 6-5, 250—Choice from Indianapolis for STEVE WRIGHT.
6. (B) **MATT MORAN**
C/G, Stanford, 6-4, 265.
7. (A) **KARL POWE**
WR, Alabama State, 6-2, 175—Choice from San Diego through Kansas City for LAWRENCE RICKS.
7. (B) **JIM HERRMANN**
DE, Brigham Young, 6-6, 265.
8. **LEON GONZALEZ**
WR, Bethune-Cookman, 5-10, 160.
9. **SCOTT STRASBURGER**
LB, Nebraska, 6-1, 220.
10. **JOE JONES**
TE, Virginia Tech, 6-4, 245.
11. **NEAL DELLOCONO**
LB, UCLA, 6-1, 220.
12. **KARL JORDAN**
LB, Vanderbilt, 6-2, 245.

1986
(Drafted Alternately, 21st, 20th, 19th, 18th)
1. **MIKE SHERRARD**
WR, UCLA, 6-2, 185.
2. **DARRYL CLACK**
RB, Arizona State, 5-10, 207.
3. **MARK WALEN**
DT, UCLA, 6-5, 265.
4. **MAX ZENDEJAS**
K, Arizona, 5-11, 184.
6. (A) **THORNTON CHANDLER**
TE, Alabama, 6-5, 238 (from Buffalo for ROD HILL).
6. (B) **STAN GELBAUGH**
QB, Maryland, 6-3, 207 (from Detroit for ANGELO KING).
6. (C) **LLOYD YANCEY**
G, Temple, 6-4, 275.
7. **JOHNNY HOLLOWAY**
DB, Kansas, 5-11, 181.
8. **TOPPER CLEMONS**
RB, Wake Forest, 5-11, 205.
9. **JOHN IONATA**
G, Florida State, 6-2, 280.
10. **BRYAN CHESTER**
G, Texas, 6-4, 260.
11. **GARTH JAX**
LB, Florida State, 6-2, 225.
12. (A) **CHRIS DULIBAN**
LB, Texas, 6-2, 216 (from Buffalo for ANTHONY DICKERSON).
13. (B) **TONY FLACK**
DB, Georgia, 6-1, 184.

1987
(Drafted Alternately, 12th, 11th)
1. **DANNY NOONAN**
DT, Nebraska, 6-4, 282.
2. **RON FRANCIS**
CB, Baylor, 5-9, 201.
3. **JEFF ZIMMERMAN**
OL, Florida, 6-3, 310.
4. **KELVIN MARTIN**
WR, Boston College, 5-9, 161.
5. **EVERETT GAY**
WR, Texas, 6-2, 204.
6. **JOE ONOSAI**
OL, Hawaii, 6-3, 283.
7. **KEVIN SWEENEY**
QB, Fresno State, 6-0, 191.
8. **KEVIN GOGAN**
T, Washington, 6-7, 295.
9. **ALVIN BLOUNT**
RB, Maryland, 5-9, 197.
10. **DALE JONES**
LB, Tennessee, 6-1, 234.
11. **JEFF WARD**
K, Texas, 5-9, 169.
12. **SCOTT ARMSTRONG**
LB, Florida, 6-1, 230.

1988
(Drafted Alternately, 11th, 14th, 13th, 12th)
1. **MICHAEL IRVIN**
WR, Miami, 6-2, 198.
2. **KEN NORTON**
LB, UCLA, 6-2, 224.
3. **MARK HUTSON**
G, Oklahoma, 6-3, 292.
4. **DAVE WIDELL**
T, Boston College, 6-6, 297.
5. **NO CHOICE/CHOICE GIVEN TO SEATTLE FOR RON ESSINK**
6. **SCOTT SECULES**
QB, Virginia, 6-3, 220.
7. **OWEN HOOVEN**
T, Oregon State, 6-8, 302.
8. **MARK HIGGS**
RB, Kentucky, 5-7, 188.
9. **BRIAN BEDFORD**
WR, California, 6-4, 209.
10. **BILLY OWENS**
DB, Pittsburgh, 6-1, 198.
11. **CHAD HENNINGS**
DE, Air Force, 6-5, 251.
12. **BEN HUMMEL**
LB, UCLA, 6-4, 234.

Cowboys vs. NFL Opponents

Atlanta Falcons

(Dallas Leads Series, 8-3)

Year	Site	Winner-Score	Att.
1966	Atlanta	Dallas, 47-14	56,990
1967	Dallas	Dallas, 37-7	54,751
1969	Atlanta	Dallas, 24-17	54,833
1970	Dallas	Dallas, 13-0	53,611
1974	Atlanta	Dallas, 24-0	52,322
1976	Atlanta	Atlanta, 17-10	54,972
1978*	Dallas	Dallas, 27-20	60,338
1981*	Atlanta	Dallas, 30-27	60,022
1985	Dallas	Dallas, 24-10	57,941
1986	Dallas	Atlanta, 37-35	62,880
1987	Dallas	Atlanta, 21-10	40,103

*NFC Divisional Playoffs

Buffalo Bills

(Dallas Leads Series, 3-1)

Year	Site	Winner-Score	Att.
1971	Buffalo	Dallas, 49-37	46,206
1976	Dallas	Dallas, 17-10	51,779
1981	Dallas	Dallas, 27-14	62,583
1984	Buffalo	Buffalo, 14-3	74,391

Chicago Bears

(Dallas Leads Series, 8-5)

Year	Site	Winner-Score	Att.
1960	Chicago	Chicago, 17-7	39,951
1962	Dallas	Chicago, 34-33	12,692
1964	Chicago	Dallas, 24-10	47,527
1968	Chicago	Dallas, 34-3	46,667
1971	Chicago	Chicago, 23-19	55,049
1973	Chicago	Dallas, 20-17	55,701
1976	Dallas	Dallas, 31-21	61,346
1977*	Dallas	Dallas, 37-7	62,920
1979	Dallas	Dallas, 24-20	64,056
1981	Dallas	Dallas, 10-9	63,499
1984	Chicago	Dallas, 23-14	63,623
1985	Dallas	Chicago, 44-0	63,855
1986	Dallas	Chicago, 24-10	57,256

*NFC Divisional Playoffs

Cincinnati Bengals

(Dallas Leads Series, 2-1)

Year	Site	Winner-Score	Att.
1973	Dallas	Dallas, 38-10	58,802
1979	Dallas	Dallas, 38-13	63,179
1985	Cinc.	Cinc., 50-24	56,936

Cleveland Browns

(Cleveland Leads Series, 15-9)

Year	Site	Winner-Score	Att.
1960	Dallas	Cleve., 48-7	28,500
1961	Cleve.	Cleve., 25-7	43,638
1961	Dallas	Cleve., 38-17	23,500
1962	Cleve.	Cleve., 19-10	44,040
1962	Dallas	Dallas, 45-21	24,226
1963	Dallas	Cleve., 41-24	28,710
1963	Cleve.	Cleve., 27-17	55,096
1964	Cleve.	Cleve., 27-6	72,062
1964	Dallas	Cleve., 20-16	37,456
1965	Cleve.	Cleve., 23-17	80,451
1965	Dallas	Dallas, 24-17	76,251
1966	Cleve.	Cleve., 30-21	84,721
1966	Dallas	Dallas, 26-14	80,259
1967	Cleve.	Dallas, 21-14	81,039
1967*	Dallas	Dallas, 52-14	70,786
1968	Dallas	Dallas, 28-7	68,733
1968*	Cleve.	Cleve., 31-20	81,497
1969	Cleve.	Cleve., 42-10	84,850
1969*	Dallas	Cleve., 38-14	69,321
1970	Cleve.	Dallas, 6-2	75,458
1974	Dallas	Dallas, 41-17	48,754
1979	Cleve.	Cleve., 26-7	80,123
1982	Dallas	Dallas, 31-14	48,267
1985	Dallas	Dallas, 20-7	61,456

*Eastern Conference Championship Game

Denver Broncos

(Dallas Leads Series, 3-2)

Year	Site	Winner-Score	Att.
1973	Denver	Dallas, 22-10	51,706
1977	Dallas	Dallas, 14-6	63,752
1978*	New O.	Dallas, 27-10	76,400
1980	Denver	Denver, 41-20	74,919
1986	Denver	Denver, 29-14	76,082

*Super Bowl XII, Jan. 15, 1978

Detroit Lions

(Dallas Leads Series 7-4)

Year	Site	Winner-Score	Att.
1960	Detroit	Detroit, 23-14	43,272
1963	Dallas	Dallas, 17-14	27,264
1968	Dallas	Dallas, 59-13	61,382
1970*	Dallas	Dallas, 5-0	73,167
1972	Dallas	Dallas, 28-24	65,378
1975	Detroit	Dallas, 36-10	79,784
1977	Dallas	Dallas, 37-0	63,160
1981	Detroit	Detroit, 27-24	79,694
1985	Detroit	Detroit, 26-21	72,985
1986	Detroit	Dallas, 31-7	73,812
1987	Detroit	Detroit, 27-17	45,325

*Divisional Playoff Game

Green Bay Packers

(Green Bay Leads Series, 8-5)

Year	Site	Winner-Score	Att.
1960	Gr. Bay	Gr. Bay, 41-7	32,294
1964	Dallas	Gr. Bay, 45-21	44,975
1965	Milw.	Gr. Bay, 13-3	48,311
1966*	Dallas	Gr. Bay, 34-27	75,504
1967*	Gr. Bay	Gr. Bay, 21-17	50,861
1968	Dallas	Gr. Bay, 28-17	74,604
1970	Dallas	Dallas, 16-3	67,182
1972	Milw.	Gr. Bay, 16-14	47,103
1975	Dallas	Gr. Bay, 19-17	64,934
1978	Milw.	Dallas, 42-14	55,256

Year	Site	Winner-Score	Att.
1980	Milw.	Dallas, 28-7	54,776
1982†	Dallas	Dallas, 37-26	63,972
1984	Dallas	Dallas, 20-6	64,222

*NFL Championship Game
†Super Bowl Tournament

Houston Oilers

(Dallas Leads Series, 4-1)

Year	Site	Winner-Score	Att.
1970	Dallas	Dallas, 52-10	50,504
1974	Houston	Dallas, 10-0	49,775
1979	Dallas	Houston, 30-24	63,897
1982	Houston	Dallas, 37-7	51,808
1985	Houston	Dallas, 17-10	49,686

Indianapolis Colts

(Dallas Leads Series, 6-3)

Year	Site	Winner-Score	Att.
1960	Dallas	Balt., 45-7	25,500
1967	Balt.	Balt., 23-17	60,238
1969	Dallas	Dallas, 27-10	63,191
1970†	Miami	Balt., 16-13	80,055
1972	Balt.	Dallas, 21-0	58,992
1976	Dallas	Dallas, 30-27	64,237
1978	Dallas	Dallas, 38-0	64,224
1981	Balt.	Dallas, 37-13	54,871
1984	Dallas	Dallas, 22-3	58,724

†Super Bowl, Jan. 17, 1971

Kansas City Chiefs

(Dallas Leads Series, 2-1)

Year	Site	Winner-Score	Att.
1970	Kan. City	Dallas, 27-16	51,158
1975	Dallas	Kan. City, 34-31	63,539
1983	Dallas	Dallas, 41-21	64,103

L.A. Raiders

(Raiders Lead Series, 3-1)

Year	Site	Winner-Score	Att.
1974	Oakland	Oakland, 27-23	45,850
1980	Oakland	Dallas, 19-13	53,194
1983	Dallas	L.A., 40-38	64,991
1986	Dallas	L.A., 17-13	61,706

Los Angeles Rams

(Series Tied, 11-11)

Year	Site	Winner-Score	Att.
1960	Dallas	L.A., 38-13	16,000
1962	L.A.	Dallas, 27-17	26,907
1967	Dallas	L.A., 35-13	75,229
1969	L.A.	L.A., 24-23	79,105
1971	Dallas	Dallas, 28-21	66,595
1973	L.A.	L.A., 37-31	81,428
1973†	Dallas	Dallas, 27-16	64,291
1975	Dallas	Dallas, 18-7	49,091
1975‡	L.A.	Dallas, 37-7	84,483
1976†	Dallas	L.A., 14-12	62,436
1978	L.A.	L.A., 27-14	65,749
1978‡	L.A.	Dallas, 28-0	67,470
1979	Dallas	Dallas, 30-6	64,462
1979†	Dallas	L.A., 21-19	64,792
1980	L.A.	L.A., 38-14	62,548
1980§	Dallas	Dallas, 34-13	64,533
1981	Dallas	Dallas, 29-17	64,649
1983§	Dallas	L.A., 24-17	43,521
1984	L.A.	Dallas, 20-13	65,403
1985†	L.A.	L.A., 20-0	66,351
1986	L.A.	L.A., 29-10	64,949
1987	L.A.	Dallas, 29-21	60,700

§Wild Card Game
†Divisional Playoff Game
‡NFC Championship Game

105

Miami Dolphins

(Miami Leads Series, 4-2)

Year	Site	Winner-Score	Att.
1971*	New O.	Dallas, 24-3	81,035
1973	Dallas	Miami, 14-7	64,100
1978	Miami	Miami, 23-16	69,414
1981	Dallas	Dallas, 28-27	64,221
1984	Miami	Miami, 28-21	74,139
1987	Dallas	Miami, 20-14	56,519

*Super Bowl VI, Jan. 16, 1972

Minnesota Vikings

(Dallas Leads Series, 10-6)

Year	Site	Winner-Score	Att.
1961	Dallas	Dallas, 21-7	20,500
1961	Minn.	Dallas, 28-0	33,070
1966	Dallas	Dallas, 28-17	64,116
1968	Dallas	Dallas, 20-7	47,644
1970	Minn.	Minn., 54-13	47,900
1971*	Minn.	Dallas, 20-12	49,100
1973†	Dallas	Minn., 27-10	64,524
1974	Dallas	Minn., 23-21	57,847
1975*	Minn.	Dallas, 17-14	48,341
1977	Minn.	Dallas, 16-10 (OT)	47,678
1977†	Dallas	Dallas, 23-8	61,968
1978	Dallas	Minn., 21-10	61,848
1979	Minn.	Dallas, 36-20	47,572
1982	Minn.	Minn., 31-27	60,007
1983	Minn.	Dallas, 37-24	60,774
1987	Dallas	Minn., 44-38 (OT)	54,229

*Divisional Playoff Game
†NFC Championship Game

New England Patriots

(Dallas Leads Series, 6-0)

Year	Site	Winner-Score	Att.
1971	Dallas	Dallas, 44-21	65,708
1975	N. Eng.	Dallas, 34-31	60,905
1978	Dallas	Dallas, 17-10	63,263
1981	N. Eng.	Dallas, 35-21	60,311
1984	Dallas	Dallas, 20-17	55,341
1987	N. Eng.	Dallas, 23-17 (OT)	60,567

New Orleans Saints

(Dallas Leads Series, 11-1)

Year	Site	Winner-Score	Att.
1967	Dallas	Dallas, 14-10	52,582
1967	New O.	Dallas, 27-10	83,437
1968	New O.	Dallas, 17-3	84,728
1969	New O.	Dallas, 21-17	79,567
1969	Dallas	Dallas, 33-17	68,282
1971	New O.	New O., 24-14	83,088
1973	Dallas	Dallas, 40-3	53,972
1976	New O.	Dallas, 24-6	61,413
1978	Dallas	Dallas, 27-7	57,920
1982	Dallas	Dallas, 21-7	64,506
1983	Dallas	Dallas, 21-20	62,136
1984	Dallas	Dallas, 30-27	50,966

New York Giants

(Dallas Leads Series, 35-14-2)

Year	Site	Winner-Score	Att.
1960	N.Y.	Tie, 31-31	55,033
1961	Dallas	N.Y., 31-10	41,500
1961	N.Y.	Dallas, 17-16	60,254
1962	Dallas	N.Y., 41-10	45,668
1962	N.Y.	N.Y., 41-31	62,694
1963	N.Y.	N.Y., 37-21	62,889
1963	Dallas	N.Y., 34-27	29,635
1964	Dallas	Tie, 13-13	33,225
1964	N.Y.	Dallas, 31-21	63,031
1965	Dallas	Dallas, 31-2	59,366
1965	N.Y.	Dallas, 38-20	62,871
1966	Dallas	Dallas, 52-7	60,010
1966	N.Y.	Dallas, 17-7	62,735
1967	Dallas	Dallas, 38-24	66,209
1968	Dallas	N.Y., 27-21	72,163
1968	N.Y.	Dallas, 28-10	62,617
1969	Dallas	Dallas, 25-3	58,964
1970	Dallas	Dallas, 28-10	57,236
1970	N.Y.	N.Y., 23-20	62,938
1971	Dallas	Dallas, 20-13	68,378
1971	N.Y.	Dallas, 42-14	62,815
1972	N.Y.	Dallas, 23-14	62,725
1972	Dallas	N.Y., 23-3	64,602
1973	Dallas	Dallas, 45-28	64,898
1973	N. Haven	Dallas, 23-10	70,128
1974	Dallas	N.Y., 14-6	46,353
1974	N. Haven	Dallas, 21-7	61,191
1975	N.Y.	Dallas, 13-7	56,511
1975	Dallas	Dallas, 14-3	53,329
1976	N.Y.	Dallas, 24-14	76,042
1976	Dallas	Dallas, 9-3	58,870
1977	Dallas	Dallas, 41-21	64,215
1977	N.Y.	Dallas, 24-10	74,532
1978	N.Y.	Dallas, 34-24	73,265
1978	Dallas	Dallas, 24-3	64,869
1979	N.Y.	Dallas, 16-14	76,490
1979	Dallas	Dallas, 28-7	63,787
1980	Dallas	Dallas, 24-3	59,126
1980	N.Y.	N.Y., 38-35	68,343
1981	Dallas	Dallas, 18-10	63,449
1981	N.Y.	N.Y., 13-10 (O.T.)	73,009
1983	Dallas	Dallas, 28-13	62,347
1983	N.Y.	Dallas, 38-20	76,142
1984	N.Y.	N.Y., 28-7	75,921
1984	Dallas	N.Y., 19-7	60,235
1985	N.Y.	Dallas, 30-29	74,981
1985	Dallas	Dallas, 28-21	62,310
1986	Dallas	Dallas, 31-28	59,804
1986	N.Y.	N.Y., 17-14	74,871
1987	N.Y.	Dallas, 16-14	73,426
1987	Dallas	Dallas, 33-24	55,730

New York Jets

(Dallas Leads Series, 4-0)

Year	Site	Winner-Score	Att.
1971	Dallas	Dallas, 52-10	66,689
1975	N.Y.	Dallas, 31-21	37,279
1978	N.Y.	Dallas, 30-7	52,532
1987	N.Y.	Dallas, 38-24	12,370

Philadelphia Eagles

(Dallas Leads Series, 36-19)

Year	Site	Winner-Score	Att.
1960	Dallas	Phil., 27-25	18,500
1961	Dallas	Phil., 43-7	25,000
1961	Phil.	Phil., 35-13	60,127
1962	Dallas	Dallas, 41-19	18,645
1962	Phil.	Phil., 28-14	58,070
1963	Phil.	Phil., 24-21	60,671
1963	Dallas	Dallas, 27-20	23,694
1964	Dallas	Phil., 17-14	55,972
1964	Phil.	Phil., 24-14	60,671
1965	Dallas	Phil., 35-24	56,249
1965	Phil.	Dallas, 21-19	54,714
1966	Dallas	Dallas, 56-7	69,372
1966	Phil.	Phil., 24-23	60,658
1967	Phil.	Phil., 21-14	60,740
1967	Dallas	Dallas, 38-17	55,834
1968	Phil.	Dallas, 45-13	60,858
1968	Dallas	Dallas, 34-14	72,083
1969	Phil.	Dallas, 38-7	60,658
1969	Dallas	Dallas, 49-14	71,509
1970	Phil.	Dallas, 17-7	59,728
1970	Dallas	Dallas, 21-17	55,736
1971	Phil.	Dallas, 42-7	65,358
1971	Dallas	Dallas, 20-7	60,178
1972	Dallas	Dallas, 28-6	55,850
1972	Phil.	Dallas, 28-7	65,720
1973	Phil.	Phil., 30-16	65,954
1973	Dallas	Dallas, 31-10	61,985
1974	Phil.	Phil., 13-10	64,088
1974	Dallas	Dallas, 31-24	43,586
1975	Phil.	Dallas, 20-17	64,889
1975	Dallas	Dallas, 27-17	57,893
1976	Dallas	Dallas, 27-7	54,052
1976	Phil.	Dallas, 26-7	55,072
1977	Phil.	Dallas, 16-10	65,507
1977	Dallas	Dallas, 24-14	60,289
1978	Dallas	Dallas, 14-7	60,525
1978	Phil.	Dallas, 31-13	64,667
1979	Dallas	Phil., 31-21	62,417
1979	Phil.	Dallas, 24-17	71,434
1980	Phil.	Phil., 17-10	70,696
1980	Dallas	Dallas, 35-27	62,548
1981†	Phil.	Phil., 20-7	70,696
1981	Phil.	Dallas, 17-14	72,111
1981	Dallas	Dallas, 21-10	64,955
1982	Dallas	Phil., 24-20	46,199
1983	Dallas	Dallas, 37-7	63,070
1983	Phil.	Dallas, 27-20	71,236
1984	Dallas	Dallas, 23-17	64,521
1984	Phil.	Dallas, 26-10	66,322
1985	Phil.	Phil., 16-14	70,114
1985	Dallas	Dallas, 34-17	54,047
1986	Phil.	Dallas, 17-14	68,572
1986	Dallas	Phil., 23-21	46,117
1987	Dallas	Dallas, 41-22	40,622
1987	Phil.	Phil., 37-20	61,630

† NFC Championship Game

Pittsburgh Steelers

(Pittsburgh Leads Series, 12-11)

Year	Site	Winner-Score	Att.
1960	Dallas	Pitts., 35-28	30,000
1961	Dallas	Dallas, 27-24	23,500
1961	Pitts.	Pitts., 37-7	17,519
1962	Dallas	Pitts., 30-28	19,478
1962	Pitts.	Dallas, 42-27	23,106
1963	Pitts.	Pitts., 27-21	19,047
1963	Dallas	Pitts., 24-19	24,136
1964	Pitts.	Pitts., 23-17	35,594
1964	Dallas	Dallas, 17-14	35,271
1965	Pitts.	Pitts., 22-13	37,804
1965	Dallas	Dallas, 24-17	57,293
1966	Dallas	Dallas, 52-21	58,453
1966	Pitts.	Dallas, 20-7	42,185
1967	Pitts.	Dallas, 24-21	39,641
1968	Dallas	Dallas, 28-7	55,069
1969	Pitts.	Dallas, 10-7	24,990
1972	Dallas	Dallas, 17-13	65,682
1975*	Miami	Pitts., 21-17	80,187
1977	Pitts.	Pitts., 28-13	49,761
1978†	Miami	Pitts., 35-31	78,656
1979	Pitts.	Pitts., 14-3	50,199
1982	Dallas	Pitts., 36-28	63,431
1985	Dallas	Dallas, 27-13	62,932

*Super Bowl X, Jan. 18, 1976
†Super Bowl XIII, Jan. 21, 1979

St. Louis Cardinals
(Dallas Leads Series, 32-18-1)

Year	Site	Winner-Score	Att.
1960	St. Louis	St. Louis, 12-10	23,128
1961	Dallas	St. Louis, 31-17	20,500
1961	St. Louis	St. Louis, 31-13	15,384
1962	Dallas	St. Louis, 28-24	16,027
1962	St. Louis	St. Louis, 52-20	14,201
1963	Dallas	St. Louis, 34-7	36,432
1963	St. Louis	Dallas, 28-24	12,695
1964	Dallas	St. Louis, 16-6	36,605
1964	St. Louis	Dallas, 31-13	28,253
1965	St. Louis	St. Louis, 20-13	32,034
1965	Dallas	Dallas, 27-13	38,499
1966	St. Louis	Tie, 10-10	50,673
1966	Dallas	Dallas, 31-17	76,965
1967	Dallas	Dallas, 46-21	68,787
1968	Dallas	Dallas, 27-10	48,206
1969	Dallas	Dallas, 24-3	62,134
1970	St. Louis	St. Louis, 20-7	50,780
1970	Dallas	St. Louis, 38-0	69,323
1971	St. Louis	Dallas, 16-13	50,486
1971	Dallas	Dallas, 31-12	66,672
1972	Dallas	Dallas, 33-24	65,218
1972	St. Louis	Dallas, 27-6	49,787
1973	Dallas	Dallas, 45-10	64,729
1973	St. Louis	Dallas, 30-3	43,946
1974	St. Louis	St. Louis, 31-28	49,885
1974	Dallas	Dallas, 17-14	64,146
1975	Dallas	Dallas, 37-31	52,417
1975	St. Louis	St. Louis, 31-17	49,701
1976	St. Louis	St. Louis, 21-17	50,317
1976	Dallas	Dallas, 19-14	62,498
1977	St. Louis	Dallas, 30-24	50,129
1977	Dallas	St. Louis, 24-17	64,038
1978	Dallas	Dallas, 21-12	62,760
1978	St. Louis	Dallas, 24-21 (OT)	48,991
1979	St. Louis	Dallas, 22-21	50,855
1979	Dallas	Dallas, 22-13	64,300
1980	St. Louis	Dallas, 27-24	50,701
1980	Dallas	Dallas, 31-21	52,567
1981	Dallas	Dallas, 30-17	63,602
1981	St. Louis	St. Louis, 20-17	49,777
1982	St. Louis	Dallas, 24-7	50,705
1983	St. Louis	Dallas, 34-17	48,532
1983	Dallas	Dallas, 35-17	60,764
1984	Dallas	St. Louis, 31-20	61,438
1984	St. Louis	Dallas, 24-17	48,721
1985	St. Louis	St. Louis, 21-10	49,347
1985	Dallas	Dallas, 35-17	54,125
1986	St. Louis	Dallas, 31-7	49,077
1986	Dallas	Dallas, 37-6	60,756
1987	St. Louis	St. Louis, 24-13	47,241
1987	Dallas	Dallas, 21-16	36,788

San Diego Chargers
(Dallas Leads Series, 3-1)

Year	Site	Winner-Score	Att.
1972	San D.	Dallas, 34-28	54,476
1980	Dallas	Dallas, 42-31	60,639
1983	San D.	San Diego, 24-23	46,192
1986	San D.	Dallas, 24-21	55,622

San Francisco 49ers
(Series Tied, 8-8-1)

Year	Site	Winner-Score	Att.
1960	Dallas	San Fran., 26-14	10,000
1963	San Fran.	San Fran., 31-24	29,563
1965	Dallas	Dallas, 39-31	39,677
1967	San Fran.	San Fran., 24-16	27,182
1969	Dallas	Tie, 24-24	62,348
1970*	San Fran.	Dallas, 17-10	59,625
1971†	Dallas	Dallas, 14-3	66,311
1972	Dallas	San Fran., 31-10	65,124
1972*	San Fran.	Dallas, 30-28	61,214
1974	Dallas	Dallas, 20-14	50,018
1977	San Fran.	Dallas, 42-35	55,848
1979	San Fran.	Dallas, 21-13	56,728
1980	Dallas	Dallas, 59-14	63,399
1981	San Fran.	San Fran., 45-14	57,574
1981†	San Fran.	San Fran., 28-27	60,525
1983	San Fran.	San Fran., 42-17	59,957

| 1985 | San Fran. | San Fran., 31-16 | 60,114 |

*Divisional Playoff Game
†NFC Championship Game

Seattle Seahawks
(Dallas Leads Series, 3-1)

Year	Site	Winner-Score	Att.
1976	Seattle	Dallas, 28-13	62,027
1980	Dallas	Dallas, 51-7	57,540
1983	Seattle	Dallas, 35-10	63,352
1986	Dallas	Seattle, 31-14	58,023

Tampa Bay Buccaneers
(Dallas Leads Series, 6-0)

Year	Site	Winner-Score	Att.
1977	Dallas	Dallas, 23-7	55,316
1980	Dallas	Dallas, 28-17	62,750
1981*	Dallas	Dallas, 38-0	64,848
1982	Dallas	Dallas, 14-9	49,578
1982†	Dallas	Dallas, 30-17	65,042
1983	Dallas	Dallas, 27-24 (OT)	63,308

*Divisional Playoff Game
†Super Bowl Tournament

Washington Redskins
(Dallas Leads Series, 31-23-2)

Year	Site	Winner-Score	Att.
1960	Wash.	Wash., 26-14	21,142
1961	Dallas	Tie, 28-28	17,500
1961	Wash.	Wash., 34-24	21,451
1962	Dallas	Tie, 35-35	15,730
1962	Wash.	Dallas, 38-10	49,888
1963	Wash.	Wash., 21-17	40,101
1963	Dallas	Dallas, 35-20	18,838
1964	Dallas	Dallas, 24-18	25,158
1964	Wash.	Wash., 28-16	49,219
1965	Dallas	Dallas, 27-7	61,577
1965	Wash.	Wash., 34-31	50,205
1966	Wash.	Dallas, 31-30	50,927
1966	Dallas	Wash., 34-31	64,198
1967	Wash.	Dallas, 17-14	50,566
1967	Dallas	Wash., 27-20	75,538
1968	Wash.	Dallas, 44-24	50,816
1968	Dallas	Dallas, 29-20	66,076
1969	Wash.	Dallas, 41-28	50,474
1969	Dallas	Dallas, 20-10	56,924
1970	Wash.	Dallas, 45-21	50,415
1970	Dallas	Dallas, 34-0	57,936
1971	Dallas	Wash., 20-16	72,000
1971	Wash.	Dallas, 13-0	53,041
1972	Wash.	Wash., 24-20	53,039
1972	Dallas	Dallas, 34-24	65,136
1972*	Wash.	Wash., 26-3	53,129
1973	Wash.	Wash., 14-7	54,314
1973	Dallas	Dallas, 27-7	64,458
1974	Wash.	Wash., 28-21	54,395
1974	Dallas	Dallas, 24-23	63,243
1975	Wash.	Wash., 30-24 (OT)	55,004
1975	Dallas	Dallas, 31-10	61,091
1976	Wash.	Dallas, 20-7	55,004
1976	Dallas	Wash., 27-14	59,916
1977	Dallas	Dallas, 34-16	62,115
1977	Wash.	Dallas, 14-7	55,031
1978	Wash.	Wash., 9-5	55,031
1978	Dallas	Dallas, 37-10	64,905
1979	Wash.	Wash., 34-20	55,031
1979	Dallas	Dallas, 35-34	62,867
1980	Wash.	Dallas, 17-3	55,045
1980	Dallas	Dallas, 14-10	58,809
1981	Wash.	Dallas, 26-10	55,045
1981	Dallas	Dallas, 24-10	64,583
1982	Wash.	Dallas, 24-10	54,633
1982*	Wash.	Wash., 31-17	55,045
1983	Dallas	Dallas, 31-30	55,045
1983	Dallas	Wash., 31-10	65,074
1984	Wash.	Wash., 34-14	55,431
1984	Dallas	Wash., 30-28	64,286
1985	Dallas	Dallas, 44-14	62,292
1985	Wash.	Dallas, 13-7	55,750
1986	Dallas	Dallas, 30-6	63,264
1986	Wash.	Wash., 41-14	55,642
1987	Dallas	Wash., 13-7	60,415
1987	Wash.	Wash., 24-20	54,882

*NFC Championship Game

Cowboys Leaders By Years

RUSHING

Year	Player	Att.	Yds.	Avg.	Long	TD	NFL/NFC Rank
1960	Dupre, L. G.	104	362	3.5	18	3	20
1961	*Perkins, Don	200	815	4.1	47	4	6
1962	Perkins, Don	222	945	4.3	35	7	5
1963	Perkins, Don	149	614	4.1	19t	7	10
1964	Perkins, Don	174	768	4.4	59	6	5
1965	Perkins, Don	177	690	3.9	43	0	7
1966	Reeves, Dan	175	757	4.3	67t	8	6
1967	Perkins, Don	201	823	4.1	30	6	6
1968	Perkins, Don	191	836	4.4	28t	4	6
1969	*Hill, Calvin	204	942	4.6	55	8	2
1970	*Thomas, Duane	151	803	5.3	47t	5	8/5
1971	Thomas, Duane	175	793	4.5	56t	11	11/7
1972	Hill, Calvin	245	1,036	4.2	26	6	7/3
1973	Hill, Calvin	273	1,142	4.2	21	6	3/2
1974	Hill, Calvin	185	844	4.6	27	7	8/3
1975	Newhouse, Robert	209	930	4.4	29	2	9/4
1976	Dennison, Doug	153	542	3.5	14	6	35/18
1977	*Dorsett, Tony	208	1,007	4.8	84t	12	9/4
1978	Dorsett, Tony	290	1,325	4.6	63t	7	3/2
1979	Dorsett, Tony	250	1,107	4.4	41	6	11/8
1980	Dorsett, Tony	278	1,185	4.3	56	11	6/6
1981	Dorsett, Tony	342	1,646	4.8	75t	4	2/2
1982	Dorsett, Tony	177	745	4.2	99t	5	2/1
1983	Dorsett, Tony	289	1,321	4.6	77	8	6/5
1984	Dorsett, Tony	302	1,189	3.9	31t	6	7/7
1985	Dorsett, Tony	305	1,307	4.3	60t	7	6/4
1986	Dorsett, Tony	184	748	4.1	33	5	19/11
1987	Walker, Herschel	209	891	4.3	60t	7	6/3

PASSING

Year	Player	Att.	Comp.	Pct.	Yds.	TD	Int.	Rating	NFL/NFC Rank
1960	LeBaron, E.	225	111	49.3	1,736	12	25	53.4	8
1961	LeBaron, E.	236	120	50.8	1,741	14	16	66.5	9
1962	LeBaron, E.	166	95	57.2	1,436	16	9	95.3	3
1963	Meredith, D.	310	167	53.9	2,381	17	18	73.2	10
1964	Meredith, D.	323	158	48.9	2,143	9	16	67.3	15
1965	Meredith, D.	305	141	46.2	2,415	22	13	79.7	8
1966	Meredith, D.	344	177	51.5	2,805	24	12	87.7	4
1967	Meredith, D.	255	128	50.2	1,834	16	16	68.6	8
1968	Meredith, D.	309	171	55.3	2,500	21	12	88.3	2
1969	Morton, C.	302	162	53.6	2,619	21	15	85.4	5
1970	Morton, C.	207	102	49.3	1,819	15	7	89.7	5/4
1971	Staubach, R.	211	126	59.7	1,882	15	4	104.8	1/1
1972	Morton, C.	339	185	54.6	2,396	15	21	65.9	15/7
1973	Staubach, R.	286	179	62.6	2,428	23	15	94.6	1/1
1974	Staubach, R.	360	190	52.8	2,552	11	15	68.5	14/7
1975	Staubach, R.	348	198	56.9	2,666	17	16	78.6	8/2
1976	Staubach, R.	369	208	56.4	2,715	14	11	79.9	8/5
1977	Staubach, R.	361	210	58.2	2,620	18	9	87.1	2/1
1978	Staubach, R.	413	231	55.9	3,190	25	16	84.9	1/1
1979	Staubach, R.	461	267	57.9	3,586	27	11	92.4	1/1
1980	White, D.	436	260	59.6	3,287	28	25	80.8	9/7
1981	White, D.	391	223	57.0	3,098	22	13	87.5	5/2
1982	White, D.	247	156	63.2	2,079	16	12	91.1	4/2
1983	White, D.	533	334	62.7	3,980	29	23	85.6	9/6
1984	White, D.	233	126	54.1	1,580	11	11	71.5	22/11
1985	White, D.	450	267	59.3	3,157	21	17	80.6	9/4
1986	Pelluer, S.	378	215	56.9	2,727	8	17	67.9	20/9
1987	White, D.	362	215	59.4	2,617	12	17	73.2	19/9

RECEIVING

Year	Player	No.	Yds.	Avg.	Long	TD	NFL/NFC Rank
1960	Doran, Jim	31	554	17.9	75t	3	21
1961	Howton, Billy	56	785	14.0	53	4	6
1962	Howton, Billy	49	706	14.4	69t	6	15
1963	Clarke, Frank	43	833	19.4	75t	10	3
1964	Clarke, Frank	65	973	15.0	49	5	3
1965	*Hayes, Bob	46	1,003	21.8	82t	12	13
1966	Hayes, Bob	64	1,232	19.3	95t	13	4
1967	Rentzel, Lance	58	996	17.2	74t	8	6
1968	Rentzel, Lance	54	1,009	18.7	65t	6	3
1969	Rentzel, Lance	43	960	22.3	75t	12	20
1970	Hayes, Bob	34	889	26.1	89t	10	45/26
1971	Garrison, Walt	40	396	9.9	36	1	23/10
1972	Hill, Calvin	43	364	8.5	33t	3	18/9
1973	Hill, Calvin	32	290	9.1	29	0	36/21
1974	Pearson, Drew	62	1,087	17.9	50t	2	3/2
1975	Pearson, Drew	46	822	17.9	46t	8	16/9
1976	Pearson, Drew	58	806	13.9	54	6	4/1
1977	Pearson, Drew	48	870	18.1	67	2	9/3
1978	Pearson, Preston	47	526	11.2	34	0	26/15
1979	Hill, Tony	60	1,062	17.7	75t	10	12/6
1980	Hill, Tony	60	1,055	17.6	58t	8	16/9
1981	Hill, Tony	46	953	20.7	63t	4	47/26
	Springs, Ron	46	359	7.8	32t	2	
1982	Hill, Tony	35	526	15.0	47	1	22/8
1983	Springs, Ron	73	589	8.1	80t	1	9/4
1984	Cosbie, Doug	60	789	13.2	36	4	28/12
1985	Hill, Tony	74	1,113	15.0	53	7	9/3
1986	Walker, Herschel	76	837	11.0	84t	2	9/4
1987	Walker, Herschel	60	715	11.9	44	1	5/4

PUNTING

Year	Player	No.	Avg.	Long	Had Blocked	NFL/NFC Rank
1960	Sherer, Dave	57	42.5	67	1	7
1961	*Green, Allen	61	36.7	53	1	14
1962	Baker, Sam	57	45.4	72	0	3
1963	Baker, Sam	71	44.2	64	0	7
1964	*Lothridge, Billy	62	40.3	75	1	15
1965	Villanueva, Danny	60	41.8	58	0	10
1966	Villanueva, Danny	65	39.2	58	1	13
1967	Villanueva, Danny	67	40.4	57	0	9
1968	Widby, Ron	59	40.9	84	0	5
1969	Widby, Ron	63	43.3	62	0	2
1970	Widby, Ron	69	41.3	59	1	10/2
1971	Widby, Ron	56	41.6	59	1	8/3
1972	*Bateman, Marv	51	38.2	61	0	24/13
1973	Bateman, Marv	55	41.6	62	2	11/7
1974	*Carrell, Duane	40	39.8	59	0	11/5
1975	*Hoopes, Mitch	68	39.4	55	1	16/9
1976	*White, Danny	70	38.4	54	2	20/9
1977	White, Danny	80	39.6	57	1	12/8
1978	White, Danny	76	40.5	56	1	8/5
1979	White, Danny	76	41.7	73	0	4/2
1980	White, Danny	71	40.9	58	0	10/5
1981	White, Danny	81	40.8	60	0	14/8
1982	White, Danny	37	41.7	56	0	8/5
1983	White, Danny	38	40.6	50	1	DNQ
1984	White, Danny	82	38.4	55	0	28/14
1985	*Saxon, Mike	81	41.9	57	1	13/8
1986	Saxon, Mike	86	40.7	58	1	15/9
1987	Saxon, Mike	68	39.5	63	0	20/10

SCORING

Year	Player	TD	PAT	FG	Tot.	NFL/NFC Rank
1960	Cone, Fred	0	21	6	39	27
1961	Clarke, Frank	9	0	0	54	22
1962	Baker, Sam	0	50	14	92	6
1963	Baker, Sam	0	38	9	65	14
1964	*VanRaaphorst, Dick	0	28	14	70	13
1965	Villanueva, Danny	0	37	16	85	10
1966	Villanueva, Danny	0	56	17	107	2
1967	Hayes, Bob	11	0	0	66	16
	Reeves, Dan	11	0	0	66	
1968	Clark, Mike	0	54	17	105	2
1969	Clark, Mike	0	43	20	103	2
1970	Clark, Mike	0	35	18	89	12/8
1971	Clark, Mike	0	47	13	86	13/7
1972	Fritsch, Toni	0	36	21	99	7/3
1973	Fritsch, Toni	0	43	18	97	11/7
1974	*Herrera, Efren	0	33	8	57	26/9
1975	Fritsch, Toni	0	38	22	104	3/2
1976	Herrera, Efren	0	34	18	88	6/4
1977	Herrera, Efren	0	39	18	93	5/2
1978	Septien, Rafael	0	46	16	94	5/2
1979	Septien, Rafael	0	40	19	97	8/3
1980	Septien, Rafael	0	59	11	92	13/6
1981	Septien, Rafael	0	40	27	122	1/1
1982	Septien, Rafael	0	28	10	58	11/5
1983	Septien, Rafael	0	57	22	123	5/5
1984	Septien, Rafael	0	33	23	102	13/6
1985	Septien, Rafael	0	42	19	99	17/8
1986	Septien, Rafael	0	43	15	88	20/9
1987	Ruzek, Roger	0	26	22	92	5/3

FIELD GOALS

Year	Player	Att.	Made	Pct.	Long	NFL/ NFC Rank
1960	Cone, Fred	13	6	.462	45	12
1961	Bielski, Dick	9	6	.667	42	13
1962	Baker, Sam	27	14	.519	53	3
1963	Baker, Sam	20	9	.450	53	12
1964	*VanRaaphorst, Dick	29	14	.483	43	8
1965	Villanueva, Danny	27	16	.593	41	7
1966	Villanueva, Danny	31	17	.548	37	8
1967	Villanueva, Danny	23	9	.391	34	14
1968	Clark, Mike	29	17	.586	50	7
1969	Clark, Mike	36	20	.555	47	5
1970	Clark, Mike	27	18	.667	43	7/4
1971	Clark, Mike	25	13	.520	48	19/9
1972	Fritsch, Toni	36	21	.583	54	18/8
1973	Fritsch, Toni	28	18	.643	37	12/4
1974	*Herrera, Efren	13	8	.615	39	11/5
1975	Fritsch, Toni	35	22	.629	43	14/8
1976	Herrera, Efren	23	18	.783	46	1/1
1977	Herrera, Efren	29	18	.621	52	12/1
1978	Septien, Rafael	26	16	.615	48	17/9
1979	Septien, Rafael	29	19	.655	51	9/4
1980	Septien, Rafael	17	11	.647	52	13/7
1981	Septien, Rafael	35	27	.771	47	4/3
1982	Septien, Rafael	14	10	.714	53	13/6
1983	Septien, Rafael	27	22	.815	47	7/3
1984	Septien, Rafael	29	23	.793	52	4/3
1985	Septien, Rafael	28	19	.679	53	18/9
1986	Septien, Rafael	21	15	.714	50	11/5
1987	Ruzek, Roger	25	22	.880	49	2/1

KICKOFF RETURNS

Year	Player	No.	Yds.	Avg.	Long	TD	NFL/ NFC Rank
1960	Franckhauser, Tom	26	526	20.2	46	0	19
1961	*Marsh, Amos	26	667	25.7	79	0	13
1962	Marsh, Amos	29	725	25.0	101t	1	10
1963	*Stiger, Jim	18	432	24.0	66	0	12
1964	*Renfro, Mel	40	1,017	25.4	65	0	7
1965	Renfro, Mel	21	630	30.0	100t	1	4
1966	Renfro, Mel	19	487	25.6	87t	1	9
1967	Garrison, Walt	20	366	18.3	36	0	23
1968	Baynham, Craig	23	590	25.7	40	0	7
1969	*Flowers, Richmond	11	283	25.7	30	0	29
1970	*Thomas, Duane	19	416	21.9	33	0	23/10
1971	Harris, Cliff	29	823	28.4	77	0	4/4
1972	Harris, Cliff	26	615	23.7	44	0	23/11
1973	**Montgomery, Mike	6	175	29.2	63	0	DNQ
1974	*Morgan, Dennis	35	823	23.5	43	0	21/11
1975	Pearson, Preston	16	391	24.4	42	0	13/7
1976	*Johnson, Butch	28	693	24.8	74	0	11/5
1977	Johnson, Butch	22	536	24.4	64	0	9/5
1978	Johnson, Butch	29	603	20.8	56	0	27/12
1979	*Springs, Ron	38	780	20.5	70	0	25/12
1980	*Jones, James	32	720	22.5	41	0	11/6
1981	Jones, James	27	517	19.1	33	0	36/17
1982	Fellows, Ron	16	359	22.4	35	0	16/9
1983	Fellows, Ron	43	855	19.9	53	0	26/12
1984	Allen, Gary	33	666	20.2	34	0	24/11
1985	*Lavette, Robert	34	682	20.1	34	0	27/13
1986	Lavette, Robert	36	699	19.4	37	0	27/12
1987	Clack, Darryl	29	635	21.9	48	0	9/7

PUNT RETURNS

Year	Player	No.	Yds.	Avg.	Long	TD	NFL/ NFC Rank
1960	Butler, Bill	13	131	10.1	46	0	2
1961	*Marsh, Amos	14	71	5.1	19	0	14
1962	Lockett, J. W.	8	45	5.6	17	0	14

Year	Player	No.	Yds.	Avg.	Long	TD	NFL/ NFC Rank
1963	*Stiger, Jim	14	141	10.1	45	0	6
1964	*Renfro, Mel	32	418	13.1	69t	1	3
1965	Renfro, Mel	24	145	6.0	35	0	9
1966	Hayes, Bob	17	106	6.2	18	0	7
1967	Hayes, Bob	24	276	11.5	69t	1	2
1968	Hayes, Bob	15	312	20.8	90t	2	1
1969	Hayes, Bob	18	179	9.9	50	0	3
1970	Hayes, Bob	15	116	7.7	34	0	20/7
1971	Harris, Cliff	17	129	7.6	35	0	11/4
1972	Harris, Cliff	19	78	4.1	21	0	21/11
1973	*Richards, Golden	21	139	6.6	46	0	23/10
1974	*Morgan, Dennis	19	287	15.1	98t	1	3/2
1975	Richards, Golden	28	288	10.3	43t	1	12/5
1976	*Johnson, Butch	45	489	10.9	55	0	8/4
1977	Johnson, Butch	50	423	8.5	38	0	20/7
1978	Johnson, Butch	51	401	7.9	23	0	18/9
1979	*Wilson, Steve	35	236	6.8	13	0	20/7
1980	*Jones, James	54	548	10.1	52	0	5/4
1981	Jones, James	33	188	5.7	17	0	28/14
1982	Fellows, Ron	25	189	7.6	17	0	18/8
1983	Hill, Rod	30	232	7.7	37	0	20/10
1984	Allen, Gary	54	446	8.3	18	0	16/8
1985	Bates, Bill	22	152	6.9	21	0	20/8
1986	Banks, Gordon	27	160	5.9	20	0	22/11
1987	*Martin, Kelvin	22	216	9.8	38	0	12/7

INTERCEPTIONS

Year	Player	No.	Yds.	Avg.	Long	TD	NFL/ NFC Rank
1960	Bishop, Don	3	13	4.3	13	0	25
	Franckhauser, Tom	3	11	3.7	9	0	25
1961	Bishop, Don	8	172	21.5	57	0	2
1962	Bishop, Don	6	134	22.3	44	0	9
1963	Green, Cornell	7	211	30.1	55	0	6
1964	*Renfro, Mel	7	110	15.7	39t	1	4
1965	Green, Cornell	3	49	16.3	43	0	27
	Livingston, Warren	3	5	1.7	5	0	27
	*Logan, Obert	3	5	1.7	3	0	27
1966	Green, Cornell	4	88	22.0	41t	1	21
1967	Green, Cornell	7	52	7.4	28	0	7
	Renfro, Mel	7	38	5.4	30	0	9
1968	Howley, Chuck	6	115	19.2	58	1	11
1969	Renfro, Mel	10	118	11.8	41	0	1
1970	*Waters, Charlie	5	45	9.0	20	0	16/9
1971	Adderley, Herb	6	182	30.3	46	0	9/4
1972	Waters, Charlie	6	132	22.0	56	1	7/3
1973	Jordan, Lee Roy	6	78	13.0	31t	1	4/2
1974	Harris, Cliff	3	8	2.7	8	0	42/20
1975	Jordan, Lee Roy	6	80	13.3	38	0	7/4
1976	Washington, Mark	4	49	12.3	22	0	24/11
1977	Harris, Cliff	5	7	1.4	7	0	16/7
1978	Barnes, Benny	5	72	14.4	38	0	25/14
1979	Hughes, Randy	2	91	45.5	68	0	93/45
	Harris, Cliff	2	35	17.5	20	0	
	Barnes, Benny	2	20	10.0	11	0	
	Lewis, D. D.	2	8	4.0	5	0	
	Kyle, Aaron	2	0	0.0	0	0	
1980	Thurman, Dennis	5	114	22.8	78t	1	24/10
	Waters, Charlie	5	78	15.6	29	0	
1981	*Walls, Everson	11	133	12.1	33	0	1/1
1982	Walls, Everson	7	61	8.7	37	0	1/1
1983	Thurman, Dennis	6	49	8.2	34	0	15/8
1984	Downs, Michael	7	126	18.0	27t	1	4/2
1985	Walls, Everson	9	31	3.4	19	0	1/1
1986	Downs, Michael	6	54	9.0	31	0	11/7
1987	Walls, Everson	5	38	7.6	30	0	7/4

t—Touchdown
*Rookie
**Did Not Qualify (Minimum 14 returns required.)

Cowboys All-Time Leaders

RUSHING

Player	Att.	Yds.	Avg.	Long	TD
1. Dorsett, Tony (1977-87)	2,755	12,036	4.4	99	72
2. Perkins, Don (1961-68)	1,500	6,217	4.1	59	42
3. Hill, Calvin (1969-74)	1,166	5,009	4.3	55	39
4. Newhouse, Robert (1972-83)	1,160	4,784	4.1	54	31
5. Garrison, Walt (1966-74)	899	3,886	4.3	41	30
6. Staubach, Roger (1969-79)	410	2,264	5.5	33	20
7. Springs, Ron (1979-84)	604	2,180	3.6	46	28
8. Marsh, Amos (1961-64)	427	2,065	4.8	71	14
9. Reeves, Dan (1965-72)	535	1,990	3.7	67	25
10. Walker, Herschel (1986-87)	360	1,628	4.5	84	19

PASSING (Min. 1500 attempts)

Player	Att.	Comp.	Pct.	Yds.	TD	Int.	Rating
1. Staubach, R. (1969-79)	2,958	1,685	57.0	22,700	153	109	83.5
2. White, Danny (1976-87)	2,908	1,732	59.6	21,685	154	129	82.0
3. Meredith, D. (1960-68)	2,308	1,170	50.7	17,199	135	111	74.7

RECEIVING

Player	No.	Yds.	Avg.	Long	TD
1. Pearson, Drew (1973-83)	489	7,822	16.0	67	48
2. Hill, Tony (1977-86)	479	7,988	16.7	75	51
3. Dorsett, Tony (1977-87)	382	3,432	9.0	91	13
4. Hayes, Bob (1965-74)	365	7,295	20.0	95	71
5. Cosbie, Doug (1979-87)	288	3,616	12.6	61	30
6. Clarke, Frank (1960-67)	281	5,214	18.6	80	50
7. DuPree, Billy Joe (1973-83)	267	3,565	13.4	42	41
8. Springs, Ron (1979-84)	222	2,029	9.1	80	10
9. Pearson, Preston (1975-80)	189	2,274	12.0	49	11
10. Rentzel, Lance (1967-70)	183	3,521	19.2	86	31

PUNTING (Min. 125)

Player	No.	Avg.	Long	Blk.
1. Baker, Sam (1962-63)	128	45.1	72	0
2. Widby, Ron (1968-71)	247	41.8	84	2
3. Saxon, Mike (1985-87)	235	40.8	63	2
4. Villanueva, Danny (1965-67)	192	40.3	58	1
5. White, Danny (1976-85)	611	40.1	73	4

INTERCEPTIONS

Player	No.	Yds.	Avg.	Long	TD
1. Renfro, Mel (1964-77)	52	626	12.0	90	3
2. Walls, Everson (1981-87)	42	391	9.3	37	0
3. Waters, Charlie (1970-78, 1980-81)	41	584	14.2	56	2
4. Thurman, Dennis (1978-85)	36	562	15.6	96	4
5. Green, Cornell (1962-74)	34	552	16.2	59	2
6. Downs, Michael (1981-87)	32	430	13.4	31	1
6. Jordan, Lee Roy (1963-76)	32	472	14.8	49	3
8. Harris, Cliff (1970-79)	29	281	9.7	60	1
9. Howley, Chuck (1961-73)	24	395	16.5	58	2
10. Bishop, Don (1960-65)	22	364	16.5	57	0

PUNT RETURNS (Min. 75 Returns)

Player	No.	Yds.	Avg.	Long	TD
1. Hayes, Bob (1965-74)	104	1,158	11.1	90	3
2. Johnson, Butch (1976-83)	146	1,313	9.0	55	0
3. Jones, James (1980-82, 1984-85)	87	736	8.5	52	0
4. Renfro, Mel (1964–77)	109	842	7.7	69	1

KICKOFF RETURNS (Min. 70 Returns)

Player	No.	Yds.	Avg.	Long	TD
1. Renfro, Mel (1964-77)	85	2,246	26.4	100	2
2. Johnson, Butch (1976-83)	79	1,832	23.2	74	0
3. Jones, James (1980-82, 1984-85)	70	1,444	20.6	41	0
4. Fellows, Ron (1981-86)	73	1,478	20.3	53	0
5. Lavette, Robert (1985-87)	74	1,453	19.6	37	0

SCORING

Player	TD	PAT	FG	Total
1. Septien, Rafael (1978-86)	—	388	162	874
2. Dorsett, Tony (1977-87)	86	—	—	516
3. Hayes, Bob (1965-74)	76	—	—	456
4. Clark, Mike (1968-71, 1973)	—	180	69	387
5. Fritsch, Toni (1971-73, 1975)	—	119	66	317
6. Clarke, Frank (1960-67)	51	—	—	306
6. Hill, Tony (1977-86)	51	—	—	306
8. Pearson, Drew (1973-83)	50	—	—	300
9. Perkins, Don (1961-68)	45	—	—	270
9. Hill, Calvin (1969-74)	45	—	—	270

FIELD GOALS (Min. 40 made)

Player	Att.	Made	Pct.	Long
1. Septien, Rafael (1978-86)	226	162	.717	53
2. Herrera, Efren (1974, 1976-77)	65	44	.677	52
3. Fritsch, Toni (1971-73, 1975)	107	66	.617	54
4. Clark, Mike (1968-71, 1973)	119	69	.580	50
5. Villanueva, Danny (1965-67)	81	42	.519	41

COMBINED YARDAGE

Player	Total	Rush.	Int. Rec.	Punt. Ret.	Kick. Ret.	Fum. Ret.
1. Dorsett, Tony (1977-87)	15,501	12,036	3,432	0	0	0	33
2. Hayes, Bob (1965-74)	9,104	70	7,295	0	1,158	581	0
3. Hill, Tony (1977-86)	8,436	84	7,988	0	268	96	0
4. Pearson, Drew (1973-83)	8,180	190	7,822	0	13	155	0
5. Perkins, Don (1961-68)	8,005	6,217	1,310	0	8	443	0

RUSHING-RECEIVING

Player	Rushing	Receiving	Total
1. Dorsett, Tony (1977-87)	12,036	3,432	15,468
2. Hill, Tony (1977-86)	84	7,988	8,072
3. Pearson, Drew (1973-83)	190	7,822	8,012
4. Perkins, Don (1961-68)	6,217	1,310	7,527
5. Hayes, Bob (1965-74)	70	7,295	7,365

Cowboys Individual Records

NOTE: The 1982 regular season was reduced from 16 games to 9 because of a players' strike. The 1987 regular season was reduced from 16 games to 15 because of a players' strike.

SCORING

TOTAL POINTS
Career
874	Rafael Septien (1978–86), 388 PATs, 162 FGs
516	Tony Dorsett (1977–87), 86 TDs

Season
123	Rafael Septien (1983), 57 PATs, 22 FGs
121	Rafael Septien (1981), 40 PATs, 27 FGs
107	Danny Villanueva (1966), 56 PATS, 17 FGs
105	Mike Clark (1968), 54 PATs, 17 FGs

Game
24	Dan Reeves (11/5/67 vs. Atlanta), 4 TDs
24	Bob Hayes (12/20/70 vs. Houston), 4 TDs
24	Calvin Hill (9/19/71 @ Buffalo), 4 TDs
24	Duane Thomas (12/18/71 vs. St. Louis), 4 TDs

Opponent/Game
24	Dick James, @ Washington (12/17/61)
24	Harold Jackson, @ L.A. Rams (10/14/73)

TOUCHDOWNS
Career
86	Tony Dorsett (1977–87)
76	Bob Hayes (1965–74)
51	Frank Clarke (1960–67)
51	Tony Hill (1977–86)

Season
16	Dan Reeves (1966), 8 run, 8 pass
14	Frank Clarke (1962), 14 pass

Game
4	Dan Reeves (11/5/67 vs. Atlanta), 2 run, 2 pass
4	Bob Hayes (12/20/70 vs. Houston), 4 pass
4	Calvin Hill (9/19/71 @ Buffalo), 4 run
4	Duane Thomas (12/18/71 vs. St. Louis), 3 run, 1 pass

Opponent/Game
4	Dick James, @ Washington (12/17/61)
4	Harold Jackson, @ L.A. Rams (10/14/73)

FIELD GOALS MADE
Career
162	Rafael Septien (1978–86), 226 attempts
69	Mike Clark (1968–71, 1973), 119 attempts
66	Toni Fritsch (1971–73, 1975), 107 attempts

Season
27	Rafael Septien (1981), 35 attempts
23	Rafael Septien (1984), 29 attempts
22	Roger Ruzek (1987), 25 attempts
22	Rafael Septien (1983), 27 attempts
22	Toni Fritsch (1975), 35 attempts

Game
5	Roger Ruzek (12/21/87 @ L.A. Rams)

Longest Field Goal
54	Toni Fritsch (9/24/72 @ N.Y. Giants)

Opponent/Game
4	Bob Khayat, @ Washington (10/9/60)
4	Tommy Davis, San Francisco (11/20/60)
4	Sam Baker, @ Philadelphia (12/5/65)
4	Fred Cox, @ Minnesota (10/18/70)
4	Jim Bakken, St. Louis (12/18/71)
4	Chris Bahr, L.A. Raiders (10/23/83)
4	Ali Haji-Sheikh, N.Y. Giants (11/4/84)

Opponent/Longest Field Goal
59	Tony Franklin, Philadelphia (11/12/79)

FIELD GOALS ATTEMPTED
Career
226	Rafael Septien (1978–86), 162 FG
119	Mike Clark (1968–71, 1973), 69 FG
107	Toni Fritsch (1971–73, 1975), 66 FG

Season
36	Toni Fritsch (1972), 21 FG
36	Mike Clark (1969), 20 FG

Game
7	Mike Clark (11/24/68 @ Chicago), 2 FG
6	Toni Fritsch (9/21/75 vs. L.A. Rams), 4 FG

Opponent/Game
7	Sam Baker, @ Philadelphia (12/5/65), 4 FG

EXTRA POINTS MADE
Career
388	Rafael Septien (1978–86)
180	Mike Clark (1968–71, 1973)

Season
59	Rafael Septien (1980)
57	Rafael Septien (1983)

Game
8	Rafael Septien (10/12/80 vs. San Francisco) Att. 8
8	Mike Clark (9/15/68 vs. Detroit) Att. 8
8	Danny Villanueva (10/9/66 vs. Philadelphia) Att. 8

Opponent/Game
7	Gerry Perry, @ St. Louis (12/9/62) Att. 7

RUSHING

TOTAL YARDS
Career
12,036	Tony Dorsett (1977–87)
6,217	Don Perkins (1961–68)
5,009	Calvin Hill (1969–74)
4,784	Robert Newhouse (1972–83)

Season
1,646	Tony Dorsett (1981), 4.8 per carry

1,325	Tony Dorsett (1978), 4.6 per carry	
1,321	Tony Dorsett (1983), 4.6 per carry	
1,307	Tony Dorsett (1985), 4.3 per carry	
1,189	Tony Dorsett (1981), 3.9 per carry	
1,185	Tony Dorsett (1980), 4.3 per carry	
1,142	Calvin Hill (1973), 4.2 per carry	
1,107	Tony Dorsett (1979), 4.4 per carry	

Game
206	Tony Dorsett (12/4/77 vs. Philadelphia) on 23 carries
183	Tony Dorsett (11/9/80 @ N.Y. Giants) on 24 carries
175	Tony Dorsett (12/6/81 @ Baltimore) on 30 carries
173	Herschel Walker (11/15/87 @ New England) on 28 carries
162	Tony Dorsett (9/21/81 @ New England) on 19 carries

Opponent/Game
232	Jim Brown, Cleveland (9/22/63)
206	Greg Bell, @ Buffalo (11/18/84)
195	Earl Campbell, Houston (11/22/79)

ATTEMPTS
Career
2,755	Tony Dorsett (1977–87)
1,500	Don Perkins (1961–68)
1,166	Calvin Hill (1969–74)
1,160	Robert Newhouse (1972–83)

Season
342	Tony Dorsett (1981)
305	Tony Dorsett (1985)
302	Tony Dorsett (1984)
290	Tony Dorsett (1978)

Game
32	Calvin Hill (11/10/74 vs. San Francisco)
31	Calvin Hill (9/16/73 @ Chicago)

Opponent/Game
32	John Riggins, Washington (10/14/84), 165 yards

TOUCHDOWNS RUSHING
Career
72	Tony Dorsett (1977–87)
42	Don Perkins (1961–68)
39	Calvin Hill (1969–74)
31	Robert Newhouse (1972–83)

Season
12	Tony Dorsett (1977)
12	Herschel Walker (1986)

Game
4	Calvin Hill (9/19/71 @ Buffalo)

Opponent/Game
3	Jim Taylor, @ Green Bay (11/13/60)
3	Dick James, @ Washington (12/17/61)

RUSHING AVERAGE
Career (700 attempts)
4.4	Tony Dorsett (1977–87), 2,755 attempts
4.3	Walt Garrison (1966–74), 899 attempts
4.3	Calvin Hill (1969–74), 1,166 attempts

Season (Qualifiers)
5.6	Amos Marsh (1962), 144-802
5.3	Duane Thomas (1970), 151-803
4.9	Herschel Walker (1986), 151-737

Game (10 attempts)
12.1	Walt Garrison (12/9/72 vs. Washington), 10-121
10.9	Amos Marsh (11/4/62 @ Washington), 10-109
10.8	Dan Reeves (12/11/66 vs. Washington), 10-108

Longest Runs
99	Tony Dorsett (1/3/83 @ Minnesota) TD
84	Tony Dorsett (12/4/77 vs. Philadelphia) TD
84	Herschel Walker (12/14/86 vs. Philadelphia) TD
77	Tony Dorsett (10/9/77 @ St. Louis) TD
77	Tony Dorsett (9/5/83 @ Washington)

Opponent/Longest Run
85	Greg Bell, @ Buffalo (11/18/84) TD

PASSING

TOTAL YARDS
Career
22,700	Roger Staubach (1969–79)
21,685	Danny White (1976–87)
17,199	Don Meredith (1960–68)

Season
3,980	Danny White (1983)
3,586	Roger Staubach (1979)
3,287	Danny White (1980)
3,190	Roger Staubach (1978)
3,157	Danny White (1985)

Game
460	Don Meredith (11/10/63 @ San Francisco), 30 of 48
406	Don Meredith (11/13/66 @ Washington), 21 of 29
394	Don Meredith (11/6/66 @ Philadelphia), 14 of 24

Opponent/Game
466	Bill Wade, Chicago (11/18/62), 28 of 46
432	Phil Simms, @ N.Y. Giants (10/6/85), 18 of 36
411	Sonny Jurgensen, @ Washington (11/28/65), 26 of 46

PASS ATTEMPTS
Career
2,958	Roger Staubach (1969–79)
2,908	Danny White (1976–87)

Season
533	Danny White (1983), 334 completions
461	Roger Staubach (1979), 267 completions
450	Danny White (1985), 267 completions
436	Danny White (1980), 260 completions

Game
49	Roger Staubach (10/26/75 @ Philadelphia), 27 completions
49	Gary Hogeboom (12/22/85 @ San Francisco), 28 completions
49	Danny White (12/13/87 @ Washington), 27 completions

Opponent/Game
52	Neil Lomax, @ St. Louis (11/11/84)
50	Phil Simms, N.Y. Giants (12/15/85)

PASS COMPLETIONS
Career
1,732	Danny White (1976–87)
1,685	Roger Staubach (1969–79)

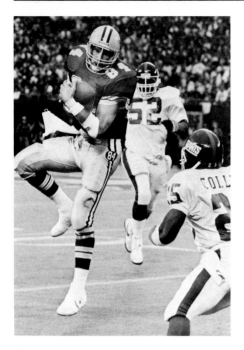

5 Don Meredith (9/18/66 vs. N.Y. Giants)
5 Don Meredith (10/9/66 vs. Philadelphia)
5 Don Meredith (9/29/68 @ Philadelphia)
5 Craig Morton (10/19/69 vs. Philadelphia)
5 Craig Morton (12/20/70 vs. Houston)
5 Danny White (10/30/83 @ N.Y. Giants)

Opponent/Game
6 Y. A. Tittle, @ N.Y. Giants (12/16/62)

PASSES HAD INTERCEPTED
Career
129 Danny White (1976–87)
111 Don Meredith (1960–68)
Season
25 Eddie LeBaron (1960), 225 attempts
25 Danny White (1980), 436 attempts
23 Danny White (1983), 533 attempts
21 Craig Morton (1972), 339 attempts
Game
5 Eddie LeBaron (9/30/60 vs. Philadelphia), 29 attempts
5 Eddie LeBaron (11/5/61 vs. St. Louis), 33 attempts
5 Danny White (11/9/80 @ N.Y. Giants), 23 attempts
5 Steve Pelluer (11/9/86 vs. L.A. Raiders), 30 attempts
Opponent/Game
6 Pete Liske, @ Philadelphia (9/26/71), 29 attempts

LOWEST INTERCEPTION RATE (Qualifiers)
Season
1.9 Roger Staubach (1971), 4 of 211
2.4 Roger Staubach (1979), 11 of 461
2.5 Roger Staubach (1977), 9 of 361
3.0 Roger Staubach (1976), 11 of 369

COMPLETION PERCENT
Career (1500 attempts)
59.6 Danny White (1976–87), 1,685 of 2,958
57.0 Roger Staubach (1969–79), 1,685 of 2,958
50.7 Don Meredith (1960–68), 1,170 of 2,308
Season (Qualifiers)
63.2 Danny White (1982), 156 of 247
62.7 Danny White (1983), 334 of 533
62.6 Roger Staubach (1973), 179 of 286
59.7 Roger Staubach (1971), 126 of 211
Game (12 or more completions)
87.5 Danny White (11/6/83 @ Philadelphia), 21 of 24
84.2 Don Meredith (9/15/68 vs. Detroit), 16 of 19
81.2 Eddie LeBaron (9/16/62 vs. Washington), 13 of 16

LONGEST PASS PLAYS
95 Don Meredith to Bob Hayes (11/13/66 vs. Washington) TD
91 Roger Staubach to Tony Dorsett (9/4/78 vs. Baltimore) TD
89 Craig Morton to Bob Hayes (10/25/70 @ Kansas City) TD

Opponent/Longest Pass Play
94 Norm Snead to Rich Houston, @ N.Y. Giants (9/24/72) TD

PASS RECEIVING

TOTAL RECEPTIONS
Career
489 Drew Pearson (1973–83)
479 Tony Hill (1977–86)
382 Tony Dorsett (1977–87)
365 Bob Hayes (1965–74)
Season
76 Herschel Walker (1986), 837 yards
74 Tony Hill (1985), 1,113 yards
73 Ron Springs (1983), 589 yards

Season
334 Danny White (1983), 533 attempts
267 Roger Staubach (1979), 461 attempts
267 Danny White (1985), 450 attempts
260 Danny White (1980), 436 attempts
231 Roger Staubach (1978), 413 attempts
Game
33 Gary Hogeboom (9/3/84 @ L.A. Rams), 47 attempts
31 Danny White (10/6/85 @ N.Y. Giants), 46 attempts
31 Danny White (11/13/83 @ San Diego), 47 attempts
30 Don Meredith (11/10/63 @ San Francisco), 48 attempts
Opponent/Game
28 Bill Wade, Chicago (11/18/62), 46 attempts
28 Kent Nix, @ Pittsburgh (10/22/67), 45 attempts
28 Joe Theismann, @ Washington (9/5/83), 38 attempts
28 Neil Lomax, St. Louis (11/28/85), 43 attempts

TOUCHDOWN PASSES
Career
154 Danny White (1976–87)
153 Roger Staubach (1969–79)
Season
29 Danny White (1983) of 334 completions
28 Danny White (1980) of 260 completions
27 Roger Staubach (1979) of 267 completions
25 Roger Staubach (1978) of 231 completions
Game
5 Eddie LeBaron (10/21/62 @ Pittsburgh)

Game
13 Lance Rentzel (11/19/67 vs. Washington), 223 yards
11 Bill Howton (11/25/62 @ Philadelphia), 102 yards
11 Ron Springs (9/21/81 @ New England), 72 yards
11 Ron Springs (10/9/83 vs. Tampa Bay), 126 yards
11 Tony Hill (9/15/85 @ Detroit), 181 yards
11 Doug Cosbie (9/15/85 @ Detroit), 159 yards
Opponent/Game
12 J. R. Wilburn, @ Pittsburgh (10/22/67), 142 yards

TOTAL RECEIVING YARDS
Career
7,988 Tony Hill (1977–86)
7,822 Drew Pearson (1973–83)
7,295 Bob Hayes (1965–74)
5,214 Frank Clarke (1960–67)
3,616 Doug Cosbie (1979–87)
Season
1,232 Bob Hayes (1966), 64 receptions
1,113 Tony Hill (1985), 74 receptions
1,087 Drew Pearson (1974), 62 receptions
1,062 Tony Hill (1979), 60 receptions
1,055 Tony Hill (1980), 60 receptions
1,043 Frank Clarke (1962), 47 receptions
1,026 Drew Pearson (1979), 55 receptions
Game
246 Bob Hayes (11/13/66 @ Washington), 9 receptions
241 Frank Clarke (9/16/62 vs. Washington), 10 receptions
223 Lance Rentzel (11/19/67 vs. Washington), 13 receptions
213 Tony Hill (11/12/79 vs. Philadelphia), 7 receptions
Opponent/Game
238 Harold Jackson, @ L.A. Rams (10/14/73), 7 receptions

TOUCHDOWNS RECEIVING
Career
71 Bob Hayes (1965–74)
51 Tony Hill (1977–86)
50 Frank Clarke (1960–67)
48 Drew Pearson (1973–83)
41 Billy Joe DuPree (1973–83)
Season
14 Frank Clarke (1962), 47 receptions
13 Bob Hayes (1966), 64 receptions
12 Lance Rentzel (1969), 43 receptions
12 Bob Hayes (1965), 46 receptions
Game
4 Bob Hayes (12/20/70 vs. Houston)
Opponent/Game
4 Harold Jackson, @ L.A. Rams (10/14/73)

RUSHING—RECEIVING
Career
15,468 Tony Dorsett (1977–87), 12,036 rushing, 3,432 receiving
8,072 Tony Hill (1977–86), 7,988 receiving, 84 rushing
8,012 Drew Pearson (1973–83), 7,822 receiving, 190 rushing
7,527 Don Perkins (1961–68), 6,217 rushing, 1,310 receiving
7,365 Bob Hayes (1965–74), 7,295 receiving, 70 rushing
Season
1,971 Tony Dorsett (1981), 1,646 rushing, 325 receiving
1,756 Tony Dorsett (1985), 1,307 rushing, 449 receiving
1,703 Tony Dorsett (1978), 1,325 rushing, 378 receiving
1,648 Tony Dorsett (1984), 1,189 rushing, 459 receiving
1,608 Tony Dorsett (1983), 1,321 rushing, 287 receiving
Game
292 Herschel Walker (12/14/86 vs. Philadelphia), 122 rushing, 170 receiving

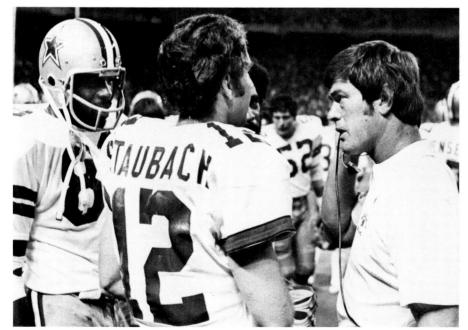

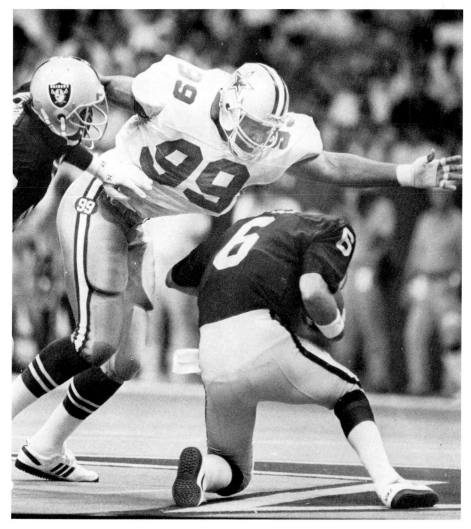

254 Tony Dorsett (9/4/78 vs. Baltimore), 147 rushing, 107 receiving
246 Bob Hayes (11/13/66 @ Washington), 246 receiving
241 Frank Clarke (9/16/62 vs. Washington), 241 receiving

COMBINED YARDAGE
Career
15,501 Tony Dorsett (1977–87), 33 return yards
9,104 Bob Hayes (1965–74), 1,739 return yards
8,436 Tony Hill (1977–86), 364 return yards
8,180 Drew Pearson (1973–83), 168 return yards
8,005 Don Perkins (1961–68), 478 return yards
Season
1,998 Amos Marsh (1962), 729 return yards
1,971 Tony Dorsett (1981), no return yards
1,757 Tony Dorsett (1978), 54 return yards
1,756 Tony Dorsett (1985), no return yards
1,627 Tony Dorsett (1984), 21 return yards
Game
292 Herschel Walker (12/14/86 vs. Philadelphia), 122 rushing, 170 receiving
285 Calvin Hill (11/16/69 @ Washington), 100 kickoff return, 150 rushing, 35 receiving

PUNTING
TOTAL PUNTS
Career
611 Danny White (1976–86)
247 Ron Widby (1968–71)
Season
86 Mike Saxon (1986), 40.7 average
82 Danny White (1984), 38.4 average
Game
11 Danny White (9/23/84 vs. Philadelphia), 40.5 average
AVERAGE YARDS
Career (125 punts)
45.1 Sam Baker (1962–63)
Season (Qualifiers)
45.4 Sam Baker (1962), 57 punts
44.2 Sam Baker (1963), 71 punts
Game (4 or more punts)
53.4 Ron Widby (11/3/68 @ New Orleans)
53.0 Marv Bateman (11/4/73 vs. Cincinnati)
LONGEST PUNT
84 Ron Widby (11/3/68 @ New Orleans)

PUNT RETURNS
TOTAL RETURNS
Career
146 Butch Johnson (1976–83)
109 Mel Renfro (1964–77)
Season
54 Gary Allen (1984), 8.3 average
54 James Jones (1980), 10.1 average
Game
9 Butch Johnson (11/15/76 vs. Buffalo)
PUNT RETURN YARDAGE
Career
1,313 Butch Johnson (1976–83)
1,158 Bob Hayes (1965–74)
Season
548 James Jones (1980), 10.1 average
489 Butch Johnson (1976), 10.9 average
446 Gary Allen (1984), 8.3 average
Game
122 Bob Hayes (12/8/68 vs. Pittsburgh), 3 returns
Longest Punt Return
98 Dennis Morgan (10/13/74 vs. St. Louis)
90 Bob Hayes (12/6/68 vs. Pittsburgh)
AVERAGE YARDS
Career (75 returns)
11.1 Bob Hayes (1965–74), 104 returns
9.0 Butch Johnson (1976–83), 146 returns
Season (Qualifiers)
20.8 Bob Hayes (1968), 15 returns
15.1 Dennis Morgan (1974), 19 returns
Game (3 returns)
40.7 Bob Hayes (12/8/68 vs. Pittsburgh), 3 for 122 yards
FAIR CATCHES
Career
38 Mel Renfro (1964–77)
38 Butch Johnson (1976–83)
Season
18 Golden Richards (1973)
16 Cliff Harris (1972)
Game
4 Golden Richards (11/16/75 @ New England)
4 Golden Richards (11/17/74 @ Washington)
4 Lance Rentzel (12/21/68 vs. Cleveland—playoff game)
4 Cliff Harris (12/23/72 @ San Francisco—playoff game)

KICKOFF RETURNS
TOTAL RETURNS
Career
85 Mel Renfro (1964–77)
79 Butch Johnson (1976–83)
Season
43 Ron Fellows (1983), 19.9 average
40 Mel Renfro (1964), 25.4 average
Game
8 Mel Renfro (10/29/64 vs. Green Bay), 156 yards
KICKOFF RETURN YARDAGE
Career
2,246 Mel Renfro (1964–77)
1,832 Butch Johnson (1976–83)
Season
1,017 Mel Renfro (1964), 25.4 average
855 Ron Fellows (1983), 19.9 average
823 Cliff Harris (1971), 28.4 average
823 Dennis Morgan (1974), 23.5 average
Game
168 Mel Renfro (11/22/64 @ Washington), 4 returns
157 Amos Marsh (10/14/62 vs. Philadelphia), 4 returns
Longest Kickoff Return
101 Amos Marsh (10/14/62 vs. Philadelphia)
101 Ike Thomas (12/4/71 vs. N.Y. Jets)
100 Mark Washington (11/22/70 @ Washington)
100 Mel Renfro (11/7/65 vs. San Francisco)
AVERAGE YARDS
Career (70 returns)
26.4 Mel Renfro (1964–77), 85 returns
23.2 Butch Johnson (1976–83), 79 returns
Season (Qualifiers)
30.0 Mel Renfro (1965), 21 returns
28.4 Cliff Harris (1971), 29 returns
Game (3 returns)
42.0 Mel Renfro (11/22/64 @ Washington), 4 for 168 yards

INTERCEPTIONS
TOTAL INTERCEPTIONS
Career
52 Mel Renfro (1964–77)
42 Everson Walls (1981–87)
41 Charlie Waters (1970–78, 1980–81)
36 Dennis Thurman (1978–85)
34 Cornell Green (1962–74)
Season
11 Everson Walls (1981), 133 yards
10 Mel Renfro (1969), 118 yards
Game
3 Herb Adderley (9/26/71 @ Philadelphia), 102 yards
3 Lee Roy Jordan (11/4/73 vs. Cincinnati), 49 yards
3 Dennis Thurman (12/13/81 vs. Philadelphia), 37 yards
INTERCEPTION YARDAGE
Career
626 Mel Renfro (1964–77)
584 Charlie Waters (1970–78, 1980–81)
Season
211 Cornell Green (1963), 7 for 30.1 average
187 Dennis Thurman (1981), 9 for 20.8 average
Game
121 Mike Gaechter (11/3/63 vs. Washington) on 2 int.
Longest Interception Return
100 Mike Gaechter (10/14/62 vs. Philadelphia)
96 Dennis Thurman (9/6/81 @ Washington)
TOUCHDOWN INTERCEPTIONS
Career
4 Dennis Thurman (1977–85)

TACKLES
TOTAL UNASSISTED TACKLES
Career
743 Lee Roy Jordan (1963–76)
Season
100 Lee Roy Jordan (1975)
Game
14 Lee Roy Jordan (10/28/73 vs. Philadelphia)
TOTAL ASSISTED TACKLES
Career
493 Lee Roy Jordan (1963–76)
Season
101 Jerry Tubbs (1960)
Game
15 Jerry Tubbs (11/27/60 vs. Chicago)
TOTAL TACKLES COMBINED
Career
1,236 Lee Roy Jordan (1963–76)
Season
167 Bob Breunig (1979)
Game
21 Lee Roy Jordan (9/26/71 vs. Philadelphia)

SACKS
TOTAL SACKS
Career
125 Harvey Martin (1973–83)
Season
23 Harvey Martin (1977)
Game
5 Jim Jeffcoat (11/10/85 @ Washington)
Opponent/Game
3½ Jerry Sherk @ Cleveland (9/24/79)
3½ John Mendenhall, Giants (9/29/74)

113

Cowboys Team Records

1960: 12 games
1961–77: 14 games
1978–81, 1983–86:
16 games

NOTE: The 1982 regular season was reduced to 9 games because of a players' strike. The 1987 season was reduced to 15 games because of a players' strike.

SCORING

MOST POINTS SCORED
Season
479   1983
Game
59   9/15/68 vs. Detroit
59   10/12/80 vs. San Francisco

FEWEST POINTS SCORED
Season
177   1960
236   1961**
308   1984*
Game
0   11/16/70 vs. St. Louis
0   11/17/85 vs. Chicago

OPPONENT/MOST POINTS SCORED
Season
402   1962
Game
54   10/18/70 @ Minnesota

OPPONENT/FEWEST POINTS SCORED
Season
186   1968
208   1978*
Game
0   9 times, last 9/4/78 vs. Baltimore

MOST POINTS, BOTH TEAMS
Game
86   9/19/71 @ Buffalo (Dallas 49, Buffalo 37)
82   11/22/87 vs. Minnesota (Vikings 44, Dallas 38 OT)

FEWEST POINTS, BOTH TEAMS
Game
8   12/12/70 @ Cleveland, (Dallas 6, Cleveland 2)

MOST DECISIVE WIN
Game
49   10/9/56 vs. Philadelphia (Dallas 56, Philadelphia 7)
46   9/15/68 vs. Detroit (Dallas 59, Detroit 13)

MOST DECISIVE LOSS
Game
44   11/17/85 vs. Chicago (Chicago 44, Dallas 0)

MOST TOUCHDOWNS SCORED
Season
60   1980
Game
8   10/9/66 vs. Philadelphia
8   9/15/68 vs. Detroit
8   10/12/80 vs. San Francisco

FEWEST TOUCHDOWNS SCORED
Season
23   1960
29   1961**
34   1984*

OPPONENT/MOST TDs SCORED
Season
52   1962
Game
7   12/9/62 @ St. Louis
7   12/8/85 @ Cincinnati

OPPONENT/FEWEST TDs SCORED
Season
22   1973
25   1978*

MOST TOUCHDOWNS BY:
RUSHING
Season
26   1980
Game
5   9/19/71 @ Buffalo
PASSING
Season
31   1962, 1983
Game
5   6 times, last 10/30/83 @ N.Y. Giants
INTERCEPTIONS
Season
4   1985
Game
2   9/9/85 vs. Washington
KO RETURNS
Season
2   1971
PUNT RETURN
Season
2   1968

FEWEST TOUCHDOWNS BY:
RUSHING
Season
6   1960
6   1961**
11   1985*
PASSING
Season
10   1964
19   1984*

OPPONENT/MOST TOUCHDOWNS BY:
RUSHING
Season
24   1960
Game
5   4 times, last 10/10/65 vs. Philadelphia
PASSING
Season
33   1962
Game
5   10/30/60 vs. Baltimore
5   11/2/69 @ Cleveland
INTERCEPTIONS
Season
6   1961
KO RETURN
Season
3   1966
PUNT RETURNS
Game
1   8 times, last 10/4/87 @ N.Y. Jets

OPPONENT/FEWEST TDs BY:
RUSHING
Season
2   1968
8   1984*
PASSING
Season
10   1970
11   1978*

MOST PATs SCORED
Season
59   1980
Game
8   9/15/68 vs. Detroit
8   10/12/80 vs. San Fran.

OPPONENT/MOST PATs SCORED
Season
49   1962
Game
7   12/9/62 @ St. Louis

MOST FGs SCORED
Season
27   1981
Game
5   12/21/87 @ L.A. Rams

SCORE BY QUARTERS
1st Quarter
28   10/19/69 vs. Philadelphia
28   12/4/71 vs. N.Y. Jets
2nd Quarter
24   9/18/66 vs. N.Y. Giants
24   10/30/66 vs. Pittsburgh
24   9/15/68 vs. Detroit
24   10/24/71 vs. New England
24   10/12/80 vs. San Francisco
3rd Quarter
21   10/30/66 vs. Pittsburgh
21   9/24/73 vs. New Orleans
21   12/7/74 vs. Cleveland
21   9/28/75 vs. St. Louis
21   10/26/80 vs. San Diego
4th Quarter
21   12/19/65 @ N.Y. Giants
21   9/15/68 vs. Detroit
21   10/6/75 @ Detroit
21   10/21/73 vs. N.Y. Giants
21   11/27/80 vs. Seattle
21   10/21/84 vs. New Orleans
21   9/15/85 @ Detroit

SCORE BY HALVES
1st Half
42   10/19/69 vs. Philadelphia
2nd Half
31   9/29/68 @ Philadelphia
31   11/17/68 vs. Washington

OPPONENT/SCORE BY QUARTERS
1st Quarter
22   12/8/85 @ Cincinnati
2nd Quarter
28   12/16/62 @ N.Y. Giants
3rd Quarter
21   12/17/61 @ Washington
21   12/8/85 @ Cincinnati
4th Quarter
21   12/9/62 @ St. Louis
21   11/28/65 @ Washington
21   11/16/70 vs. St. Louis
21   11/5/72 @ San Diego
21   9/13/87 @ St. Louis

OPPONENT/SCORE BY HALVES
1st Half
34   10/18/70 @ Minnesota
34   10/14/73 @ L.A. Rams
34   11/23/86 at Washington

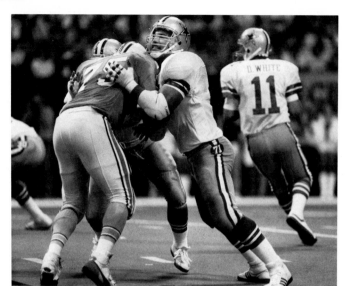

2nd Half
38   12/9/62 @ St. Louis

SCORE BY QUARTERS, BOTH TEAMS
1st Quarter
35   10/19/69 vs. Philadelphia
2nd Quarter
38   11/10/75 vs. Kansas City
38   10/23/83 vs. L.A. Raiders
3rd Quarter
35   9/28/75 vs. St. Louis
4th Quarter
35   10/21/73 vs. N.Y. Giants

SCORE BY HALVES, BOTH TEAMS
1st Half
55   10/23/83 vs. L.A. Raiders
2nd Half
52   9/28/75 vs. St. Louis

FIRST DOWNS

MOST FIRST DOWNS
Season
342   1978, 1983
Game
39   9/15/85 @ Detroit

FEWEST FIRST DOWNS
Season
180   1960
211   1965**
321   1981*
Game
8   10/16/60 vs. Cleveland
8   11/12/61 @ Pittsburgh
8   12/10/61 @ St. Louis
8   11/29/64 vs. Green Bay
8   11/1/70 vs. Philadelphia

OPPONENT/MOST FIRST DOWNS
Season
312   1985
Game
31   10/23/83 vs. L.A. Raiders
31   12/8/85 @ Cincinnati

OPPONENT/FEWEST FIRST DOWNS
Season
199   1974
232   1978*
Game
5   11/6/66 @ Philadelphia
5   10/20/74 vs. Philadelphia

MOST FIRST DOWNS, BOTH TEAMS
Season
648   1985
Game
55   10/1/67 vs. L.A. Rams

MOST FIRST DOWNS BY:
RUSHING
Season
147   1974
Game
19   12/6/81 @ Baltimore
PASSING
Season
208   1985
Game
23   11/10/63 @ San Francisco
PENALTY
Season
33   1985
Game
6   10/9/83 vs. Tampa Bay

FEWEST FIRST DOWNS BY:
RUSHING
Season
57   1960

87   1965**
93   1984*
Game
0   11/16/70 vs. St. Louis
PASSING
Season
95   1970
158   1981*
Game
3   8 times, last 9/23/74 @ Philadelphia
PENALTY
Season
9   1961
9   1962**
9   1971**
22   1979*

OPPONENT/MOST FIRST DOWNS BY:
RUSHING
Season
122   1961
Game
17   9/30/84 @ Chicago
PASSING
Season
193   1985
Game
21   11/18/62 vs. Chicago
21   11/20/83 vs. Kansas City
21   11/11/84 vs. St. Louis
PENALTY
Season
34   1987
Game
7   10/4/87 vs. N.Y. Jets

OPPONENT/FEWEST FIRST DOWNS BY:
RUSHING
Season
52   1969
82   1983*
PASSING
Season
94   1977
128   1978*
PENALTY
Season
10   1969
18   1981*

TOTAL YARDS

MOST NET YARDS GAINED
Season
5,968   1979
Game
652   10/6/66 vs. Philadelphia
583   9/4/78 vs. Baltimore
578   9/30/73 vs. St. Louis

FEWEST NET YARDS GAINED
Season
3,153   1960
3,704   1964**
5,320   1984*
Game
126   12/10/61 @ St. Louis

OPPONENT/MOST NET YARDS GAINED
Season
5,608   1985
Game
570   12/8/85 @ Cincinnati
529   10/25/81 vs. Miami

OPPONENT/FEWEST NET YARDS GAINED

Season
3,213 1977
4,009 1978**

Game
63 10/24/65 @ Green Bay
80 12/10/67 vs. Philadelphia

MOST NET YARDS, BOTH TEAMS

Season
11,386 1983

Game
995 10/25/81 vs. Miami
926 11/10/63 @ San Francisco

RUSHING

MOST YARDS RUSHING

Season
2,783 1978

Game
354 12/6/81 @ Baltimore

FEWEST YARDS RUSHING

Season
1,049 1960
1,608 1965**
1,714 1984*

Game
26 11/2/87 vs. N.Y. Giants

OPPONENT/MOST YARDS RUSHING

Season
2,242 1960
2,226 1984*

Game
289 10/22/61 vs. Philadelphia

OPPONENT/FEWEST YARDS RUSHING

Season
1,050 1969
1,499 1983*

Game
7 10/30/66 vs. Pittsburgh

MOST YARDS RUSHING, BOTH TEAMS

Season
5,760 1981

Game
510 12/6/81 @ Baltimore
466 10/22/61 vs. Philadelphia

MOST ATTEMPTS RUSHING

Season
630 1981

Game
66 12/6/81 @ Baltimore

FEWEST RUSHING ATTEMPTS

Season
311 1960
416 1961**
447 1986*

Game
16 11/7/65 vs. San Francisco
16 11/17/85 vs. Chicago

OPPONENT/MOST ATTEMPTS RUSHING

Season
510 1984

Game
54 10/11/70 vs. Atlanta

OPPONENT/FEWEST ATTEMPTS RUSHING

Season
313 1969
410 1983*

Game
12 10/16/83 vs. Philadelphia
12 9/24/67 vs. N.Y. Giants
12 10/30/66 vs. Pittsburgh

PASSING

MOST NET YARDS PASSING

Season
3,861 1985

Game
452 9/15/85 @ Detroit

FEWEST NET YARDS PASSING

Season
2,013 1964
3,104 1980*

Game
−10 10/24/65 @ Green Bay

OPPONENT/MOST NET YARDS PASSING

Season
3,928 1983

Game
437 11/18/62 vs. Chicago

OPPONENT/FEWEST NET YARDS PASSING

Season
1,562 1977
2,288 1980*

Game
−1 10/24/65 @ Green Bay
−1 12/21/75 vs. N.Y. Jets

MOST GROSS YARDS PASSING

Season
4,236 1985

Game
481 9/15/85 @ Detroit

FEWEST GROSS YARDS PASSING

Season
2,388 1960
2,445 1970**
3,356 1980*

Game
42 10/24/65 @ Green Bay

OPPONENT/MOST GROSS YARDS PASSING

Season
4,365 1983

Game
466 11/18/62 vs. Chicago

OPPONENT/FEWEST GROSS YARDS PASSING

Season
1,991 1977
2,730 1978*

Game
−15 12/21/75 @ N.Y. Jets

MOST PASS ATTEMPTS

Season
604 1984

Game
62 9/15/85 @ Detroit

FEWEST PASS ATTEMPTS

Season
297 1970
439 1981*

Game
11 10/21/73 vs. N.Y. Giants
11 10/11/70 vs. Atlanta

OPPONENT/MOST PASS ATTEMPTS

Season
558 1983

Game
59 11/20/83 vs. Kansas City

OPPONENT/FEWEST PASS ATTEMPTS

Season
293 1960
326 1961**
432 1978*

Game
10 10/3/71 vs. Washington
10 10/22/73 vs. Miami

MOST PASS COMPLETIONS

Season
346 1983

Game
40 9/15/85 @ Detroit

FEWEST PASS COMPLETIONS

Season
149 1970
251 1978*

Game
4 10/11/70 vs. Atlanta

OPPONENT/MOST PASS COMPLETIONS

Season
299 1983

Game
33 11/20/83 vs. Kansas City

OPPONENT/FEWEST PASS COMPLETIONS

Season
146 1960
154 1977**
202 1978*

Game
2 12/21/75 @ N.Y. Jets

DEFENSE, MOST QB SACKS

Season
62 1985

Game
12 11/20/66 @ Pittsburgh
12 9/29/85 @ Houston

OPPONENT/DEFENSE, MOST QB SACKS

Season
68 1964

Game
11 11/16/86 @ San Diego

INTERCEPTIONS

MOST PASSES INTERCEPTED

Season
37 1981

Game
7 9/30/60 vs. Philadelphia
7 9/26/71 @ Philadelphia

FEWEST PASSES INTERCEPTED

Season
13 1974, 1979

OPPONENT/MOST PASSES INTERCEPTED

Season
33 1960

Game
5 9/30/60 vs. Philadelphia
5 11/5/61 vs. St. Louis
5 11/9/80 @ N.Y. Giants
5 12/2/84 @ Philadelphia
5 11/9/86 vs. L.A. Raiders

OPPONENT/FEWEST PASSES INTERCEPTED

Season
10 1977
13 1979*

PENALTIES

MOST PENALTIES

Season
131 1987

Game
16 10/4/87 @ N.Y. Jets
15 10/18/81 vs. L.A. Rams
15 11/15/87 @ New England

FEWEST PENALTIES

Season
47 1961
96 1978**

Game
0 12/10/61 @ St. Louis
0 11/23/80 vs. Washington

OPPONENT/MOST PENALTIES

Season
108 1985

Game
14 10/9/83 vs. Tampa Bay

OPPONENT/FEWEST PENALTIES

Season
38 1961
70 1979*

Game
0 10/21/62 @ Pittsburgh
0 12/5/65 @ Philadelphia

MOST YARDS PENALIZED

Season
1,091 1987

Game
161 11/2/70 @ Washington
159 10/13/68 vs. Philadelphia

FEWEST YARDS PENALIZED

Season
427 1961
704 1978*

Game
0 12/10/61 @ St. Louis
0 11/23/80 vs. Washington

OPPONENT/MOST YARDS PENALIZED

Season
990 1985

Game
185 10/9/83 vs. Tampa Bay
166 10/9/77 @ St. Louis

OPPONENT/FEWEST YARDS PENALIZED

Season
362 1961
704 1979*

Game
0 10/21/62 @ Pittsburgh
0 12/5/65 @ Philadelphia

BOTH TEAMS, FEWEST YARDS PENALIZED

Season
789 1961

1,549 1979*

Game
10 12/10/61 @ St. Louis

PUNTING

MOST PUNTS

Season
108 1984

Game
11 9/23/84 vs. Philadelphia

OPPONENT/MOST PUNTS

Season
108 1978

Game
11 9/30/62 @ L.A. Rams
11 9/15/74 @ Atlanta
11 11/15/76 vs. Buffalo
11 11/22/84 vs. New England

HIGHEST AVERAGE

Season
45.4 1962

Game (4 punts)
53.4 11/3/68 vs. New Orleans

OPPONENT/HIGHEST AVERAGE

Season
45.5 1961

Game (4 punts)
54.3 10/17/65 @ Cleveland

PUNT RETURNS

MOST PUNT RETURNS

Season
63 1978

Game
9 11/15/76 vs. Buffalo

MOST PUNT RETURN YARDS

Season
573 1974**
556 1980*

Game
122 12/8/68 vs. Pittsburgh

OPPONENT/MOST PUNT RETURNS

Season
55 1984

Game
8 11/4/84 vs. N.Y. Giants

OPPONENT/MOST PUNT RETURN YARDS

Season
588 1983

Game
109 11/16/70 vs. St. Louis

KICKOFF RETURNS

MOST KICKOFF RETURNS

Season
70 1983

Game
9 10/18/70 @ Minnesota

MOST KICKOFF RETURN YARDS

Season
1,376 1971**
1,351 1983*

Game
260 11/7/65 vs. San Francisco

OPPONENT/MOST KICKOFF RETURNS

Season
78 1966, 1983*

Game
10 9/15/68 vs. Detroit

OPPONENT/MOST KICKOFF RETURN YARDS

Season
1,806 1983

Game
261 11/6/66 @ Philadelphia

FUMBLES

MOST FUMBLES

Season
46 1961**
45 1981*

Game
7 10/11/71 vs. N.Y. Giants

MOST FUMBLES LOST

Season
21 1961, 1971, 1979

Game
5 11/13/68 @ New Orleans
5 10/11/71 vs. N.Y. Giants
5 11/10/75 vs. Kansas City

OPPONENT/MOST FUMBLES

Season
44 1973
43 1981*

Game
7 11/28/65 @ Washington
7 11/10/75 vs. Kansas City

OPPONENT/MOST FUMBLES LOST

Season
25 1971**
21 1983*

Game
5 10/11/71 vs. N.Y. Giants
5 9/16/73 @ Chicago
5 10/12/80 vs. San Francisco
5 10/23/83 vs. L.A. Raiders

*16-game record
**14-game record

Miscellaneous Records

Individual

Most Consecutive Passes Completed
14—Steve Pelluer (vs. Seattle, Nov. 27, 1986).

Most Consecutive Passes Without Interception
166—Don Meredith (began vs. Philadelphia, Dec. 5, 1965, ended vs. St. Louis, Oct. 16, 1966).

Most Consecutive Games Rush for TD
6—Tony Dorsett in 1977.
6—Tony Dorsett in 1980.

Most Consecutive Games Catch TD Pass
7—Frank Clarke (final game of 1961 season, first six games in '62).
7—Bob Hayes (final three games of 1965 season, first four games in 1966).

Most Consecutive Games Intercept Pass
5—Don Bishop in 1961.

Most Consecutive PATs
99—Mike Clark (last 17 in 1969, all 35 in 1970 and all 47 in 1971).

Most Consecutive Games at Least One Pass Catch
72—Tony Hill (final 12 games of 1981 season, all of 1982, 1983, 1984 and 1985, first 13 games of 1986).

Most Consecutive FG
9—Rafael Septien (began vs. New England, Sept. 21, 1981, ended vs. Miami, Oct. 25, 1981).

Most Consecutive Games Kick FG
10—Mike Clark (final nine games of 1969 season, first game in 1970).
10—Toni Fritsch, twice (final seven games of 1972 season, first three games in 1973; first 10 games in 1975).

Most Seasons Played
14—Bob Lilly (1961–74)
　　Lee Roy Jordan (1963–76)
　　Jethro Pugh (1965–78)
13—Cornell Green (1962–74)
　　Dave Edwards (1963–75)
　　D. D. Lewis (1968, 1970–81)
　　Ed Jones (1974–78, 1980–87)
　　Randy White (1975–87)

Most Consecutive Games Played
196—Bob Lilly (from 1961 through 1974)
168—Cornell Green (1962–74)
165—Tom Rafferty (1976–86)

Team

*Consecutive Winning Seasons
20—(1966–85)

*Consecutive Playoff Appearances
9—(1975–83)

Consecutive Season–Opening Victories
17—(1965–81)

All-Time Texas Stadium Record
103-33—(1971–87, regular season and playoffs)

Longest Home Winning Streak
18 games—(began Sept. 21, 1980 vs. Tampa Bay, ended Sept. 13, 1982 vs. Pittsburgh).

Most Consecutive Games Intercept Pass
28—Every game in 1962 and 1963.

Most Consecutive PATs
162—1969, 1970, 1971, 1972, 1973.

Most Consecutive Games Without Losing Fumble
3—1973, 1974, 1975, 1976 and 1977.
*NFL record

PAT Record

21 of 23 in 1960—last 17 straight.	37 of 38 in 1974—first 4, last 33.
29 of 29 in 1961—all 29.	38 of 40 in 1975—last 34.
50 of 51 in 1962—first 33, last 17.	34 of 34 in 1976—all 34.
38 of 40 in 1963—first 32.	39 of 41 in 1977—first 14, last 16.
28 of 30 in 1964—last 23.	46 of 48 in 1978—first 8, last one.
37 of 38 in 1965—last 24.	40 of 45 in 1979—first one, last 26.
56 of 56 in 1966—all 56.	59 of 60 in 1980—first 52, last 7.
41 of 44 in 1967—first 8, last 1.	40 of 40 in 1981—all 40.
54 of 54 in 1968—all 54.	28 of 28 in 1982—all 28.
43 of 44 in 1969—first 26, last 17.	57 of 59 in 1983—first 13, last 20.

35 of 35 in 1970—all 35.	33 of 34 in 1984—first 17, last 16.
50 of 50 in 1971—all 50.	42 of 43 in 1985—first 28, last 14.
36 of 36 in 1972—all 36.	43 of 43 in 1986—all 43.
45 of 46 in 1973—first 24, last 21.	37 of 37 in 1987—all 37.

Largest Margin of Victory

1. 49 points, (56-7) vs. Philadelphia, 1966
2. 46 points, (59-13) vs. Detroit, 1968
3. 45 points, (52-7) vs. N.Y. Giants, 1966
　 45 points, (59-14) vs. San Francisco, 1980
5. 44 points, (51-7) vs. Seattle, 1980
6. 42 points, (52-10) vs. Houston, 1970
　 42 points, (52-10) vs. N.Y. Jets, 1971
8. 38 points, (52-14) vs. Cleveland, 1967 (Eastern Conference Championship Game)
　 38 points, (38-0) vs. Baltimore, 1978
　 38 points, (38-0) vs. Tampa Bay, 1982 (1981 NFC Divisional Playoff)
11. 37 points, (40-3) vs. New Orleans, 1973
　 37 points, (37-0) vs. Detroit, 1977
13. 35 points, (49-14) vs. Philadelphia, 1969
　 35 points, (42-7) vs. Philadelphia, 1971
　 35 points, (45-10) vs. St. Louis, 1973
16. 34 points, (34-0) vs. Washington, 1970

Largest Margin of Defeat

1. 44 points, (44-0) vs. Chicago, 1985
2. 41 points, (48-7) vs. Cleveland, 1960
　 41 points, (54-13) vs. Minnesota, 1970
4. 38 points, (45-7) vs. Baltimore, 1960
　 38 points, (38-0) vs. St. Louis, 1970
6. 36 points, (43-7) vs. Philadelphia, 1961
7. 34 points, (41-7) vs. Green Bay, 1960
8. 32 points, (52-20) vs. St. Louis, 1962
　 32 points, (42-10) vs. Cleveland, 1969
10. 31 points, (45-14) @ San Francisco, 1981

Cowboys Longest Plays

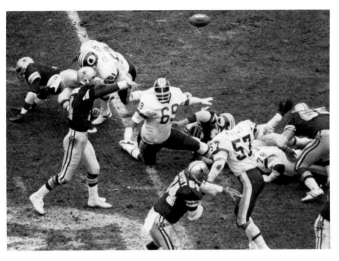

LONG RUNS FROM SCRIMMAGE
99—Tony Dorsett @ Minnesota, Jan. 3, 1983 (TD).
84—Herschel Walker vs. Philadelphia, Dec. 14, 1986 (TD).
84—Tony Dorsett vs. Philadelphia, Dec. 4, 1977 (TD).
77—Tony Dorsett vs. St. Louis, Oct. 9, 1977 (TD).
77—Tony Dorsett @ Washington, Sept. 5, 1983.
75—Tony Dorsett vs. New England, Sept. 21, 1981 (TD).
73—Amos Bullocks vs. Chicago, Nov. 18, 1962 (TD).
71—Amos Marsh vs. New York, Oct. 15, 1961.
70—Amos Marsh vs. Washington, Nov. 4, 1962.
68—Les Shy vs. Philadelphia, Oct. 9, 1966.
67—Dan Reeves vs. Washington, Dec. 11, 1966 (TD).
64—Jim Stiger vs. Washington, Nov. 22, 1964.
63—Tony Dorsett vs. New Orleans, Nov. 19, 1978.
62—Kelvin Edwards vs. Philadelphia, Oct. 11, 1987 (TD).
60—Tony Dorsett vs. Atlanta, Oct. 27, 1985 (TD).
60—Herschel Walker @ New England, Nov. 15, 1987 (TD).
59—James Jones vs. Baltimore, Dec. 6, 1981 (TD).
59—Don Perkins vs. Pittsburgh, Sept. 27, 1964.
59—Scott Laidlaw vs. Washington, Nov. 23, 1978.
56—Frank Clarke vs. New Orleans, Nov. 12, 1967.
56—Duane Thomas vs. New England, Oct. 24, 1971 (TD).
56—Tony Dorsett vs. N.Y. Giants, Nov. 9, 1980.

LONG FORWARD PASSES
95—Don Meredith to Bob Hayes vs. Washington, Nov. 13, 1966 (TD).
91—Roger Staubach to Tony Dorsett vs. Baltimore, Sept. 4, 1978 (TD).
89—Craig Morton to Bob Hayes vs. Kansas City, Oct. 25, 1970 (TD).
86—Craig Morton to Lance Rentzel vs. Philadelphia, Nov. 1, 1970 (TD).
85—Eddie LeBaron to Amos Marsh vs. L.A. Rams, Sept. 30, 1962 (TD).
85—Roger Staubach to Bob Hayes vs. N.Y. Giants, Dec. 12, 1971 (TD).
84—Don Meredith to Pete Gent vs. Pittsburgh, Oct. 30, 1966 (TD).
84—Steve Pelluer to Herschel Walker vs. Philadelphia, Dec. 14, 1986 (TD).

LONG PUNTS
84—Ron Widby vs. New Orleans, Nov. 3, 1968.
75—Billy Lothridge vs. New York, Oct. 11, 1964.
75—Sam Baker vs. L.A. Rams, Sept. 30, 1962.
73—Danny White vs. L.A. Rams, Oct. 14, 1979.
71—Billy Lothridge vs. St. Louis, Sept. 12, 1964.
71—Sam Baker vs. New York, Dec. 16, 1962.

LONG PUNT RETURNS
98—Dennis Morgan vs. St. Louis, Oct. 13, 1974 (TD).
90—Bob Hayes vs. Pittsburgh, Dec. 8, 1968 (TD).
69—Bob Hayes vs. St. Louis, Nov. 23, 1967 (TD).
69—Mel Renfro vs. Green Bay, Nov. 29, 1964 (TD).
68—Gary Allen vs. Kansas City, Nov. 20, 1983 (TD).
63—Bob Hayes vs. New York, Dec. 15, 1968 (TD).
55—Butch Johnson vs. Philadelphia, Dec. 5, 1976.
52—James Jones vs. Washington, Nov. 23, 1980.
51—Mel Renfro vs. Cleveland, Oct. 4, 1964.
50—Bob Hayes vs. Washington, Nov. 16, 1969.

LONG KICKOFF RETURNS
101—Amos Marsh vs. Philadelphia, Oct. 14, 1962 (TD).
101—Ike Thomas vs. New York Jets, Dec. 4, 1971 (TD).
100—Mark Washington vs. Washington, Nov. 22, 1970 (TD).
100—Mel Renfro vs. San Francisco, Nov. 7, 1965 (TD).
97—Thomas Henderson vs. St. Louis, Sept. 28, 1975 (TD).
89—Ike Thomas vs. L.A. Rams, Nov. 25, 1971 (TD).
87—Mel Renfro vs. Pittsburgh, Oct. 30, 1966 (TD).

LONG INTERCEPTION RETURNS
100—Mike Gaechter vs. Philadelphia, Oct. 14, 1962 (TD).
96—Dennis Thurman vs. Washington, Sept. 6, 1981.
90—Mel Renfro vs. St. Louis, Oct. 4, 1965 (TD).
86—Mike Gaechter vs. Washington, Nov. 3, 1963.

LONG FUMBLE RETURNS
97—Chuck Howley vs. Atlanta, Oct. 2, 1966 (TD).
86—Michael Downs vs. Houston, Dec. 13, 1982 (TD).
84—Don Bishop vs. St. Louis, Oct. 28, 1962 (TD).
72—Benny Barnes vs. San Francisco, Oct. 11, 1981 (TD).
63—Jim Ridlon vs. Philadelphia, Dec. 6, 1964 (TD).

LONG RETURNS OF FIELD-GOAL ATTEMPTS
94—Jerry Norton vs. St. Louis, Dec. 9, 1962 (TD).
62—Ron Fellows vs. New Orleans, Sept. 25, 1983 (TD).
60—Mike Gaechter vs. Washington, Nov. 28, 1965 (TD).
60—Obert Logan vs. New York, Dec. 19, 1965 (TD).
    *Playoff Game

Cowboys Big Days

RUSHING
(includes all 100-yard days)

206—Tony Dorsett vs. Philadelphia, Dec. 4, 1977 (23 carries).
183—Tony Dorsett @ N.Y. Giants, Nov. 9, 1980 (24 carries).
175—Tony Dorsett @ Baltimore, Dec. 6, 1981 (30 carries).
173—Herschel Walker @ New England, Nov. 15, 1987 (28 carries).
162—Tony Dorsett @ New England, Sept. 21, 1981 (19 carries).
159—Tony Dorsett vs. L.A. Rams, Oct. 18, 1981 (27 carries).
159—Tony Dorsett @ Houston, Sept. 29, 1985 (23 carries).
154—Tony Dorsett vs. St. Louis, Sept. 24, 1978 (21 carries).
153—Tony Dorsett @ Minnesota, Jan. 3, 1983 (16 carries).
153—Calvin Hill vs. San Francisco, Nov. 10, 1974 (32 carries).
152—Tony Dorsett vs. New Orleans, Nov. 19, 1978 (25 carries).
151—Tony Dorsett @ Washington, Sept. 5, 1983 (14 carries).
150—Calvin Hill @ Washington, Nov. 16, 1969 (27 carries).
149—Tony Dorsett @ Green Bay, Nov. 12, 1978 (23 carries).
147—Tony Dorsett vs. Baltimore, Sept. 4, 1978 (15 carries).
145—Tony Dorsett @ Minnesota, Oct. 7, 1979 (21 carries).
141—Tony Dorsett @ Minnesota, Oct. 2, 1983 (26 carries).
141—Tony Dorsett @ St. Louis, Oct. 9, 1977 (14 carries).
140—Calvin Hill vs. Philadelphia, Oct. 20, 1974 (26 carries).
138—Calvin Hill @ New Orleans, Sept. 28, 1969 (23 carries).
137—Herschel Walker vs. St. Louis, Dec. 27, 1987 (25 carries).
137—Don Perkins vs. St. Louis, Oct. 28, 1962 (24 carries).
137—Don Perkins vs. N.Y. Giants, Oct. 11, 1964 (17 carries).
134—Duane Thomas @ Kansas City, Oct. 25, 1970 (20 carries).
133—Don Perkins @ Green Bay, Oct. 24, 1965 (22 carries).
132—Tony Dorsett @ Washington, Sept. 6, 1981 (20 carries).
130—Calvin Hill @ Chicago, Sept. 16, 1973 (31 carries).
129—Tony Dorsett vs. St. Louis, Sept. 13, 1981 (16 carries).
124—Robert Newhouse @ St. Louis, Dec. 16, 1973 (19 carries).
124—Tony Dorsett vs. New Orleans, Sept. 25, 1983 (16 carries).
123—Don Perkins vs. Cleveland, Dec. 3, 1961 (20 carries).
123—Duane Thomas vs. Washington, Dec. 6, 1970 (19 carries).
123—Calvin Hill vs. N.Y. Giants, Oct. 21, 1973 (23 carries).
122—Herschel Walker vs. Philadelphia, Dec. 14, 1986 (6 carries).
122—Tony Dorsett vs. Miami, Oct. 25, 1981 (24 carries).
122—Scott Laidlaw vs. Washington, Nov. 23, 1978 (16 carries).
122—Tony Dorsett vs. St. Louis, Nov. 16, 1980 (26 carries).
121—Walt Garrison vs. Washington, Dec. 9, 1972 (10 carries).
121—Tony Dorsett @ N.Y. Jets, Dec. 17, 1978 (29 carries).
120—Herschel Walker vs. St. Louis, Oct. 26, 1986 (26 carries).
120—Robert Newhouse @ Seattle, Oct. 3, 1976 (19 carries).
120—Calvin Hill @ St. Louis, Dec. 3, 1972 (20 carries).
119—Tony Dorsett vs. Cincinnati, Sept. 30, 1979 (20 carries).
117—Tony Dorsett @ Detroit, Sept. 14, 1986 (23 carries).
117—Tony Dorsett @ Seattle, Dec. 4, 1983 (26 carries).
117—Tony Dorsett vs. Buffalo, Nov. 9, 1981 (28 carries).
117—Amos Marsh vs. Cleveland, Dec. 2, 1962 (17 carries).

117—Calvin Hill @ Philadelphia, Sept. 20, 1970 (25 carries).
117—Calvin Hill vs. Atlanta, Oct. 11, 1970 (29 carries).
116—Tony Dorsett vs. Cleveland, Nov. 25, 1982 (20 carries).
115—Tony Dorsett vs. Washington, Nov. 22, 1981 (23 carries).
115—Duane Thomas vs. Houston, Dec. 20, 1970 (17 carries).
114—Dan Reeves @ Cleveland, Sept. 17, 1967 (18 carries).
113—Tony Dorsett vs. Pittsburgh, Oct. 13, 1985 (21 carries).
112—Duane Thomas vs. N.Y. Jets, Dec. 4, 1971 (14 carries).
111—Don Perkins vs. Cleveland, Nov. 24, 1966 (23 carries).
111—Don Perkins vs. Atlanta, Nov. 5, 1967 (21 carries).
111—Calvin Hill vs. Washington, Dec. 9, 1972 (24 carries).
111—Tony Dorsett @ N.Y. Giants, Sept. 10, 1978 (24 carries).
111—Tony Dorsett vs. St. Louis, Oct. 21, 1979 (20 carries).
110—Tony Dorsett @ Philadelphia, Dec. 2, 1984 (22 carries).
110—Calvin Hill vs. Washington, Dec. 9, 1973 (27 carries).
109—Amos Marsh @ Washington, Nov. 4, 1962 (10 carries).
109—Don Perkins @ Washington, Sept. 29, 1963 (25 carries).
109—Calvin Hill vs. New Orleans, Nov. 9, 1969 (13 carries).
108—Herschel Walker @ L.A. Rams, Dec. 21, 1987 (23 carries).
108—Don Perkins vs. Minnesota, Sept. 24, 1961 (17 carries).
108—Don Perkins @ Pittsburgh, Oct. 21, 1962 (20 carries).
108—Dan Reeves vs. Washington, Dec. 11, 1966 (10 carries).
108—Calvin Hill vs. Pittsburgh, Oct. 8, 1972 (23 carries).
108—Robert Newhouse @ N.Y. Jets, Dec. 21, 1975 (19 carries).
108—Robert Newhouse @ St. Louis, Sept. 2, 1979 (18 carries).
108—Tony Dorsett vs. Chicago, Sept. 16, 1979 (20 carries).
108—Tony Dorsett vs. N.Y. Giants, Dec. 2, 1979 (29 carries).
108—Tony Dorsett vs. Kansas City, Nov. 20, 1983 (18 carries).
107—Tony Dorsett vs. Seattle, Nov. 27, 1980 (24 carries).
105—Tony Dorsett vs. New Orleans, Dec. 19, 1982 (25 carries).
104—Tony Dorsett vs. Indianapolis, Oct. 28, 1984 (24 carries).
104—Duane Thomas @ Washington, Nov. 22, 1970 (16 carries).
104—Scott Laidlaw vs. Philadelphia, Sept. 12, 1976 (19 carries).
103—Don Perkins @ Washington, Nov. 17, 1968 (13 carries).
103—Calvin Hill @ Washington, Oct. 8, 1973 (21 carries).
103—Tony Dorsett vs. L.A. Rams, Oct. 14, 1979 (24 carries).
102—Walt Garrison vs. N.Y. Giants, Oct. 27, 1969 (16 carries).
102—Tony Dorsett vs. St. Louis, Nov. 24, 1983 (17 carries).
101—Tony Dorsett vs. L.A. Raiders, Nov. 9, 1986 (22 carries).
101—Tony Dorsett vs. Philadelphia, Dec. 13, 1981 (28 carries).
101—Duane Thomas @ St. Louis, Nov. 7, 1971 (26 carries).
101—Preston Pearson vs. Green Bay, Oct. 19, 1975 (15 carries).
101—Robert Newhouse @ Green Bay, Nov. 12, 1978 (18 carries).
100—Calvin Hill @ Philadelphia, Nov. 19, 1972 (15 carries).
100—Calvin Hill @ Philadelphia, Oct. 28, 1973 (25 carries).
100—Tony Dorsett vs. Tampa Bay, Sept. 21, 1980 (20 carries).
100—Tony Dorsett @ Philadelphia, Oct. 20, 1985 (20 carries).

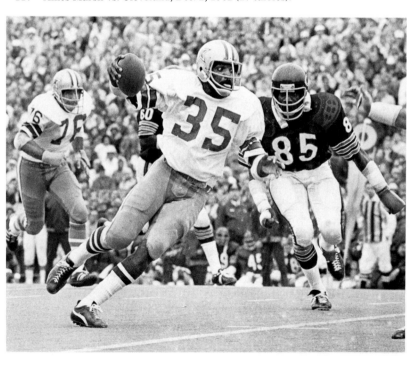

RECEIVING
246—Bob Hayes @ Washington, Nov. 13, 1966 (9 catches).
241—Frank Clarke vs. Washington, Sept. 16, 1962 (10 catches)
223—Lance Rentzel vs. Washington, Nov. 19, 1967 (13 catches).
213—Tony Hill vs. Philadelphia, Nov. 12, 1979 (7 catches).
195—Bob Hayes vs. N.Y. Giants, Sept. 18, 1966 (6 catches).
190—Frank Clarke @ San Francisco, Nov. 10, 1963 (8 catches).
188—Drew Pearson @ Detroit, Oct. 6, 1975 (6 catches).
187—Bob Hayes vs. Houston, Dec. 20, 1970 (6 catches).
181—Tony Hill @ Detroit, Sept. 15, 1985 (11 catches).
177—Bob Hayes vs. Philadelphia, Oct. 10, 1965 (8 catches).
170—Herschel Walker vs. Philadelphia, Dec. 14, 1986 (9 catches).
170—Bob Hayes @ Philadelphia, Oct. 22, 1967 (7 catches).
168—Frank Clarke @ N.Y. Giants, Oct. 20, 1963 (4 catches).
164—Mike Renfro @ San Francisco, Dec. 22, 1985 (9 catches).
161—Drew Pearson @ Philadelphia, Sept. 23, 1974 (10 catches).
161—Tony Hill vs. Atlanta, Oct. 27, 1985 (10 catches).

PASSING
460—Don Meredith @ San Francisco, Nov. 10, 1963 (30 of 48).
406—Don Meredith @ Washington, Nov. 13, 1966 (21 of 29).
394—Don Meredith @ Philadelphia, Nov. 6, 1966 (14 of 24).
389—Gary Hogeboom @ San Francisco, Dec. 22, 1985 (28 of 49).
377—Danny White vs. Tampa Bay, Oct. 9, 1983 (29 of 44).
362—Danny White vs. Atlanta, Oct. 27, 1985 (27 of 47).
359—Danny White @ Washington, Dec. 13, 1987 (27 of 49).
358—Don Meredith vs. N.Y. Giants, Sept. 18, 1966 (14 of 24).
354—Danny White vs. Miami, Oct. 25, 1981 (22 of 32).
349—Craig Morton vs. Houston, Dec. 20, 1970 (13 of 17).
347—Danny White vs. Pittsburgh, Sept. 13, 1982 (25 of 36).
345—Eddie LeBaron vs. Pittsburgh, Sept. 24, 1960 (15 of 28).
343—Gary Hogeboom @ L.A. Rams, Sept. 3, 1984 (33 of 47).
342—Danny White @ N.Y. Giants, Oct. 6, 1985 (31 of 46).
341—Danny White vs. Minnesota, Nov. 26, 1987 (25 of 41).
339—Steve Pelluer @ N.Y. Giants, Nov. 2, 1986 (28 of 38).
339—Roger Staubach vs. Baltimore, Sept. 26, 1976 (22 of 28).
336—Roger Staubach vs. Washington, Dec. 16, 1979 (24 of 42).
327—Danny White vs. Washington, Dec. 9, 1984 (22 of 42).

Cowboys Individual Playoff Records

SCORING

TOTAL POINTS
18 Craig Baynham (12/24/67 vs. Cleveland), 3 TDs
18 Preston Pearson (1/4/76 @ L.A. Rams), 3 TDs
13 Toni Fritsch (1/4/76 @ L.A. Rams) (kicker)
13 Efren Herrera (12/26/77 vs. Chicago) (kicker)
13 Rafael Septien (1/16/83 vs. Green Bay) (kicker)

TOUCHDOWNS
3 Craig Baynham (12/24/67 vs. Cleveland), 2 runs, 1 pass
3 Preston Pearson (1/4/76 @ L.A. Rams), 3 passes

FIELD GOALS MADE
3 Toni Fritsch (12/23/72 @ San Francisco)
3 Toni Fritsch (1/4/76 @ L.A. Rams)
3 Efren Herrera (12/26/77 vs. Chicago)
3 Rafael Septien (1/9/83 vs. Tampa Bay and 1/16/83 vs. Green Bay)

LONGEST FIELD GOAL
50 Rafael Septien (1/16/83 vs. Green Bay)

FIELD GOALS ATTEMPTED
5 Efren Herrera (1/15/78 vs. Denver), 2 FGs

EXTRA POINTS ATTEMPTED–MADE
7-7 Danny Villanueva (12/24/67 vs. Cleveland)

RUSHING

RUSHING YARDS
160 Tony Dorsett (12/28/80 vs. L.A. Rams), 22 carries

RUSHING ATTEMPTS
30 Duane Thomas (12/26/70 vs. Detroit)

TOUCHDOWNS RUSHING
2 Don Perkins (12/24/67 vs. Cleveland)
2 Craig Baynham (12/24/67 vs. Cleveland)
2 Tony Dorsett (12/26/77 vs. Chicago)

RUSHING AVERAGE (Min. 10 Attempts)
7.2 Tony Dorsett (12/28/80 vs. L.A. Rams), 22-160
6.9 Calvin Hill (12/23/72 @ San Francisco), 18-125
6.4 Don Perkins (1/1/67 vs. Green Bay), 17-108

LONGEST RUN
53 Tony Dorsett (1/7/79 @ Los Angeles)

PASSING

PASSING YARDS
330 Danny White (12/26/83 vs. L.A. Rams), 32 of 53
322 Danny White (1/4/81 @ Atlanta), 25 of 39
312 Danny White (1/9/83 vs. Tampa Bay), 27 of 45
246 Roger Staubach (12/28/75 @ Minnesota), 15 of 24

PASS ATTEMPTS
53 Danny White (12/26/83 vs. L.A. Rams), 32 completions
45 Danny White (1/9/83 vs. Tampa Bay), 27 completions
43 Danny White (1/4/86 @ L.A. Rams), 24 completions
39 Danny White (1/4/81 @ Atlanta), 25 completions
37 Roger Staubach (12/19/76 vs. L.A. Rams), 15 completions

PASS COMPLETIONS
32 Danny White (12/26/83 vs. L.A. Rams), 53 attempts
27 Danny White (1/9/83 vs. Tampa Bay), 45 attempts
25 Danny White (1/4/81 @ Atlanta), 39 attempts
24 Danny White (1/4/86 @ L.A. Rams), 43 attempts
23 Danny White (1/16/83 vs. Green Bay), 36 attempts

TOUCHDOWN PASSES
4 Roger Staubach (1/4/76 @ L.A. Rams)

PASSES HAD INTERCEPTED
4 Roger Staubach (12/30/73 vs. Minnesota)

COMPLETION PERCENTAGE (Min. 12 completions)
68.0 Roger Staubach (1/15/78 vs. Denver), 17 of 25
66.7 Danny White (1/10/82 @ San Francisco), 16 of 24
64.1 Danny White (1/4/81 @ Atlanta), 25 of 39

LONGEST COMPLETION
86 Don Meredith to Bob Hayes (12/24/67 vs. Cleveland), TD
83 Roger Staubach to Drew Pearson (12/23/73 vs. L.A.), TD

MOST TIMES SACKED
7 Roger Staubach (12/23/73 vs. L.A. Rams)
7 Roger Staubach (1/18/76 vs. Pittsburgh)

PASS RECEIVING

RECEPTIONS
9 Tony Hill (12/26/83 vs. L.A. Rams), 115 yards
8 Tony Dorsett (1/4/86 @ L.A. Rams), 80 yards

RECEIVING YARDS
144 Bob Hayes (12/24/67 vs. Cleveland), 5 receptions
142 Tony Hill (1/16/83 vs. Green Bay), 7 receptions

TOUCHDOWNS RECEIVING
3 Preston Pearson (1/4/76 @ L.A. Rams)

RUSHING—RECEIVING
188 Tony Dorsett (12/28/80 vs. L.A. Rams), 160 rushing, 28 receiving
167 Duane Thomas (1/3/71 vs. San Francisco), 143 rushing, 24 receiving

COMBINED YARDAGE
285 Bob Hayes (12/24/67 vs. Cleveland), 5/144 receiving, 3/141 punt returns

PUNTING

PUNTS
9 Ron Widby (1/17/71 vs. Baltimore), 38.6 average

PUNT AVERAGE
46.9 Mike Saxon (1/4/86 @ L.A. Rams), 7 punts

PUNT RETURNS

PUNT RETURNS
5 James Jones (12/28/80 vs. L.A. Rams)

PUNT RETURN YARDAGE
141 Bob Hayes (12/24/67 vs. Cleveland), 3 returns

LONGEST PUNT RETURN
68 Bob Hayes (12/24/67 vs. Cleveland)

PUNT RETURN AVERAGE (3 returns)
47.0 Bob Hayes (12/24/67 vs. Cleveland), 3 for 141 yards

FAIR CATCHES
4 Lance Rentzel (12/21/68 @ Cleveland)
4 Cliff Harris (12/23/72 @ San Francisco)

KICKOFF RETURNS

KICKOFF RETURNS
5 Mel Renfro (1/1/67 vs. Green Bay), 124 yards

KICKOFF RETURN YARDAGE
124 Mel Renfro (1/1/67 vs. Green Bay), 5 returns

LONGEST KICKOFF RETURN
48 Thomas Henderson (1/18/76 vs. Pittsburgh)

KICKOFF RETURN AVERAGE (4 returns)
24.8 Mel Renfro (1/1/67 vs. Green Bay), 5 for 124 yards

INTERCEPTIONS

INTERCEPTIONS
3 Charlie Waters (12/26/77 vs. Chicago)
3 Dennis Thurman (1/4/86 vs. Green Bay)

INTERCEPTION RETURN YARDAGE
68 Thomas Henderson (1/8/79 @ L.A. Rams), on 1 interception

LONGEST INTERCEPTION RETURN
68 Thomas Henderson (1/8/79 @ L.A. Rams)

MISCELLANEOUS INDIVIDUAL RECORDS

MOST GAMES PLAYED
27—D. D. Lewis
26—Larry Cole
25—Charlie Waters
23—Robert Newhouse
23—Jethro Pugh

MOST SUPER BOWLS PLAYED
5—Larry Cole, Cliff Harris, D. D. Lewis, Charlie Waters, Rayfield Wright

MOST CONSECUTIVE PASSES WITHOUT INTERCEPTION
99—Roger Staubach (began vs. Minnesota, 12/25/71, ended vs. Minnesota, 12/30/73).

MOST CONSECUTIVE GAMES RUSHING FOR TD
3—Duane Thomas (began vs. Minnesota, ended 1/16/72 after Super Bowl victory).
3—Tony Dorsett (began 12/26/77 vs. Chicago, ended 12/30/78 vs. Atlanta).

MOST CONSECUTIVE GAMES CATCH TD PASS
2—Golden Richards (vs. Minnesota, 1/1/78 and vs. Denver, 1/15/78).
2—Drew Pearson (vs. Los Angeles, 12/28/80 and vs. Atlanta, 1/4/81).
2—Tony Hill (vs. Tampa Bay, 1/2/82 and @ San Francisco, 1/10/82).

MOST CONSECUTIVE GAMES INTERCEPT PASS
3—Mel Renfro (vs. Detroit, 12/26/70; vs. San Francisco, 1/3/71; and vs. Baltimore, 1/17/71).
3—Randy Hughes (vs. Denver, 1/15/78; vs. Atlanta, 12/30/78; and vs. Los Angeles, 1/7/79).

MOST CONSECUTIVE GAMES AT LEAST ONE PASS CATCH
16—Drew Pearson (began vs. Los Angeles, 12/23/73, ended 1/4/86 @ L.A. Rams)

MOST CONSECUTIVE GAMES KICK FG
7—Toni Fritsch (started vs. San Francisco, 12/23/72, ended after 1/18/76, vs. Pittsburgh).

MOST CONSECUTIVE FIELD GOALS MADE
15—Rafael Septien (began vs. Pittsburgh 1/21/79, ended @ Washington 1/22/83).

Cowboys Team Playoff Records

SCORING
MOST POINTS SCORED
52   12/24/67 vs. Cleveland
(Dallas 52, Cleveland 14)
FEWEST POINTS SCORED
0   1/4/86 vs. L.A. Rams
(L.A. Rams 20, Dallas 0)
OPPONENT/MOST POINTS SCORED
38   12/28/69 vs. Cleveland
(Cleveland 38, Dallas 14)
OPPONENT/FEWEST POINTS SCORED
0   12/26/70 vs. Detroit
(Dallas 5, Detroit 0)
0   1/7/79 @ L.A. Rams
(Dallas 28, L.A. Rams 0)
0   1/2/82 vs. Tampa Bay
(Dallas 38, Tampa Bay 0)
MOST DECISIVE WIN
38   1/2/82 vs. Tampa Bay
(Dallas 38, Tampa Bay 0)
38   12/24/67 vs. Cleveland
(Dallas 52, Cleveland 14)
MOST DECISIVE LOSS
24   12/28/69 vs. Cleveland
(Cleveland 38, Dallas 14)
MOST POINTS COMBINED
66   12/24/67 vs. Cleveland
(Dallas 52, Cleveland 14)
66   1/21/79 vs. Pittsburgh
(Pittsburgh 35, Dallas 31)

FIRST DOWNS
MOST FIRST DOWNS
29   12/28/80 vs. L.A. Rams
29   1/9/83 vs. Green Bay
FEWEST FIRST DOWNS
8   12/31/72 @ Washington
OPPONENT/MOST FIRST DOWNS
26   1/10/82 @ San Francisco
22   12/28/69 vs. Cleveland
OPPONENT/FEWEST FIRST DOWNS
7   12/26/70 vs. Detroit
MOST FIRST DOWNS BY:
Rushing
19   12/28/80 vs. L.A. Rams
Passing
20   12/26/83 vs. L.A. Rams
Penalty
2   8 times, last 1/10/82 @ San Francisco
FEWEST FIRST DOWNS BY:
Rushing
2   1/22/83 @ Washington
Passing
3   12/26/70 vs. Detroit
3   12/31/72 @ Washington
OPPONENT/MOST FIRST DOWNS BY:
Rushing

14   12/30/73 vs. Minnesota
Passing
17   12/28/69 vs. Cleveland
17   1/10/82 @ San Francisco
Penalty
4   1/17/71 vs. Baltimore
OPPONENT/FEWEST FIRST DOWNS BY:
Rushing
1   1/4/76 @ L.A. Rams
Passing
1   1/15/78 vs. Denver

TOTAL YARDS
MOST NET YARDS GAINED
528   12/28/80 vs. L.A. Rams
FEWEST NET YARDS GAINED
153   12/30/73 vs. Minnesota
OPPONENT/MOST NET YARDS GAINED
466   1/16/83 vs. Green Bay
393   1/10/82 @ San Francisco
OPPONENT/FEWEST NET YARDS GAINED
118   1/4/76 @ L.A. Rams

RUSHING
MOST YARDS RUSHING
345   1/2/82 vs. Tampa Bay
338   12/28/80 vs. L.A. Rams
FEWEST YARDS RUSHING
61   1/4/86 @ L.A. Rams
OPPONENT/MOST YARDS RUSHING
269   1/4/86 @ L.A. Rams
OPPONENT/FEWEST YARDS RUSHING
22   1/4/76 vs. L.A. Rams

PASSING
MOST NET YARDS PASSING
310   1/4/81 @ Atlanta
FEWEST NET YARDS PASSING
22   12/26/70 vs. Detroit
OPPONENT/MOST NET YARDS PASSING
308   1/16/83 vs. Green Bay
OPPONENT/FEWEST NET YARDS PASSING
35   12/30/78 vs. Atlanta
MOST GROSS YARDS PASSING
330   12/26/83 vs. L.A. Rams
FEWEST GROSS YARDS PASSING
38   12/26/70 vs. Detroit
OPPONENT/MOST GROSS YARDS PASSING
322   1/16/83 vs. Green Bay
320   1/4/81 @ Atlanta
OPPONENT/FEWEST GROSS YARDS PASSING
50   1/4/86 vs. L.A. Rams
MOST PASS ATTEMPTS

53   12/26/83 vs. L.A. Rams
45   1/9/83 vs. Tampa Bay
FEWEST PASS ATTEMPTS
14   12/25/71 @ Minnesota
14   12/24/77 vs. Chicago
OPPONENT/MOST PASS ATTEMPTS
40   1/3/71 vs. San Francisco
OPPONENT/FEWEST PASS ATTEMPTS
18   12/31/72 @ Washington
MOST PASS COMPLETIONS
32   12/26/83 vs. L.A. Rams
27   1/9/83 vs. Tampa Bay
FEWEST PASS COMPLETIONS
4   12/26/70 vs. Detroit
OPPONENT/MOST COMPLETIONS
22   1/10/82 @ San Francisco
20   12/28/69 vs. Cleveland
OPPONENT/FEWEST PASS COMPLETIONS
6   1/4/86 @ L.A. Rams
DEFENSE, MOST QB SACKS
8   12/31/67 @ Green Bay, (76 yards)
OPPONENT/DFNS., MOST QB SACKS
7   12/23/73 vs. L.A. Rams
7   1/18/76 vs. Pitt. (52 yds.)

INTERCEPTIONS
MOST PASSES INTERCEPTED BY COWBOYS
5   1/7/79 @ L.A. Rams
OPPONENT/MOST PASSES INTERCEPTED BY
4   12/21/68 @ Cleveland
4   12/30/73 vs. Minnesota

PENALTIES
MOST PENALTIES
12   1/15/78 vs. Denver
FEWEST PENALTIES
2   7 times, last 1/18/76 vs. Pittsburgh
OPPONENT/MOST PENALTIES
10   1/2/82 vs. Tampa Bay
8   1/19/76 vs. L.A. Rams
8   1/15/78 vs. Denver
OPPONENT/FEWEST PENALTIES
0   3 times, last 1/18/76 vs. Pittsburgh
MOST YARDS PENALIZED
133   1/17/71 vs. Baltimore
FEWEST YARDS PENALIZED
10   12/24/67 vs. Cleveland
10   12/25/71 @ Minnesota
OPPONENT/MOST YARDS PENALIZED
94   12/19/76 @ L.A. Rams

PUNTING

MOST PUNTS
9   1/17/71 vs. Baltimore
FEWEST PUNTS
2   12/24/67 vs. Cleveland
2   12/28/80 vs. L.A. Rams
OPPONENT/MOST PUNTS
8   3 times, last 1/1/78 vs. Minnesota
OPPONENT/FEWEST PUNTS
1   12/28/69 vs. Cleveland
HIGHEST COWBOYS AVERAGE
46.9   1/4/86 @ L.A. Rams
HIGHEST OPPONENT AVERAGE
48.8   12/26/70 vs. Detroit

PUNT RETURNS
MOST PUNT RETURNS
5   1/1/78 vs. Minnesota
5   12/28/80 vs. L.A. Rams
5   1/19/83 vs. Tampa Bay
MOST PUNT RETURN YARDS
155   12/24/67 vs. Cleveland
OPPONENT/MOST PUNT RETURNS
6   12/26/70 vs. Detroit
6   1/11/81 @ Philadelphia
OPPONENT/MOST PUNT RETURN YARDS
69   1/11/81 @ Philadelphia

KICKOFF RETURNS
MOST KICKOFF RETURNS
6   4 times, last 1/16/83 vs. Green Bay
MOST KICKOFF RETURN YARDS
173   1/16/83 vs. Green Bay
OPPONENT/MOST KICKOFF RETURNS
8   1/4/76 @ L.A. Rams
8   12/26/77 vs. Chicago
OPPONENT/MOST KICKOFF RETURN YARDS
188   12/25/71 @ Minnesota

FUMBLES
MOST FUMBLES
6   12/30/78 vs. Atlanta
6   1/15/78 vs. Denver
MOST FUMBLES LOST
3   12/23/72 @ San Francisco
3   12/28/74 vs. Atlanta
3   1/4/86 @ L.A. Rams
OPPONENT/MOST FUMBLES
5   1/17/71 vs. Baltimore
5   12/23/72 @ San Francisco
5   1/1/78 @ Minnesota
OPPONENT/MOST FUMBLES LOST
4   1/17/71 @ Baltimore
4   1/15/78 vs. Denver
3   1/10/82 @ San Francisco

Cowboys Longest Plays / Playoffs

LONG RUNS FROM SCRIMMAGE
53 yards—Tony Dorsett vs. L.A. Rams .... January 7, 1979
48 yards—Calvin Hill vs. San Francisco .... December 23, 1972
32 yards—Ron Springs vs. Los Angeles .... December 28, 1980
29 yards—Roger Staubach vs. Washington .... December 31, 1972
29 yards—Tony Dorsett vs. Pittsburgh .... January 21, 1979
27 yards—Billy Joe DuPree vs. Los Angeles .... January 30, 1979
26 yards—Tony Dorsett vs. L.A. Rams .... December 30, 1979
26 yards—Tony Dorsett vs. Tampa Bay .... January 2, 1982

LONG FORWARD PASSES
86 yards—Don Meredith to Bob Hayes vs. Cleveland (TD) .... December 24, 1967
83 yards—Roger Staubach to Drew Pearson vs. L.A. Rams (TD) .... December 23, 1973
68 yards—Don Meredith to Frank Clarke vs. Green Bay (TD) .... January 1, 1967
51 yards—Don Meredith to Bob Hayes vs. Minnesota (TD) .... January 5, 1969
50 yards—Roger Staubach to Drew Pearson vs. Minnesota (TD) .... December 28, 1975
49 yards—Drew Pearson to Tony Hill vs. Green Bay .... January 16, 1983
45 yards—Roger Staubach to Butch Johnson vs. Denver (TD) .... January 15, 1978

LONG PUNT RETURNS
68 yards—Bob Hayes vs. Cleveland .... December 24, 1967
63 yards—Golden Richards vs. Minnesota (TD) .... December 30, 1973
44 yards—Butch Johnson vs. L.A. Rams .... December 19, 1976
43 yards—James Jones vs. L.A. Rams .... December 28, 1980

LONG KICKOFF RETURNS
89 yards—Rod Hill vs. Green Bay .... January 16, 1983
48 yards—Thomas Henderson vs. Pittsburgh .... January 18, 1976
34 yards—Cliff Harris vs. Minnesota .... December 30, 1973
33 yards—Cliff Harris vs. San Francisco .... December 23, 1972
33 yards—James Jones vs. L.A. Rams .... December 28, 1980
33 yards—Ron Fellows vs. L.A. Rams .... December 26, 1983

LONG INTERCEPTION RETURNS
68 yards—Thomas Henderson vs. L.A. Rams (TD) .... January 7, 1979
60 yards—Cornell Green vs. Cleveland (TD) .... December 24, 1967
41 yards—Chuck Howley vs. Miami .... January 16, 1972
39 yards—Dennis Thurman vs. Green Bay (TD) .... January 16, 1983
31 yards—Dennis Thurman vs. Tampa Bay .... January 2, 1982
30 yards—Cliff Harris vs. Minnesota .... December 25, 1971
27 yards—Mark Washington vs. Denver .... January 15, 1978
26 yards—Chuck Howley vs. Minnesota .... December 25, 1971

LONG FUMBLE RETURNS
44 yards—Chuck Howley vs. Cleveland (TD) .... December 21, 1968
37 yards—Mike Hegman vs. Pittsburgh (TD) .... January 21, 1979
21 yards—Randy Hughes vs. Denver .... January 15, 1978
20 yards—Charlie Waters vs. Detroit .... December 26, 1970
15 yards—D. D. Lewis vs. Chicago .... December 26, 1977

Cowboys Big Days/Playoffs

100 YARD RUSHING GAMES
160 yards—Tony Dorsett vs. L.A. Rams .... December 28, 1980
143 yards—Duane Thomas vs. San Francisco .... January 3, 1971
135 yards—Duane Thomas vs. Detroit .... December 26, 1970
125 yards—Calvin Hill vs. San Francisco .... December 23, 1972
110 yards—Tony Dorsett vs. Tampa Bay .... January 9, 1983
108 yards—Don Perkins vs. Green Bay .... January 1, 1967
101 yards—Tony Dorsett vs. L.A. Rams .... January 7, 1979

PASSING
330 yards—Danny White vs. L.A. Rams .... December 26, 1983
322 yards—Danny White vs. Atlanta .... January 4, 1981
312 yards—Danny White vs. Tampa Bay .... January 9, 1983
246 yards—Roger Staubach vs. Minnesota .... December 28, 1975
243 yards—Don Meredith vs. Minnesota .... January 5, 1969
238 yards—Don Meredith vs. Green Bay .... January 1, 1967
228 yards—Roger Staubach vs. Pittsburgh .... January 21, 1979
225 yards—Danny White vs. Green Bay .... January 16, 1983
220 yards—Roger Staubach vs. L.A. Rams .... January 4, 1976
217 yards—Danny White @ L.A. Rams .... January 4, 1986
212 yards—Don Meredith vs. Cleveland .... December 24, 1967

RECEIVING
144 yards—Bob Hayes vs. Cleveland .... December 24, 1967
142 yards—Tony Hill vs. Green Bay .... January 16, 1983
136 yards—Billy Parks vs. San Francisco .... December 23, 1972
123 yards—Preston Pearson vs. L.A. Rams .... January 4, 1976
115 yards—Tony Hill vs. L.A. Rams .... December 26, 1983
102 yards—Frank Clarke vs. Green Bay .... January 1, 1967
 91 yards—Drew Pearson vs. Minnesota .... December 28, 1975
 90 yards—Drew Pearson vs. Atlanta .... January 4, 1981

The Last Time . . .

400 Yards Total Offense
BY COWBOYS—428 @ Washington, 12/13/87
  Playoffs—456 vs. Tampa Bay, 1/9/83
BY OPPONENT—422, St. Louis, 12/27/87
  Playoffs—456 vs. Green Bay, 1/16/83

500 Yards Total Offense
BY COWBOYS—554 @ Detroit, 9/15/85
  Playoffs—528 vs. L.A. Rams, 12/28/80
BY OPPONENT—570 @ Cincinnati, 12/8/85
  Playoffs—N.A.

300 Yards Passing in Game by Player
BY COWBOYS—Danny White, 359, @ Washington, 12/13/87
  Playoffs—Danny White, 330 vs. L.A. Rams, 12/26/83
BY OPPONENT—Neil Lomax, St. Louis, 314, 12/27/87
  Playoffs—Lynn Dickey, Green Bay, 332, 1/16/83

4 Touchdown Passes Thrown in Game by Player
BY COWBOYS—Danny White, vs. Minnesota, 11/26/87
  Playoffs—Roger Staubach, @ L.A. Rams, 1/4/76
BY OPPONENT—Dan Marino @ Miami, 12/17/84
  Playoffs—Terry Bradshaw, Pittsburgh, 1/21/79

100 Yards Rushing in Game by Player
BY COWBOYS—Herschel Walker, 137 vs. St. Louis, 12/27/87
  Playoffs—Tony Dorsett, 110, vs. Tampa Bay, 1/9/83
BY OPPONENT—Gerald Riggs, Atlanta, 119, 12/6/87
  Playoffs—John Riggins, 140, @ Washington, 1/22/83

3 Touchdowns Rushing in Game by Player
BY COWBOYS—Ron Springs (1, 4, 1) vs. St. Louis, 9/13/81
  Playoffs—N.A.
BY OPPONENT—Dick James (5, 3, 39) @ Washington, 12/17/61
  Playoffs—Larry Schreiber (1, 1, 1) @ San Francisco, 12/23/72

3 Touchdown Catches in Game by Player
BY COWBOYS—Mike Renfro (8, 14, 18) vs. Minnesota, 11/26/87
  Playoffs—Preston Pearson (18, 15, 19) @ L.A. Rams, 1/4/76
BY OPPONENT—Mark Clayton (41, 39, 63) @ Miami, 12/17/84
  Playoffs—N.A.

3 Touchdowns in Game by Player
BY COWBOYS—Mike Renfro (3 receive) vs. Minnesota, 11/26/87
  Playoffs—Preston Pearson (3 receive) @ L.A. Rams, 1/4/76
BY OPPONENT—Gerald Willhite (2 receive, 1 rush) @ Denver, 10/5/86
  Playoffs—Larry Schreiber (3 run) @ San Francisco, 12/23/72

4 Touchdowns in Game by Player
BY COWBOYS—Duane Thomas (3 run, 1 receive) vs. St. Louis, 12/18/71
  Playoffs—N.A.
BY OPPONENT—Harold Jackson (4 receive) @ L.A. Rams, 10/14/73
  Playoffs—N.A.

3 Interceptions in Game by Player
BY COWBOYS—Dennis Thurman vs. Philadelphia, 12/13/81
  Playoffs—Dennis Thurman vs. Green Bay, 1/16/83
BY OPPONENT—Terry Kinard, @ N.Y. Giants, 9/20/87
  Playoffs—N.A.

Punt Returned for TD
BY COWBOYS—Gary Allen, 68 yards, vs. Kansas City, 11/20/83
  Playoffs—Golden Richards, 63 yards vs. Minnesota, 12/30/73
BY OPPONENT—Michael Harper, @ N.Y. Jets, 78 yards, 10/4/87
  Playoffs—N.A.

Kickoff Return for TD
BY COWBOYS—Thomas Henderson, 97 yards, vs. St. Louis, 9/28/75
  Playoffs—N.A.
BY OPPONENT—Roy Green, 106 yards, St. Louis, 10/21/79
  Playoffs—Vic Washington, 97 yards, @ San Francisco, 12/23/72

Interception Returned for TD
BY COWBOYS—Ron Francis, 18 yards, @ New England, 11/15/87
  Playoffs—Dennis Thurman, 39 yards, vs. Green Bay, 1/16/83
BY OPPONENT—LeRoy Irvin, @ L.A. Rams, 50 yards, 12/7/86
  Playoffs—Darryl Grant, @ Washington, 10 yards, 1/22/83

Fumble Returned for TD
BY COWBOYS—Jim Jeffcoat, recovered in end zone, vs. New

Orleans, 10/21/84
  Playoffs—Mike Hegman, 37 yards, vs. Pittsburgh, 1/21/79
BY OPPONENT—Robert Moore, Atlanta, 20 yards, 12/6/87
  Playoffs—Hugh Green, vs. Tampa Bay, 60 yards, 1/9/83

Punt Blocked for TD
BY COWBOYS—Everson Walls, @ Cincinnati (Penn runs 46 yards), 12/8/85
  Playoffs—N.A.
BY OPPONENT—Miles McPherson, @ San Diego (Derrie Nelson runs 21 yards), 11/13/83
  Playoffs—N.A.

50 Points Scored in a Game
BY COWBOYS—Dallas 51, Seattle 7, 11/27/80
  Playoffs—Dallas 52, Cleveland 14, 12/24/67
BY OPPONENT—@ Cincinnati 50, Dallas 24, 12/8/85
  Playoffs—N.A.

40 Points Scored in a Game
BY COWBOYS—Dallas 41, Philadelphia 22, 10/11/87
  Playoffs—N.A.
BY OPPONENT—Minnesota 44, Dallas 38 (OT), 11/26/87
  Playoffs—N.A.

Shutout Scored
BY COWBOYS—Dallas 38, Baltimore 0, 9/4/78
  Playoffs—Dallas 38, Tampa Bay 0, 1/2/82
BY OPPONENT—Chicago 44, Dallas 0, 11/17/85
  Playoffs—@ L.A. Rams 20, Dallas 0, 1/4/86

Safety Scored
BY COWBOYS—John Dutton tackled Pisarcik in end zone, @ Philadelphia, 12/2/84
  Playoffs—Randy White tackled V. Ferragamo in end zone, vs. L.A. Rams, 12/30/79
BY OPPONENT—Gary Jeter, @ L.A. Rams, tackled Pelluer in end zone, 12/7/86
  Playoffs—Reggie Harrison, blocked punt out of end zone, Pittsburgh, 1/18/76

PAT Missed
BY COWBOYS—Rafael Septien, vs. Philadelphia, 11/24/85
  Playoffs—Rafael Septien, @ Atlanta, 1/4/81
BY OPPONENTS—Dave Jacobs, Philadelphia, 10/11/87
  Playoffs—Jan Stenerud, Green Bay, 1/16/83

Field Goal Blocked
BY COWBOYS—Michael Downs, vs. Minnesota, 11/26/87
  Playoffs—Aaron Mitchell, @ Philadelphia, 1/11/81
BY OPPONENTS—Clyde Simmons, @ Philadelphia, 10/25/87
  Playoffs—Frank Nunley, @ San Francisco, 1/2/72

Punt Blocked
BY COWBOYS—Bruce Livingston, vs. Philadelphia, 10/11/87
  Playoffs—N.A.
BY OPPONENT—Jody Schulz, Philadelphia, 12/14/86
  Playoffs—Reggie Harrison, Pittsburgh, 1/18/76

100 Yards Receiving in Game by Player
BY COWBOYS—Mike Renfro, 100, vs. Minnesota, 11/26/87
  Playoffs—Tony Hill, 115 yards, vs. L.A. Rams, 12/26/83
BY OPPONENT—Roy Green, 112 yards, J. T. Smith, 102, St. Louis, 12/27/87
  Playoffs—James Lofton, 109 yards, Green Bay, 1/16/83

PAT Blocked
BY COWBOYS—Robert Williams, vs. Philadelphia, 10/11/87
  Playoffs—Rod Hill vs. Green Bay, 1/16/83
BY OPPONENT—Vernon Maxwell, Indianapolis, 10/28/84
  Playoffs—Carl Eller, Minnesota, 1/1/78

400 Yards Passing
BY COWBOYS—406, Don Meredith, @ San Francisco, 11/10/63
  Playoffs—N.A.
BY OPPONENT—432, Phil Simms, @ N.Y. Giants, 10/6/85
  Playoffs—N.A.

200 Yards Rushing
BY COWBOYS—206, Tony Dorsett, vs. Philadelphia, 12/4/77
  Playoffs—N.A.
BY OPPONENT—206, Greg Bell, @ Buffalo, 11/18/84
  Playoffs—248, Eric Dickerson, @ L.A. Rams, 1/4/86

Cowboys All-Time Results

All-Time Regular Season
Record: 240-141-6
Playoff Record: 20-15

*Designates Home Games

1960 (0-11-1)
Tom Landry, Head Coach

L	*28	Pittsburgh (30,000)	35
L	*25	Philadelphia (18,500)	27
L	14	Washington (21,142)	26
L	*7	Cleveland (28,500)	48
L	10	St. Louis (23,128)	12
L	*7	Baltimore (25,500)	45
L	*13	Los Angeles (16,000)	38
L	7	Green Bay (32,294)	41
L	*14	San Francisco (10,000)	26
L	7	Chicago (39,951)	17
T	31	New York (55,033)	31
L	14	Detroit (43,272)	23
	177		369

1961 (4-9-1)
Tom Landry, Head Coach

W	*27	Pittsburgh (23,500)	24
W	*21	Minnesota (20,500)	7
L	7	Cleveland (43,638)	25
W	28	Minnesota (33,070)	0
L	*10	New York (41,500)	31
L	*7	Philadelphia (25,000)	43
W	17	New York (60,254)	16
L	*17	St. Louis (20,500)	31
L	7	Pittsburgh (17,519)	37
T	*28	Washington (17,500)	28
L	13	Philadelphia (60,127)	35
L	17	Cleveland (23,500)	38
L	13	St. Louis (15,384)	31
L	24	Washington (21,451)	34
	236		380

1962 (5-8-1)
Tom Landry, Head Coach

T	*35	Washington (15,730)	35
L	*28	Pittsburgh (19,478)	30
W	27	Los Angeles (26,907)	17
L	10	Cleveland (44,040)	19
W	*41	Philadelphia (18,645)	19
W	42	Pittsburgh (23,106)	27
L	*24	St. Louis (16,027)	28
W	38	Washington (49,888)	10
L	*10	New York (45,668)	41
L	*33	Chicago (12,692)	34
L	14	Philadelphia (58,070)	28
W	*45	Cleveland (24,226)	21
L	20	St. Louis (14,102)	52
L	31	New York (62,694)	41
	398		402

1963 (4-10)
Tom Landry, Head Coach

L	*7	St. Louis (36,432)	34
L	*24	Cleveland (28,710)	41
L	17	Washington (40,101)	21
L	21	Philadelphia (60,671)	24
W	*17	Detroit (27,264)	14
L	21	New York (62,889)	37
L	21	Pittsburgh (19,047)	27
W	*35	Washington (18,838)	20
L	24	San Francisco (29,563)	31
W	*27	Philadelphia (23,694)	20
L	17	Cleveland (55,096)	27
L	*27	New York (29,653)	34
L	*19	Pittsburgh (24,136)	24
W	28	St. Louis (12,695)	24
	305		378

1964 (5-8-1)
Tom Landry, Head Coach

L	*6	St. Louis (36,605)	16
W	*24	Washington (25,158)	18
L	17	Pittsburgh (35,594)	23
L	6	Cleveland (72,062)	27
T	*13	New York (33,324)	13
L	*16	Cleveland (37,456)	20
W	31	St. Louis (28,253)	13
W	24	Chicago (47,527)	10

W	31	New York (63,031)	21
L	*14	Philadelphia (55,972)	17
L	16	Washington (49,219)	28
L	*21	Green Bay (44,975)	45
L	14	Philadelphia (60,671)	24
W	*17	Pittsburgh (35,271)	14
	250		289

1965 (7-7)
Tom Landry, Head Coach

W	*31	New York (59,366)	2
W	*27	Washington (61,577)	7
L	13	St. Louis (32,034)	20
L	*24	Philadelphia (56,249)	35
L	17	Cleveland (80,451)	23
L	3	Green Bay (48,311)	13
L	13	Pittsburgh (37,804)	22
W	*39	San Francisco (39,677)	31
W	*24	Pittsburgh (57,293)	17
L	*17	Cleveland (76,251)	24
L	31	Washington (50,205)	34
W	21	Philadelphia (54,714)	19
W	*27	St. Louis (38,499)	13
W	38	New York (62,871)	20
	325		280

PLAYOFF BOWL GAME (Miami)

L	3	Baltimore (65,569)	35

1966 (10-3-1)
Tom Landry, Head Coach

W	*52	New York (60,010)	7
W	*28	Minnesota (64,116)	17
W	47	Atlanta (56,990)	14
W	*56	Philadelphia (69,372)	7
T	10	St. Louis (50,673)	10
L	21	Cleveland (84,721)	30
W	*52	Pittsburgh (58,453)	21
L	23	Philadelphia (60,658)	24
W	31	Washington (50,927)	30
W	20	Pittsburgh (42,185)	7
W	*26	Cleveland (80,259)	14
W	*31	St. Louis (76,965)	17
L	*31	Washington (64,198)	34
W	17	New York (62,735)	7
	445		239

1966 CHAMPIONSHIP GAME (Dallas)

L	27	Green Bay (75,504)	34

1967 (9-5)
Tom Landry, Head Coach

W	21	Cleveland (81,039)	14
W	*38	New York (66,209)	24
L	*13	Los Angeles (75,229)	35
W	17	Washington (50,566)	14
W	*14	New Orleans (64,128)	10
W	24	Pittsburgh (39,641)	21
L	14	Philadelphia (69,740)	21
W	*37	Atlanta (74,751)	7
W	27	New Orleans (83,437)	10
L	*20	Washington (75,538)	27
W	*46	St. Louis (68,787)	21
L	17	Baltimore (60,238)	23
W	*38	Philadelphia (55,834)	17
W	16	San Francisco (27,182)	24
	342		268

1967 EASTERN CHAMPIONSHIP GAME (Dallas)

W	52	Cleveland (70,786)	14

1967 CHAMPIONSHIP GAME (Green Bay)

L	17	Green Bay (50,861)	21

1968 (12-2)
Tom Landry, Head Coach

W	*59	Detroit (61,382)	13
W	*28	Cleveland (68,733)	7
W	45	Philadelphia (60,858)	13
W	27	St. Louis (48,296)	10
W	*34	Philadelphia (72,083)	14
W	20	Minnesota (47,644)	7
L	*17	Green Bay (74,604)	28
W	17	New Orleans (84,728)	3
L	*21	New York (72,163)	27
W	44	Washington (50,816)	24
W	34	Chicago (46,667)	3
W	*29	Washington (66,076)	20

W	*28	Pittsburgh (55,069)	7
W	28	New York (62,617)	10
	431		186

1968 EASTERN CHAMPIONSHIP GAME (Cleveland)

L	20	Cleveland (81,497)	31

PLAYOFF BOWL GAME (Miami)

W	17	Minnesota (22,961)	13

1969 (11-2-1)
Tom Landry, Head Coach

W	*24	St. Louis (62,134)	3
W	21	New Orleans (79,567)	17
W	38	Philadelphia (60,658)	7
W	24	Atlanta (54,833)	17
W	*49	Philadelphia (71,509)	14
W	*25	New York (58,964)	3
L	10	Cleveland (84,850)	42
W	*33	New Orleans (68,282)	17
W	41	Washington (50,474)	28
L	23	Los Angeles (79,105)	24
T	*24	San Francisco (62,348)	24
W	10	Pittsburgh (24,990)	7
W	*27	Baltimore (63,191)	10
W	*20	Washington (56,924)	10
	369		223

1969 EASTERN CHAMPIONSHIP GAME (Dallas)

W	14	Cleveland (69,321)	38

PLAYOFF BOWL GAME (Miami)

L	0	Los Angeles (31,151)	31

1970 (10-4)
Tom Landry, Head Coach

W	17	Philadelphia (59,728)	7
W	*28	N.Y. Giants (57,239)	10

L	7	St. Louis (50,780)	20
W	*13	Atlanta (53,611)	0
L	13	Minnesota (47,900)	54
W	27	Kansas City (51,158)	16
W	*21	Philadelphia (55,736)	17
L	20	N.Y. Giants (62,928)	23
L	*0	St. Louis (69,323)	38
W	45	Washington (50,415)	21
W	*16	Green Bay (67,182)	3
W	*34	Washington (57,936)	0
W	6	Cleveland (75,458)	2
W	*52	Houston (50,504)	10
	299		221

1970 DIVISIONAL PLAYOFF (Dallas)

W	5	Detroit (73,167)	0

1970 NFC CHAMPIONSHIP GAME (San Francisco)

W	17	San Francisco (59,625)	10

SUPER BOWL V (Miami)

L	13	Baltimore (80,055)	16

1971 (11-3)
Tom Landry, Head Coach

W	49	Buffalo (46,206)	37
W	42	Philadelphia (65,358)	7
L	*16	Washington (72,000)	20
W	*20	N.Y. Giants (68,378)	13
L	14	New Orleans (83,088)	24
W	*44	New England (65,708)	21
L	19	Chicago (55,049)	23
W	16	St. Louis (50,486)	13
W	*20	Philadelphia (60,178)	7
W	13	Washington (53,041)	0
W	*28	Los Angeles (66,595)	21
W	*52	N.Y. Jets (66,689)	10
W	42	N.Y. Giants (62,815)	14

W *31 St. Louis (66,672) 12
  406 222
1971 DIVISIONAL PLAYOFF
(Minnesota)
W 20 Minnesota (49,100) 12
1971 NFC CHAMPIONSHIP GAME
(Dallas)
W 14 San Francisco (66,311) 3
SUPER BOWL VI (New Orleans)
W 24 Miami (81,035) 3

1972 (10-4)
Tom Landry, Head Coach
W *28 Philadelphia (55,850) 6
W 23 N.Y. Giants (62,725) 14
L 13 Green Bay (47,103) 16
W *17 Pittsburgh (65,682) 13
W 21 Baltimore (58,992) 0
L 20 Washington (53,039) 24
W *28 Detroit (65,378) 24
W 34 San Diego (54,476) 28
W *33 St. Louis (65,218) 24
W 28 Philadelphia (65,720) 7
L *10 San Francisco (65,124) ... 31
W 27 St. Louis (49,797) 6
W *34 Washington (65,136) 24
L *3 N.Y. Giants (64,602) 23
  319 240

1972 DIVISIONAL PLAYOFF
(San Francisco)
W 30 San Francisco (61,214) 28
1972 NFC CHAMPIONSHIP GAME
(Washington)
L 3 Washington (53,129) 26

1973 (10-4)
Tom Landry, Head Coach
W 20 Chicago (55,701) 17
W *40 New Orleans (53,972) 3
W *45 St. Louis (64,815) 10
L 7 Washington (54,314) 14
L 31 Los Angeles (61,428) 37
W *45 N.Y. Giants (64,898) 28
L 16 Philadelphia (65,954) 30

W *38 Cincinnati (58,802) 10
W 23 N.Y. Giants (70,128) 10
W *31 Philadelphia (61,985) 10
L *7 Miami (64,100) 14
W 22 Denver (51,706) 10
W *27 Washington (65,458—†) ... 7
W 30 St. Louis (43,946) 3
  382 203
1973 DIVISIONAL PLAYOFF (Dallas)
W 27 Los Angeles (64,291) 16
1973 NFC CHAMPIONSHIP GAME
(Dallas)
L 10 Minnesota (64,524) 27

1974 (8-6)
Tom Landry, Head Coach
W 24 Atlanta (52,322) 0
L 10 Philadelphia (64,088) 13
L *6 N.Y. Giants (45,841) 14
L *21 Minnesota (57,847) 23
L 28 St. Louis (49,885) 31
W *31 Philadelphia (43,586) 24
W 21 N.Y. Giants (61,918) 7
W *17 St. Louis (64,146) 14
W *20 San Francisco (50,018) ... 14
W 21 Washington (54,395) 28
W 10 Houston (49,775) 0
W *24 Washington (63,243) 23
W *41 Cleveland (48,754) 17
L 23 Oakland (45,850) 27
  297 235

1975 (10-4)
Tom Landry, Head Coach
W *18 Los Angeles (49,091) 7
W *37 St. Louis (52,417) (OT) . 31
W 36 Detroit (79,784) 10
W 13 N.Y. Giants (56,511) 7
L *17 Green Bay (64,934) 19
W 20 Philadelphia (64,889) 17
L 24 Washington (55,004) (OT) . 30
L *31 Kansas City (53,539) 34
W 34 New England (60,905) 31
W *27 Philadelphia (57,893) 17
W *14 N.Y. Giants (53,329) 3

L 17 St. Louis (49,701) 31
W *31 Washington (61,091) 10
W 31 N.Y. Jets (37,279) 21
  350 268
1975 DIVISIONAL PLAYOFF
(Minnesota)
W 17 Minnesota (48,341) 14
1975 NFC CHAMPIONSHIP GAME
(Los Angeles)
W 37 Los Angeles (84,483) 7
SUPER BOWL X (Miami)
L 17 Pittsburgh (80,187) 21

1976 (11-3)
Tom Landry, Head Coach
W *27 Philadelphia (54,052) 7
W 24 New Orleans (61,413) 6
W *30 Baltimore (64,237) 27
W 28 Seattle (62,027) 13
W 24 N.Y. Giants (76,042) 14
L 17 St. Louis (50,317) 21
W *31 Chicago (61,346) 21
W 20 Washington (55,004) 7
W *9 N.Y. Giants (58,870) 3
W *17 Buffalo (51,779) 10
L 10 Atlanta (54,992) 17
W *19 St. Louis (62,498) 14
W 26 Philadelphia (55,072) 7
L *14 Washington (59,916) 27
  296 194

1976 DIVISIONAL PLAYOFF
(Dallas)
L 12 Los Angeles (62,436) 14

1977 (12-2)
Tom Landry, Head Coach
W 16 Minnesota (47,678) (OT) .. 10
W *41 N.Y. Giants (64,215) 21
W *23 Tampa Bay (55,316) 7
W 30 St. Louis (50,129) 24
W *34 Washington (62,115) 16
W 16 Philadelphia (65,507) 10
W *37 Detroit (63,160) 0
W 24 N.Y. Jets (74,532) 10

L *17 St. Louis (64,038) 24
L 13 Pittsburgh (49,761) 28
W 14 Washington (55,031) 7
W *24 Philadelphia (60,289) 14
W 42 San Francisco (55,848) ... 35
W *14 Denver (63,752) 6
  345 212
1977 DIVISIONAL PLAYOFF
(Dallas)
W 37 Chicago (62,920) 7
1977 NFC CHAMPIONSHIP GAME
(Dallas)
W 23 Minnesota (61,968) 6
SUPER BOWL XII (New Orleans)
W 27 Denver (76,400) 10

1978 (12-4)
Tom Landry, Head Coach
W *38 Baltimore (64,224) 0
W 34 N.Y. Giants (73,265) 24
L 14 Los Angeles (65,749) 27
W *21 St. Louis (62,760) 12
L 5 Washington (55,031) 9
W *24 N.Y. Giants (63,420) 3
W 24 St. Louis (48,991) (OT) 21
W *14 Philadelphia (60,525) 7
L *10 Minnesota (61,848) 21
L 16 Miami (69,414) 23
W 42 Green Bay (55,256) 14
W *27 New Orleans (57,920) 7
W *37 Washington (64,905) 10
W *17 New England (63,263) 10
W 31 Philadelphia (64,667) 13
W 30 N.Y. Jets (52,632) 7
  384 208
1978 DIVISIONAL PLAYOFF
(Dallas)
W 27 Atlanta (60,338) 20
1978 NFC CHAMPIONSHIP GAME
(Los Angeles)
W 28 Los Angeles (67,470) 0
SUPER BOWL XIII (Miami)
L 31 Pittsburgh (78,656) 35

1979 (11-5)
Tom Landry, Head Coach
W 22 St. Louis (50,855) 21
W 21 San Francisco (56,728) ... 13
W *24 Chicago (64,056) 20
L 7 Cleveland (80,123) 26
W *38 Cincinnati (63,179) 13
W 36 Minnesota (47,572) 20
W *30 Los Angeles (64,462) 6
W *22 St. Louis (64,300) 13
L 3 Pittsburgh (50,199) 14
W 16 New York (76,490) 14
L *21 Philadelphia (62,417) 31
L 20 Washington (55,031) 34
L *24 Houston (63,897) 30
W *28 New York (63,787) 7
W 24 Philadelphia (71,434) 17
W *35 Washington (62,867) 34
  371 313
1979 DIVISIONAL PLAYOFF
(Dallas)
L 19 Los Angeles (64,792) 21

1980 (12-4)
Tom Landry, Head Coach
W 17 Washington (55,045) 3
L 20 Denver (74,919) 41
W *28 Tampa Bay (62,750) 17
W 28 Green Bay (54,776) 7
W *24 N.Y. Giants (59,126) 3
W *59 San Francisco (63,399) 14
L 10 Philadelphia (70,696) 17
W *42 San Diego (60,639) 31
W 27 St. Louis (50,701) 24
L 35 N.Y. Giants (68,343) 38
W *31 St. Louis (52,567) 21
W *14 Washington (58,809) 10
W *51 Seattle (57,540) 7
W 19 Oakland (53,194) 13
L 14 Los Angeles (65,154) 38
W *35 Philadelphia (62,548) 27
  454 311
1980 NFC WILD CARD PLAYOFF
(Dallas)
W 34 Los Angeles (64,533) 13
1980 DIVISIONAL PLAYOFF
(Atlanta)
W 30 Atlanta (60,022) 27
1980 NFC CHAMPIONSHIP GAME
(Philadelphia)
L 7 Philadelphia (70,696) 20

1981 (12-4)
Tom Landry, Head Coach
W *17 Washington (55,045) 3

W	*30	St. Louis (63,602)	17
W	35	New England (60,311) ...	21
W	*18	N.Y. Giants (63,449)	10
L	17	St. Louis (49,777)	20
L	14	San Francisco (57,574) ...	45
W	*29	Los Angeles (64,649) ...	17
W	*28	Miami (64,221)	27
W	17	Philadelphia (72,111)	14
W	*27	Buffalo (62,583)	14
L	24	Detroit (79,694)	27
W	*24	Washington (64,583)	10
W	*10	Chicago (63,499)	9
W	37	Baltimore (54,871)	13
W	*21	Philadelphia (64,955) ...	10
L	10	N.Y. Giants (73,009) (OT) .	13
	358		270

1981 DIVISIONAL PLAYOFF
(Dallas)
W 38 Tampa Bay (64,848) 0
1981 NFC CHAMPIONSHIP GAME
(San Francisco)
L 27 San Francisco (60,525) 28

1982 (6-3)
Tom Landry, Head Coach
L	*28	Pittsburgh (63,431)	36
W	24	St. Louis (50,705)	7
		Minnesota—canceled	
		*N.Y. Giants—canceled	
		*Washington—canceled	
		Philadelphia—canceled	
		Cincinnati—canceled	
		N.Y. Giants—canceled	
		*St. Louis—canceled	
		San Francisco—canceled	
W	*14	Tampa Bay (49,578)	9
W	*31	Cleveland (46,267)	14
W	24	Washington (54,633)	10
W	37	Houston (51,808)	7
W	*21	New Orleans (64,506)	7
	479		360

L	*20	Philadelphia (46,199)	24
L	27	Minnesota (60,007)	31
	226		145

1982 SUPER BOWL TOURNAMENT —ROUND 1
W *30 Tampa Bay (65,042) 17
1982 SUPER BOWL TOURNAMENT —ROUND 2
W *37 Green Bay (63,972) 26
1982 SUPER BOWL TOURNAMENT —ROUND 3
L 17 Washington (55,045) 31

1983 (12-4)
Tom Landry, Head Coach
W	31	Washington (55,045)	30
W	34	St. Louis (48,532)	17
W	*28	N.Y. Giants (62,347)	13
W	*21	New Orleans (62,136) ...	20
W	37	Minnesota (60,774)	24
W	*27	Tampa Bay (63,308) (OT)	24
W	*37	Philadelphia (63,070) ...	7
L	*38	L.A. Raiders (64,991)	40
W	38	N.Y. Giants (76,142)	20
W	27	Philadelphia (71,236)	20
L	23	San Diego (46,192)	24
W	*41	Kansas City (64,103)	21
W	*35	St. Louis (60,764)	17
W	35	Seattle (63,352)	10
L	*10	Washington (65,074)	31
L	17	San Francisco (59,957) ...	42
	479		360

1983 NFC WILD CARD GAME
(Dallas)
L 17 L.A. Rams (43,521) 24

1984 (9-7)
Tom Landry, Head Coach
W 20 L.A. Rams (65,403) 13
L 7 N.Y. Giants (75,921) 28

W	*23	Philadelphia (64,521)	17
W	*20	Green Bay (64,222)	6
W	23	Chicago (63,623)	14
L	*20	St. Louis (61,438)	31
L	14	Washington (55,431)	34
W	*30	New Orleans (50,966) (OT)	27
W	*22	Indianapolis (58,724)	3
L	*7	N.Y. Giants (60,235)	19
W	24	St. Louis (48,721)	17
L	3	Buffalo (74,391)	14
W	*20	New England (55,341) ...	17
L	26	Philadelphia (66,322)	10
L	*28	Washington (64,286)	30
L	21	Miami (74,139)	28
	308		308

1985 (10-6)
Tom Landry, Head Coach
W	*44	Washington (62,292)	14
L	21	Detroit (72,985)	26
W	*20	Cleveland (61,456)	7
W	17	Houston (49,686)	10
W	30	N.Y. Giants (74,981)	29
W	*27	Pittsburgh (62,932)	13
L	14	Philadelphia (70,114)	16
L	10	St. Louis (49,347)	21
W	13	Washington (55,750)	7
L	*0	Chicago (63,855)	44
W	*34	Philadelphia (54,047)	17
W	*35	St. Louis (54,125)	17
L	24	Cincinnati (56,936)	50
W	*28	N.Y. Giants (62,310)	21
W	16	San Francisco (60,114)	31
	357		333

1985 DIVISIONAL PLAYOFF
(Anaheim)
L 0 L.A. Rams (66,351) 20

1986 (7-9)
Tom Landry, Head Coach
W	*31	N.Y. Giants (59,804)	28
W	31	Detroit (73,812)	7
L	*35	Atlanta (62,880)	37
W	31	St. Louis (49,077)	7
L	14	Denver (76,082)	29
W	*30	Washington (63,264)	6
W	17	Philadelphia (68,572)	14
W	*37	St. Louis (60,756)	6
L	14	N.Y. Giants (74,871)	17
L	*13	L.A. Raiders (61,706)	17
W	24	San Diego (55,622)	21
L	14	Washington (55,642)	41
L	*14	Seattle (58,023)	31
L	10	L.A. Rams (64,949)	29
L	*21	Philadelphia (46,117)	23
L	*10	Chicago (57,256)	24
	346		337

1987 (7-8)
Tom Landry, Head Coach
L	13	St. Louis (47,241)	24
W	16	N.Y. Giants (73,426)	14
		*Buffalo—cancelled	
W	38	N.Y. Jets (12,370)	24
W	*41	Philadelphia (40,622)	22
L	*7	Washington (60,415)	13
L	20	Philadelphia (61,630)	37
W	*33	N.Y. Giants (55,730)	24
L	17	Detroit (45,325)	27
W	23	New England (60,567) OT .	17
L	*14	Miami (56,519)	20
L	*38	Minnesota (54,229) OT ..	44
L	*10	Atlanta (40,103)	21
L	20	Washington (54,882)	24
W	29	L.A. Rams (60,700)	21
W	*21	St. Louis (36,788)	16
	340		348

Cowboys All-Time Pre-Season Results

DAL.   OPP.

1960 (1-5)
10 San Francisco (22,000) @ Seattle 16
13 St. Louis (14,000) @ San Antonio 20
10 Baltimore (40,000) @ Dallas 14
14 New York (10,663) @ Louisville 3
14 Los Angeles (13,500) @ Pendleton 49
23 Green Bay (20,121) @ Minn. 28

1961 (2-3)
38 Minnesota (4,954) @ Sioux Falls 13
7 Green Bay (30,000) @ Dallas 30
10 N.Y. (21,500) @ Albuquerque 28
35 Baltimore (19,000) @ Norman 24
10 S.F. (22,130) @ Sacramento 24

1962 (0-5)
7 Green Bay (54,500) @ Dallas 31
24 Detroit (77,683) @ Cleveland 35
10 Baltimore (14,000) @ Roanoke 24
7 S.F. (20,000) @ Sacramento 26
26 Minnesota (12,500) @ Atlanta 45

1963 (3-2)
17 Los Angeles (70,675) @ L.A. 14
10 Green Bay (53,121) @ Dallas 31
17 Los Angeles (29,349) @ Portland 20
37 S.F. (9,927) @ Bakersfield 24
27 Detroit (51,218) @ New Orleans 17

1964 (1-4)
6 Los Angeles (57,450) @ L.A. 17
34 S.F. (24,679) @ Portland 23
16 Los Angeles (30,565) @ Portland 25
3 Green Bay (60,057) @ Dallas 35
6 Chicago (35,000) @ New Orleans 21

1965 (2-3)
0 Los Angeles (31,579) @ L.A. 9
7 S.F. (24,837) @ Portland 27
21 Green Bay (67,954) @ Dallas 12
17 Minn. (41,500) @ Birmingham 57
34 Chicago (33,525) @ Tulsa 21

1966 (5-0)
24 San Francisco (28,899) @ S.F. 13
20 Los Angeles (44,217) @ L.A. 10
21 Green Bay (75,504) @ Dallas 3
20 Detroit (31,250) @ Tulsa 10
28 Minnesota (58,316) @ Dallas 24

1967 (2-3)
6 Los Angeles (57,595) @ L.A. 20
30 San Francisco (31,212) @ S.F. 24
3 Green Bay (78,087) @ Dallas 20
30 Houston (53,125) @ Houston 17
7 Baltimore (58,492) @ Dallas 33

1968 (3-3)
24 Chicago (14,578) @ Canton 30
16 San Francisco (27,530) @ S.F. 14
42 Los Angeles (65,978) @ L.A. 10
27 Green Bay (72,014) @ Dallas 31
33 Houston (52,289) @ Houston 19
10 Baltimore (69,520) @ Dallas 16

1969 (4-2)
17 Los Angeles (87,381) @ L.A. 24
20 San Francisco (33,894) @ S.F. 17
31 Green Bay (73,764) @ Dallas 13
14 Houston (55,310) @ Houston 11
25 N.Y. Jets (74,771) @ Dallas 9
7 Baltimore (58,975) @ Dallas 23

1970 (1-5)
20 San Diego (39,392) @ San Diego 10
10 Los Angeles (64,646) @ L.A. 17
34 Green Bay (72,389) @ Dallas 35
21 Houston (46,548) @ Houston 37
0 Kansas City (69,055) @ Dallas 13
21 New York Jets (55,297) @ Dallas 29

1971 (6-0)
45 Los Angeles (87,187) @ L.A. 21

36 New Orleans (73,560) @ Dallas 21
16 Cleveland (69,099) @ Dallas 15
28 Houston (49,078) @ Houston 20
27 Baltimore (22,921) @ Baltimore 14
24 Kansas City (74,035) @ Dallas 17

1972 (6-1)
20 College All-Stars (54,162) @ Chi. 7
26 Houston (65,405) @ Dallas 24
27 Los Angeles (66,051) @ L.A. 13
30 New Orleans (81,070) @ N.O. 7
34 N.Y. Jets (65,386) @ Dallas 27
10 Kansas City (79,592) @ K.C. 20
16 Oakland (62,607) @ Dallas 10

1973 (4-2)
24 Los Angeles (75,461) @ L.A. 7
26 Oakland (53,723) @ Oakland 27
24 New Orleans (61,022) @ Dallas 14
24 Houston (46,942) @ Houston 27
27 Kansas City (57,468) @ Dallas 16
26 Miami (61,378) @ Dallas 23

1974 (3-3)
7 Oakland (41,049) @ Oakland 27
13 Los Angeles (46,468) @ L.A. 6
19 Houston (53,148) @ Dallas (OT) 13
7 N. Orleans (56,563) @ N. Orleans 16
25 Kansas City (43,492) @ Dallas 16
15 Pittsburgh (43,900) @ Dallas 41

1975 (2-4)
7 Los Angeles (62,843) @ L.A. 35
20 Kansas City (35,630) @ K.C. 26
13 Minnesota (45,395) @ Dallas 16
17 Houston (46,951) @ Houston 14
20 Oakland (39,562) @ Dallas 31
17 Pittsburgh (43,186) @ Dallas 16

1976 (3-3)
14 Oakland (52,391) @ Oakland 17
14 Los Angeles (60,158) @ L.A. 26
9 Denver (54,567) @ Dallas 13
36 Detroit (30,340) @ Memphis 16
20 Pittsburgh (64,264) @ Dallas 10
26 Houston (58,844) @ Dallas (OT) 20

1977 (3-3)
34 San Diego (59,504) @ Dallas 14
17 Seattle (58,789) @ Seattle (OT) 23
14 Miami (56,820) @ Dallas 20
23 Baltimore (54,835) @ Dallas 21
14 Houston (49,777) @ Houston 23
30 Pittsburgh (49,824) @ Dallas 0

1978 (3-1)
41 San Francisco (63,736) @ Dallas 24
21 Denver (74,619) @ Denver 14

13 Houston (62,242) @ Dallas 27
16 Pittsburgh (59,747) @ Dallas 13

1979 (3-2)
13 Oakland (20,648) @ Canton, Ohio 20
7 Denver (61,192) @ Dallas 6
17 Seattle (59,803) @ Seattle 27
16 Houston (62,803) @ Dallas 13
16 Pittsburgh (64,543) @ Dallas 14

1980 (1-3)
17 Green Bay (54,876) @ Dallas 14
19 Los Angeles (63,283) @ Anaheim 16
20 Houston (63,658) @ Dallas 13
10 Pittsburgh (62,795) @ Dallas 31

1981 (2-2)
17 Green Bay (55,087) @ Dallas 21
21 Los Angeles (61,459) @ Anaheim 33
24 Pittsburgh (63,504) @ Dallas 14
28 Green Bay (63,799) @ Dallas 20

1982 (3-1)
10 Buffalo (48,612) @ Dallas 14
26 San Diego (49,182) @ San Diego 16
36 New England (50,113) @ Dallas 21
20 Houston (60,150) @ Dallas 14

1983 (3-1)
20 Miami (46,826) @ Dallas 17
30 L.A. Rams (54,268) @ Los Angeles 7
7 Pittsburgh (62,164) @ Dallas 24
34 Houston (54,363) @ Dallas 31

1984 (3-1)
31 Green Bay (43,371) @ Dallas 17
24 San Diego (50,740) @ San Diego 13
10 Pittsburgh (55,658) @ Dallas 20
31 Houston (53,877) @ Dallas 24

1985 (4-0)
27 Green Bay (41,847) @ Dallas 3
27 San Diego (48,596) @ San Diego (OT) 24
15 Chicago (49,540) @ Dallas 13
20 Houston (53,812) @ Dallas 10

1986 (0-5)
6 Chicago (82,699) @ London 17
0 San Diego (47,744) @ San Diego 20
19 L.A. Raiders (52,153) @ L.A. 24
28 Pittsburgh (54,299) @ Dallas 41
14 Houston (62,239) @ Dallas 17

1987 (1-3)
0 San Diego (48,020) @ San Diego 29
13 S. Fran. (57,598) @ S. Fran. 3
10 L.A. Raiders (46,666) @ Dallas 34
13 Houston (47,043) @ Dallas 18

128